Generational Change

Generational Change

Closing the Test Score Gap

Edited by Paul E. Peterson

ROWMAN & LITTLEFIELD PUBLISHERS, INC.
Lanham • Boulder • New York • Toronto • Oxford

ROWMAN & LITTLEFIELD PUBLISHERS, INC.

Published in the United States of America
by Rowman & Littlefield Publishers, Inc.
A wholly owned subsidary of The Rowman & Littlefield Publishing Group, Inc.
4501 Forbes Boulevard, Suite 200, Lanham, Maryland 20706
www.rowmanlittlefield.com

PO Box 317
Oxford
OX2 9RU, UK

British Library Cataloguing in Publication Information Available

Library of Congress Cataloging-in-Publication Data

Generational change : closing the test score gap / edited by Paul E. Peterson.
       p.   cm.
    Includes bibliographical references.
    ISBN 0-7425-4608-X (cloth : alk. paper)—ISBN 0-7425-4609-8
    (pbk. : alk. paper)
 1. Educational equalization—United States.   2. Academic
achievement—United States.   3. African Americans—Education—United States.
 4. United States—Race relations.
 I. Peterson, Paul E.
 LC213.2.G455   2006
 379.2'6'0973—dc22   2005020328

Printed in the United States of America

∞ ™ The paper used in this publication meets the minimum requirements of
American National Standard for Information Sciences—Permanence of Paper for
Printed Library Materials, ANSI/NISO Z39.48–1992.

Contents

1

Toward the Elimination of Race Differences in Educational Achievement

Paul E. Peterson, Harvard University

> We are mindful . . . that a "core purpose of the Fourteenth Amendment was to do away with all governmentally imposed discrimination based on race." . . . Accordingly, race-conscious admissions policies must be limited in time. . . .
>
> However compelling their goals, [racial classifications] are potentially so dangerous that they . . . must have a logical end point.
>
> It has been 25 years since Justice Powell first approved the use of race to further an interest in student body diversity. . . . Since that time, the number of minority applications with high grades and test scores has indeed increased. . . . We expect that 25 years from now, the use of racial preferences will no longer be necessary.
>
> —Justice Sandra Day O'Connor, *Grutter v. Bollinger* [2003], 30–31.

Strong words, these are, especially when spoken with all the authority of the Supreme Court of the United States. After centuries of slavery, a century of legal segregation, and a half-century of deep racial divide, Justice Sandra Day O'Connor, in 2003, proclaimed the Court's expectation that, in little more than a generation, it shall no longer allow racial distinctions. The context for an announcement that affirmative action would eventually be banned was a decision handed down in a suit filed against the University of Michigan law school, which had been giving preference to minority students in its admission procedures. The Court agreed to allow the practice to continue, thereby reaffirming the result in the *Bakke* case, decided in 1978, in which Justice

1

Lewis F. Powell, Jr. outlawed racial quotas but permitted racial preferences to achieve greater ethnic diversity.

O'Connor departed from the opinion in *Bakke* in one important respect: She established a term limit to racial preferences. Perpetual racial preferences, even in the name of diversity, were said to be potentially too pernicious to withstand legal scrutiny. The length of the term: twenty-five years, a number chosen for no explicit reason other than the length of time between the *Bakke* case and the Michigan one then being decided. But even though no substantive reason was given, the Court implicitly announced its expectation that it should take no longer than a generation to erase differences in black and white educational achievement.

One year previously, in 2002, an even more stringent term limit had been established. The U.S. Congress passed, and President George W. Bush signed into law, No Child Left Behind (NCLB), which mandated that all children reach a certain standard of proficiency within twelve years. Annual progress toward this goal has to be made by every school—and by disadvantaged groups within the school, including African Americans and Hispanics. Though not exactly calling for an end to ethnic differentiation in test score performance—some groups might still be more proficient than others, even if all pass the minimum threshold—the designers of NCLB once again articulated a grand vision: Within a half generation, existing disparities are to be greatly narrowed.

Presidents have a weakness for articulating grand and far-reaching goals that are never achieved. Lyndon Johnson declared a war on poverty, Richard Nixon announced one on cancer, Jimmy Carter did the same for U.S. dependence on foreign energy, and George W. Bush pursued a genuine war on terrorism. Yet we still have poverty, cancer, foreign energy dependence, and terrorist activities. Nor is the Supreme Court, normally more cautious, exempt from unwarranted proclamations. *Brown* was to end segregation, and *Baker v. Carr* to equalize the vote. While historic decisions, their stated goals have never been entirely fulfilled.

Is O'Connor, otherwise one of the most cautious members of the Supreme Court, just another politically inspired visionary? Perhaps, except for one detail: There is nothing to prevent the Court, in twenty-some years, from declaring an end to affirmative action, whatever the disparities in racial achievement—on the stated grounds that perpetual racial classification is *ipso facto* pernicious.

So the gauntlet has been thrown down. If we are to construct a race-neutral, equal-opportunity society, where each individual is to be rewarded according to merit but where opportunity is equally open to Blacks and Whites alike, we need to erase the achievement gap within a generation. Is this realistic?

The evidence contained in the chapters that follow indicates that the task can be accomplished, if the political will is there to achieve it. Although the difference between the educational achievement of black and white high schoolers is large, and of no less magnitude today than it was thirty years ago, the gap need not be perpetuated for still another generation. *Indeed, had the pace of change for African American seventeen-year-olds continued at the same rate after 1990 as it had been in the preceding generation, the test gap would by now be closed.*

Unfortunately, the gap opened instead, a disconcerting development. To alter the direction of change once again, one cannot simply return to the 1980s. Instead, a combination of education policies—some espoused by liberals, others by conservatives—is needed: revitalized preschool education, further school desegregation, greater student accountability, and more control by black families over the educational experiences of their children. The remainder of this chapter connects the findings contained in the ensuing essays to the steps that must be trod, if the world the Supreme Court has envisioned is to be realized.

MEASURING THE MAGNITUDE OF THE CHALLENGE

I begin with an apology. This chapter sets to one side the important question of changes in Hispanic and Asian achievement, as well as the achievement of other ethnic groups, not because these topics are not important but because of the lesser quality of the available information on changes in their achievement level since 1970. In-migration rates for many of these ethnic groups have been large, and any comparisons over time are complicated by the arrival of new, poorly educated, often impoverished families. My focus is thus concentrated on changes in achievement levels of black and white students.

The Measuring Stick

Measuring achievement is an art to which a good deal of scientific expertise has been devoted. One does not learn much simply from adding up the average number of correct answers to a math or reading test by a group—seventy correct answers out of a hundred, for example. Obviously, the number of correct answers depends on the difficulty of the questions being posed and the circumstances under which the test is administered. To obtain a standard measuring tool that allows for comparisons across time and among groups, psychometricians have created tests in which the performance of large groups of students will take the shape of a normal distribution (a bell curve, as it is known in psychometric circles), with the scores of most students bulged around the test-score average and smaller numbers of scores scattered out toward the upper and lower extremes of the distribution. When so designed, one can measure similar group differences in test performance in terms of standard deviations, the amount by which scores are spread around their average.

A difference in test score performance of a full standard deviation is considered very large. For example, if fourth graders and eighth graders take the same test, the eighth grader will score, on average, about a little more than one (1.0) standard deviation higher. A full standard deviation is also roughly the size of the difference in the math performance of high school students in the United States and Japan, a large gap that has worried American educators for years. The decline in SAT (college-entrance exam) test scores that took place during the 1970s was just one third of a full standard deviation. Yet it was deemed big enough to provoke urgent calls for educational reform in the late seventies.

The performances of black and white students in the United States are best measured by the federally sponsored long-term trend National Assessment of Educational Progress (NAEP), a periodic survey of student performance of nine-, thirteen-, and seventeen-year-olds in reading and math that has been administered since about 1970. The survey is not a perfect measuring tool.[1] For many years, tests were administered only at four-year intervals, and the year the math test was given did not coincide with the testing year for reading. Nonetheless, NAEP has been administered to a representative sample of the U.S. school population at a given age and has been designed to yield a bell curve that allows for comparisons of trends over time. The best available measure of educational progress, it is widely considered to be the "nation's report card."

White Performance

The word *progress* is not quite accurate. Overall, the trends in the performance of white students, as measured by NAEP, have not been impressive, especially given the country's prosperity and increasing investment in elementary and secondary public education (see figures 1.1, 1.2, and 1.3).

Younger white students are performing at a somewhat higher level than their peers of earlier generations, but these gains do not hold through high school, where gains are just barely discernable. American schools—especially high schools—are troubled institutions. But even though the gains of white students have been uneven and modest, they still outperformed their black peers by a wide margin in 2004. The difference in the black and white math scores at the age of thirteen was 80 percent of a standard deviation.[2] Put concretely, the average white fourth grader was doing only a little

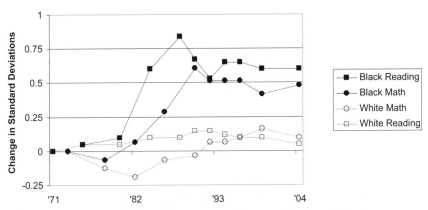

Figure 1.1   Change in Math and Reading Performance of Black and White Seventeen-Year-Olds on the National Assessment of Educational Progress, 1970–2004

Note: Initial score set to zero; subsequent scores constitute changes in standard deviations relative to the initial score. The standard deviation used here is the average standard deviation from years 1970–1999 (31.3 in math and 41.8 in reading).

Source: National Center for Education Statistics, "NAEP 2004 Trends in Academic Progress."

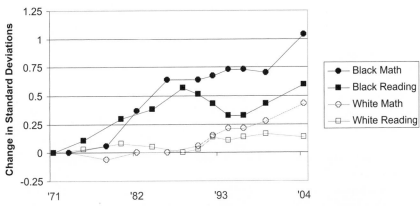

Figure 1.2   Change in Math and Reading Performance of Black and White Thirteen-Year-Olds on the National Assessment of Educational Progress, 1970–2004

Note: Initial score set to zero; subsequent scores constitute changes in standard deviations relative to the initial score. The standard deviation used here is the average standard deviation from years 1970–1999 (32.7 in math and 36.9 in reading).

Source: National Center for Education Statistics, "NAEP 2004 Trends in Academic Progress."

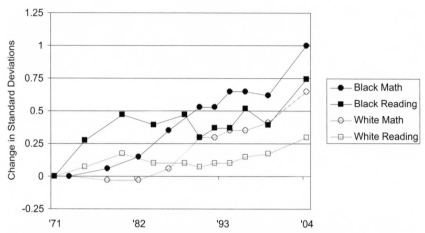

Figure 1.3   Change in Math and Reading Performance of Black and White Nine-Year-Olds on the National Assessment of Educational Progress, 1970–2004

Note: Initial score set to zero; subsequent scores constitute changes in standard deviations relative to the initial score. The standard deviation used here is the average standard deviation from years 1970–1999 (33.9 in math and 40.5 in reading).

Source: National Center for Education Statistics, "NAEP 2004 Trends in Academic Progress."

less well than the average black eighth grader. The reading score difference was not this large—but it was still 60 percent of a standard deviation.

Test-Score Importance

Why should we care about differences in student responses to multiple choice questions? Aren't these test biased, arbitrary, and capricious, with little meaning for real life outcomes, such as future earnings and other life prospects? Not so. On average, you will do much better in life if you have a test score elevated by one standard deviation than if you come from a family where parental income is this much higher. Those who think family background largely determines life outcomes will be impressed by the evidence that it is no more important than a person's test score performance as a junior in high school.[3]

So important are achievement levels that, when black high school students score as well as their white peers, their hourly earnings later in life are roughly the same.[4] This rough equality was not the case in 1964, but its realization by the 1990s is crucial to O'Connor's utopia. If the disparities in achievement can be eliminated, there is hope that many other race differences can be greatly reduced as well. In the words of scholars Christopher Jencks and Meredith Phillips:

But if racial equality is America's goal, reducing the black-white test score gap would probably do more to promote this goal than any other strategy that commands broad political support. Reducing the test score gap is probably both necessary and sufficient for substantially reducing racial inequality in educational attainment and earnings.[5]

NO EASY TASK

If erasing the test-score gap is both necessary and sufficient for achieving O'Connor's vision, that only defines the task. It does not make the job a simple one. In fact conventional wisdom, among conservative and liberal thinkers alike, sees little hope that the gap can be eliminated apart from wrenching changes well outside the boundaries of what is currently regarded as politically acceptable.

Conservative Skeptics

Consider the argument advanced by conservative writers Richard Herrnstein and Charles Murray in their widely read *The Bell Curve*, published only nine years prior to *Grutter v. Bollinger*.[6] In their view, intelligence is determined in large part by genetic inheritance. Nothing much can be altered after the first years of life, with perhaps ages five or six being the latest moment that effective intervention can take place. Intelligence, in turn, has a decisive impact on educational achievement. They place weight on the fact that what one knows at age six is highly correlated with what one knows at age sixteen. In their view, one learns easily, if one has the brains. If not, learning is more arduous—and accomplishments fewer.

Liberal Skeptics

The argument advanced in *The Bell Curve* was harshly criticized by liberal scholars and public school apologists. But, except for the hereditary factor, the typical liberal explanation for ethnic differences is as deterministic as the one set forth by Herrnstein and Murray. The argument goes much as follows: Deprivations, past and present, have, on average, left children within certain ethnic groups unequipped to learn, to achieve, to attain success in modern, industrial societies. For them, special provision—affirmative action, if you will—must be made, if the egalitarian goals of a democratic society are to survive. Consider, for example, the claim advanced recently by Richard Rothstein, once the influential education columnist for the *New York Times* and now a Senior Fellow at the left-leaning Economic Policy Institute:

Americans have come to the conclusion that the achievement gap is the fault of
"failing schools." . . . This . . . perspective, however, is misleading and dangerous. It ignores how social class characteristics in a stratified society like ours
may actually influence learning in school. . . . For example parents of different
social classes often have different styles of childrearing. . . . Differences in wealth
. . . are also likely to be important. . . .

[Taken together, these] social class characteristics [are] probably so powerful
that schools cannot overcome [them], no matter how well trained are their
teachers and no matter how well designed are their instructional programs and
climates.[7]

From Rothstein's vantage point, the achievement gap will persist as long
as the United States remains a socially stratified society, where groups have
differential access to health, housing, income, wealth, and appropriate childrearing practices. If that is so, it will take massive change engineered by a
cultural or sociopolitical revolution of the first magnitude to erase ethnic differences in achievement. A new sociopolitical order is needed to transfer
wealth and income to an extent quite outside the American tradition. If such
massive change were possible, schools could perhaps be left out of the equation. But only utopians can believe such sociopolitical changes are likely to
occur in one generation. When penning the Court opinion in *Bollinger*, it is
doubtful that Sandra Day O'Connor had this in mind.

To repeat, the task is undoubtedly large. Some, as we have seen, have
declared it Sisyphean—unless one makes dramatic alterations in the genetic
code, family life, or the social order. Is there, then, any reason to think the
Supreme Court vision anything other than mere fantasy or, even worse, a
dangerous deception?

The Reasons for Optimism

The best reason to think otherwise is that the United States was at one
point moving steadily forward toward the elimination of the racial gap in
student achievement. Between the early 1970s and 1988, the NAEP scores of
nine-year-old African American students climbed by almost half a standard
deviation in reading and, by 1990, it increased by more than half a standard
deviation in math (see figure 1.3). Test scores of black students in the older
age cohorts trended upward at an even steeper pace. As can be seen in figure
1.1, the most marked gains were for African American seventeen-year-olds,
whose reading scores climbed by 84 percent of a standard deviation between
1971 and 1988 and whose math results improved by 61 percent between 1973
and 1990.[8] As mentioned previously, had the pace of change for African
American seventeen-year-olds continued at the same rate after 1990 as it had
in the preceding generation, the test gap would by now be closed.

Despite a decade of strong economic growth, this did not happen.

Between 1988 and 2004, the achievement of black seventeen-year-olds instead fell by 24 percent of a standard deviation in reading and, after 1990, by 13 percent of a standard deviation in math. Meanwhile, the scores of white seventeen-year-olds remained essentially unchanged. In short, the gap in the final year of schooling, after having closed steadily over a two-decade period, began to open up once again.

The same pattern is evident when one considers the number of years of education received by white and black Americans. As Derek Neal points out in chapter 2, the differences between white and black educational attainment among young adults, both male and female, narrowed decade by decade between 1940 and 1990. But after 1990, he says, "there has been no further closing of these gaps."

The picture for the nine-year-old African Americans is much more encouraging (see figure 1.3). Between 1990 and 2004, their test scores continued to rise by nearly 44 and 47 percent of a standard deviation in reading and math, respectively. The gains were especially steep after 2000 as school accountability systems were being introduced.

The gains by young African American children should be celebrated, if for no other reason than that they clearly demonstrate the malleability of student test-score performance. Hereditary factors cannot explain the rapid closing of the test score gap over a short period of time. And changes in black family life did not need to be wholesale for noticeable gains to be achieved. In short, the pessimists on both the right and left wings of the political spectrum are hard put to explain the progress that once was being made. And if such gains occurred once, there is no reason to think they cannot happen again.

WHY THE TEST SCORE GAP CLOSED— AND THEN OPENED AGAIN FOR SEVENTEEN-YEAR-OLDS

The causes for the narrowing—and then the reopening—of the test score gap among older black students have remained a mystery, partly because their timing runs so contrary to common expectations about what is necessary to achieve racial progress. Consider the milieu in which the test gap closed most rapidly—the 1980s, a decade not normally chosen as the equal opportunity moment in American history. A conservative Republican president, Ronald Reagan, criticized affirmative action, called for higher educational standards, and placed no particular emphasis on reducing racial disparities. Nor was the economic context much better than the overt political one. For the first half of the decade, the economy was lethargic, and poverty rates among families with young children were climbing. Meanwhile, the federal government, in the midst of a large fiscal crisis, was cutting back its level of financial support to local school districts.

In the 1990s, by contrast, equal opportunities were everywhere available. The economy grew more rapidly than in any other postwar decade, black employment opportunities improved, poverty rates fell, and African American leaders were welcomed into the White House with open arms. Although some lower federal courts were placing limits on affirmative action policy, the executive branch of government was actively supporting its extension. Why, then, was this the decade the test-score gap reopened?

A team of researchers led by David Grissmer, in an important article published in 1996, considered the evidence for alternative explanations for the closing of the gap during the 1980s.[9] In their view, changes in family background explained about a third of the reduction in the race gap. Equally or more important were school and societal factors, including opportunities to receive preschool education, smaller size classes, school desegregation, and greater opportunities for African Americans in American society. They gave less attention to the reopening of the gap, since it had only begun to appear at the time of their investigation, but they expressed concern that it might be caused by rising violence among young African Americans.

Although the explanations offered by the Grissmer team deserve careful attention, the topic seems in need of further consideration, especially since stagnation and decline, especially at the high school level, continued after they concluded their research. I turn to that task now. In brief, I suggest that the gains made by young black children have been due primarily to the growing educational capacities of the African American family. The rise and fall of adolescent test scores, however, are due to broader social and cultural changes in society. In the future, the country needs to strengthen its preschool education, encourage further desegregation, hold students accountable, and give black parents greater choice.

Family Background

Family life is known to play a more important role in explaining a child's educational achievement than any school-related factors. Analyses have repeatedly found that mother's education, father's education, the number of siblings in the family (fewer is better), family income, family health care, the number of books in the home, and other, less easily measured characteristics (such as parental relationships with the child) together have a major impact on student achievement. Of all these factors, the educational attainment of the mother seems to be the single most important, because it so directly affects the care the child receives at home.[10]

As Derek Neal points out in chapter 2, differences in black and white family resources remain very large. Still, as can be seen in table 1.1, the family

Table 1.1.   Changes in the Characteristics of Black Families, 1970–2000

Characteristic	1970	1980	1990	2000
Percentage of adults with a high school diploma[a]	33.7	51.2	66.2	78.5
Percentage of adults who completed 4 years of college	4.5	7.9	11.3	16.5
Median household income (in constant 2001 dollars)	24,789	25,788	28,135	34,616
Percentage of children below the poverty level	41.5	42.1	44.2	30.9
Birth rates (per 1,000 adult women)[b]	25.3	21.3	22.4	17.0
Infant mortality rates (per 1,000 births)[b]	32.6	22.2	18	14.1
Average number of children per family[c]	2.48	2.05	1.93	1.85
Percentage of children under 18 living with both parents	58	42	38	36
Percentage of children under 18 living with one parent	32	46	55	53

[a] *Note:* may include recipients of GED.
[b] *Note:* for birth and infant mortality rates: before 1980, based on race of birth; 1980 and after, based on race of mother.
[c] *Note:* approximation.
Sources: National Center for Health Statistics and U.S. Census Bureau.

context in which black children were growing up improved markedly between 1970 and 1990. The percentage of black adults who had a high school degree almost doubled. The percentage who had completed four years of college more than doubled—from 5 percent to 11 percent. Black infant mortality rates were cut by almost one half, indicating that health care for black children was improving as well.

These educational and health gains are offset by a mixed economic picture and by an increase in the number of single-parent families. Black median household income, stagnant during the 1970s, rose by only 9 percent during the next decade. Much of this deterioration in the economic well-being of black families was due to the rise in the number of households headed by a single parent. The percentage of black children living in households headed by two parents dropped from 58 percent in 1970 to 38 percent in 1990.

Still, changes in the most critical factors affecting student achievement were favorable. Trends in black parental education, health care provision, and family size were definitely positive, helping to boost test scores.

In 1990, the educational climate of the family continued to improve. The percentage of black adults with high school diplomas or its GED equivalent reached 79 percent of the population by 2000. College diplomas continued a steady upward trajectory—to 17 percent of the black population. Economically, trends within the black community became decidedly better in the

1990s than they had been in the earlier two decades. Black unemployment fell from 11 percent to 5 percent between 1992 and 2000.[11] Household income for black Americans rose by 23 percent in constant 2001 dollar terms between 1990 and 2000.

Continuing improvements in African American family life translated into higher levels of achievement for their nine-year-old children. Between 1990 and 2004, their reading and math scores both climbed by nearly 50 percent of a standard deviation (figure 1.3). These results are consistent with the findings Roland Fryer and Steven Levitt report in chapter 4. Drawing on data from the nationwide Early Childhood Longitudinal Study, they found that the test scores of very young African Americans (four-year-olds) who were soon to enter kindergarten in 1998 were equivalent to those of white children from similar family backgrounds. This striking finding reveals a clear gain in the educational preparation of young black children since the 1980s, when, according to earlier research, black preschoolers trailed white peers by a larger margin. The finding supports the conclusion that black families are becoming more similar to white families, providing a basis for the optimism expressed in the O'Connor opinion.

The gains by young African American children are not being sustained as they "progress" through school, however. By age thirteen, the gains between 1990 and 2004 have slipped to 9 percent of a standard deviation in reading, though they remained a sizable 40 percent of a standard deviation in math (figure 1.2). But, as mentioned previously, it is the results for the seventeen-year-olds that are the most shocking. After having registered sizable gains by 1988, the test scores of these older adolescents, as of 2004, had dropped by 24 percent of a standard deviation in reading, and, after 1990, by 13 percent of a standard deviation in math (figure 1.1). Contrary to the old adage, the tree, by age seventeen, was not growing in the direction the nine-year-old twig had been bent. To explain this phenomenon one must look beyond the family to broader forces within schools and society.

School Policies

Schools changed in three important ways over the past thirty-five years. Kindergarten and other preschool education were expanded to include a broader segment of the population. More teachers were hired, thereby reducing the size of the typical class. And schools were desegregated, particularly in the South. Of the three factors, school desegregation is the one that contributed the most to gains in student achievement.

Preschool Education

Between 1960 and 1990, preschool enrollment rates increased by as much as 23 percentage points for five-year-olds, and by an even greater amount among four-year-olds.[12] The leading innovation of the period was the federally sponsored Head Start program, which served children from low-income families, particularly those living in minority communities.

Studies have shown that the potential impact of well-designed, resource-rich preschool programs can have a substantial effect on student achievement. But as Ron Haskins points out in chapter 3, Head Start and other, state-run preschool programs often lack an educational focus. Under the control of the social-work community, they have taken socialization as their primary mission, emphasizing playgroup relationships rather than the acquisition of basic skills. As a result, there is little evidence that they have had significant long-term impact on the educational performance of the children participating in them. Haskins's conclusions are quite consistent with those reached by the Grissmer team, who estimated that the spread of preschool programs raised NAEP scores by at best a trivial amount—about 4 to 7 hundredth of a percent of a standard deviation, annually.[13]

Even this may well be a high-end estimate, especially when one considers the Fryer-Levitt findings in chapter 4. As mentioned previously, they found that black and white four-year-olds had similar test scores in the late 1990s once family background characteristics were taken into account. But the test-score gap increased after the child entered kindergarten and first grade, a disconcerting change that cannot be explain by family background characteristics. Something in school was adversely affecting black performance relative to that of their white peers. If this was true in earlier decades as well, then it is difficult to attribute NAEP gains to the spread of kindergarten and other preschool education.

This does not mean that preschool education is necessarily harmful to black children. On the contrary, there is good evidence that they benefit from well-designed, effectively administered, educationally focused programs. But such programs do not yet exist on a large scale.

School Resources

Nor is there much evidence that the larger investment in elementary and secondary education has yielded much of an achievement dividend. This, despite the fact that per pupil expenditures on public elementary and secondary education in the United States grew (in real dollars that are adjusted for inflation) from $4,500 in 1970 to nearly $9,500 in 2000, a 111 percent increase which more than doubled the nation's public investment in its schools. Growth during the 1970s was at a 27 percent clip; during the 1980s, it was at a 33 percent rate; and during the 1990s, growth continued by another 24 percent.[14] In other words, the growth rate was fairly constant throughout the entire period. Per pupil expenditures did not vary significantly by ethnic group during this period, so it may be assumed that the overall increase in educational investment applied more or less equally to black and white students alike.[15]

As Derek Neal points out in chapter 2, there is little evidence that these increases in school expenditure translated into higher student performance. The finding is less surprising than it seems. For one thing, much of the school dollar is spent on transportation, food lunch programs, health services, ancillary services, compliance with federal and state regulations, and other activities that have little direct connection to student learning. Much of the remainder has been allocated toward augmenting the number of teachers relative to the number of pupils.

Class Size

The sheer number of teachers increased dramatically in the closing decades of the twentieth century. The average of number of pupils per teacher fell from 22.5 in 1970 to seventeen in 1990, a number that remained essentially unchanged through 1998.[16] Put more concretely, in 1998, there were nearly three teachers for every fifty students (as compared to around two teachers for fifty students in 1970). To pay for the extra teacher, without reducing teacher salaries, required a near 50 percent increase in expenditure. The decline in class size seems to have been about the same for black and white students alike.[17]

Grissmer and his colleagues believe that "smaller classes are clearly a viable candidate for explaining some part of the black NAEP gains and some part of the reduction in the black-white gap."[18] This view is supported by an often-cited Tennessee experiment that found positive effects of class size reduction on the achievement of black students in kindergarten and first grade.[19] However, other studies have been unable to replicate consistently the Tennessee findings.[20] In California, for example, class size was reduced significantly without registering any material gains in student performance.[21] Moreover, in 1990, class size stopped falling, but the scores of both white and black nine-year-olds continued to rise. In short, there is scant evidence that black gains were materially affected by changes in class size.

Teacher Salaries

Had more money been allocated to higher salaries for teachers, and had that money been allocated in such a way as to attract high-quality young people into the teaching profession, it is possible that achievement gains could have been realized with the great increase in public expenditure that occurred during the latter part of the twentieth century.[22] But despite the 111 percent increase in school expenditure between 1970 and 2000, teacher salaries in inflation-adjusted dollars remained surprisingly constant. Overall, teacher salaries just kept pace with the wages of all other workers in the United States. As compared to other college graduates, teacher salaries fell—from roughly being 20 percent lower than the average college graduates' salary in 1970 to being 30 percent lower by 2000.[23]

Because average teacher salaries remained fairly constant relative to other occupations, there is little reason to expect gains in student performance from enhanced teacher quality. On the contrary, quality was slipping over the time period, especially at the high school level, because the highest-quality women teachers in 2000 were being paid much less relative to the average teacher salary than their counterparts had been paid in the early 1960s.[24]

More importantly, teachers are paid according to a standardized schedule that today (unlike the past) includes both elementary and secondary teachers. That schedule is subject to a collective bargaining process in which teacher unions play a major role. Except in unusual circumstances, unions oppose differentiated pay—whether for high-quality teaching, hardship conditions, special need for subject matter coverage (math, science, computer science, and so forth), or any other purpose a school administration might deem appropriate. Since there is little connection between teacher pay and school productivity, the great increase in school expenditure has had little impact on student performance.

School Desegregation

The benefits from racial integration may have been greater. Racial segregation dropped noticeably during the seventies, and shortly thereafter test scores rose noticeably.[25] David Armor points out in chapter 5 that desegregation could have positive effects either as the result of increasing interracial contact or by reducing the negative cultural concomitants of extreme racial isolation, a point I develop further below. Armor finds some evidence that extreme concentrations have negative impacts, a finding reinforced by the recent, well-designed study by Hanushek and his coauthors.[26] Yet after carefully reviewing patterns of desegregation state by state, Armor does not find consistently positive benefits from desegregated settings. The benefits should be much more apparent, given the length of time the intervention has been in place. The final word on this subject is certainly yet to be written. But, clearly, racial segregation cannot account for the recent decline of the test scores of high schoolers. Since 1990, there has been little change in the degree of racial separation.[27]

Broader Social and Cultural Changes

Brown, by inducing broader changes in the racial climate of the country, could nonetheless have contributed to the earlier gains in black student performance that took place during the 1980s. As the Grissmer team put it: "These changes may have signaled to black parents and students nationwide, and also to their teachers, that black children's education was a national priority."[28] Such broad social cultural changes can have more dramatic impacts on adolescents than on either older adults or young children. Adults are settled in their ways, and families shelter children from broad social forces. But teenagers, eager to assert their independence and eager to develop and sustain friendships among their peers, respond to the changing fads and fancies of the time. Style changes in popular music, clothing, and eating habits first sweep through teenage culture and only later penetrate into adult society. Even the acquisition of partisan political identification is age dependent. In moments of change, it is the first-time voter—typically the young adult emerging from adolescence—that is most likely to swing with momentary changes in the public mood. It was the new voter, more than any other, who brought Franklin Delano Roosevelt to power in 1932, Ronald Reagan to office in 1980, and revived the Democratic party under Bill Clinton in 1992.

The civil rights movement, especially, was a young person's political stimulant, one that excited hope for the future in a generation of young black Americans unlike any that had preceded it. The young civil rights movement demanded equal rights and equal opportunities, the chance to perform on an equal playing field. Initially, the movement encountered intense resistance, especially in the South, but it broke down with stronger federal interventions to desegregate schools in the early seventies. Finally, with the election in 1976 of Jimmy Carter, a southerner who nonetheless won support in the South from Whites and Blacks alike, equal opportunity seemed at hand, giving energy and hope to young black Americans.

Initially, the role models for young black Americans were hard-working, well-educated political leaders, such as Thurgood Marshall and Martin Luther King, Jr., whose life and accomplishments implied that success came only from hard work, sacrifice and struggle. The message was reinforced by Ronald Reagan's emphasis on individual responsibility. It was during these years that black adolescent test scores shot up at a faster rate than did the scores of younger children, reaching their high-water mark in 1988. In reading, the black-white test gap among seventeen-year-olds closed by more than one-half during the 1970s and 1980s, even while that of black nine-year-olds was closing by only a third.

After 1988, new cultural influences became dominant. The most noteworthy African American success stories were to be found not in the business community but in the world of entertainment—sports figures, rap musicians, TV personalities, and Hollywood film stars. Rewards seemed to go at least as frequently to the provocative and outrageous as to the hard-working and responsible.

Meanwhile, affirmative action and racial preferences gradually received broader acceptance. Before the 1978 *Bakke* decision, affirmative action was contested ground. *Bakke* itself said that racial quotas could not be imposed. But by permitting other forms of affirmative action under the rubric of diversity, special arrangements for minorities spread through the political, educational, and workforce worlds. Even the Reagan administration's Department of Justice took the position that racial background should be used to help define district boundaries (for the quite cynical reason that, by doing so, Democrats were concentrated in particular districts, giving Republicans more opportunity elsewhere). Unfortunately, racial districting meant that black candidates typically ran in all-black electoral districts, forcing them to pitch their appeals to a distinctive constituency instead of building broader white-black coalitions. Pulled to the political extreme, black political leaders could not rise to higher office, a U.S. Senate seat, the gubernatorial chair, or other statewide position. With no highly visible elected leaders available, the door was left open to flamboyant civil rights activists, most notably Jesse Jackson and Al Sharpton, to provide political role models for the young black adults of the 1990s.

The distinction between diversity and quotas drawn by Powell in *Bakke* became a distinction without a difference. During the Bush and Clinton administrations, minority contractors were given bidding advantages on federal contracts, an advantage often exploited by large corporate interests who teamed up with minority firms organized for the purpose. Also, specific numerical targets were used to determine whether colleges and businesses had complied with civil rights laws. Despite the *Bakke* decision, the University of Michigan decided that it could legally give a specific numerical advantage to those from minority backgrounds in its college admission procedures. It was hardly the only institution of higher learning to do so. Equal rights had been transformed into special arrangements.

All of these steps may have been at first necessary to create a level playing field for African Americans. All may have initially provided the equal opportunity that stimulated learning among black adolescents during the 1980s. But for how long could these practices be sustained without undermining the very advances that the civil rights movement had generated? Was Sandra Day O'Connor correct in saying that affirmative action, if perpetuated for too long, becomes pernicious? Have the unanticipated consequences already begun? Is the drop in black achievement after 1988 rooted in political and cultural changes that at first seemed to foster it?

The answer to this difficult question remains murky. For one thing, there are competing explanations for the decline in black adolescent test scores. The one set forth in Derek Neal's chapter focuses on the rising violence of the early 1990s, a period when the homicide rate among black male teenagers doubled. Between 1988 and 1993, murder victimization rates among black males aged fourteen to seventeen increased from 43 to 76 per 100,000. For those aged eighteen to twenty-four, the increase was from 109 to 184 per 100,000. With higher levels of violence, the incarceration rates of young black males, especially those without a high school education, escalated to a new high. This more violent world, aggravated by the increasing use of extreme drugs (especially "crack"), could have suppressed adolescent achievement.

Neal's findings are significant, but it should also be noted that after reaching their high-water mark in 1993, black male youth victimization rates quickly reversed direction, so that by 2000 it was back down to lower than its 1988 level—twenty-six per 100,000 for the younger age group, one hunderd per 100,000 for the older one.[29] Yet black adolescent achievement continued to slip throughout the 1990s and beyond.

What did not change during the nineties and the beginning of the twenty-first century were other debilitating changes in youth culture that have undermined student learning. Hollywood films, youth-oriented television, the recording industry, and popular fashions have continued to express open hostility to the school, the teacher, the classroom, and the hard-working nerd. The street-smart, the rebellious, the drug-dependent, the gang leader, and the drop-out remained the celebrated, the anti-heroes now worthy of hero worship.

That culture penetrates into the neighborhood school by means of the adolescent peer group. Although these forces are at work in their most debilitating form within the central-city school, they are not limited to this milieu. As Harvard scholar Ronald Ferguson has shown, the peer pressures that dissuade black high schoolers from studying are prevalent even among adolescents from middle- and upper-middle-income families.[30] Too often, high performance is acceptable only if it does not require much work. Though similar pressures are undoubtedly present within white youth culture as well, the anti-educational pressures are more intense for African Americans.[31]

These broad social forces are undoubtedly more powerful than any government policy, even one with as broad implications as affirmative action. The danger remains, though, that the longer affirmative action policy remains in place, the more certainly it reinforces a culture that does not place the responsibility for success squarely on the shoulders of the individual. If rewards are allocated according to something other than merit, a youth culture will notice and respond accordingly. It must be hoped that progress will be made toward closing the test gap before the policy, by itself, creates a continuing need for its own perpetuation.

TWO STEPS FORWARD

Two kinds of policies—school accountability and school choice—have been proposed to help achieve that end. Both contain the promise of isolating learning in school from more debilitating influences in the larger society. Can either succeed?

School and Student Accountability

In 2002, with the passage of NCLB, the federal government has asked states to test all students annually in reading, math, and science in grades three through eight and, again, in tenth grade. Each school must show progress on these tests toward a state-determined level of proficiency. It is too soon to evaluate the consequences of the federal law. But a number of pioneering states and school districts had previously established their own accountability programs. In chapter 6, Margaret Raymond and Eric Hanushek report that NAEP math scores in these pioneering states rose more rapidly than in states without accountability systems.[32] However, the gains for black students trailed those for white students, so these accountability systems, though they fostered gains for all students, did not help close the test-score gap.

This may not be the end of the story, however. Unlike most of the early state accountability programs studied by Raymond-Hanushek, the federal law requires progress by students of all ethnic groups, African Americans included. By requiring a more specific focus on black achievement than early accountability systems, the new legislation may be focusing school energies where they are most badly needed. This, along with favorable trends in black family life, could help explain the recent rapid rise in the test scores among nine-year-old African Americans.

Unfortunately, NCLB, for all of its promise, has serious missing links. Its sanctions for nonperformance lack bite. It is more focused on elementary and middle school than on the high school, where educational problems are concentrated. More importantly, the law does not hold students accountable for their own performance. NCLB instead reinforces the image that students are objects to be manipulated, not people who need to acquire a sense of discipline, responsibility, and self-respect.

Holding students accountable is particularly important as they enter middle and high school. Given the strength of the anti-learning peer group culture, only well-defined measures are likely to be effective. If students are held to an externally determined standard, and if that standard is substantially meaningful, in the sense that it can affect job prospects and higher education opportunities, then students, guided by teachers, parents, and friends, can be motivated to reach higher levels of achievement. To be effective, the test must have multiple performance levels that can challenge students across the ability range. Although minimal standards may be effective for challenging those with the most limited skills, only a multiplicity of performance levels, each with their own rewards, are likely to change the learning culture of the high school. Once such standards are put into place, teachers become coaches instead of regulators, friends may turn into helpmates rather than competitors, and parents may be utilized as sources of information rather than contact points to be avoided.

Such graduation examinations are well known in many European countries. Students are expected to pass examinations in particular subjects at specific levels, if they are to receive certificates of accomplishment that carry significant weight in colleges and job markets. In the United States, the New York State regency exam has functioned in a similar way. In other states, even less demanding tests have generated higher levels of student achievement.[33] If NCLB is to achieve its goals, it needs to be revised so as to hold students themselves accountable.

School Choice

Student accountability will be even more effective, if parents are given more choice over the school their child attends. According to market theory, school voucher programs that cover the cost of schooling at the public or private school of a family's choice can be expected to yield large educational dividends. When parents select the school their child attends, schools must compete for students. Effective schools are in demand, while ineffective ones lose students and eventually disappear, unless they upgrade their offerings. Currently, private schools are the closest available approximation to this theoretical ideal.

Given market theory, it is surprising that Patrick Wolf in chapter 7 finds little evidence that a private school education yields much of a dividend for white students. The educational benefits from private schooling—higher test scores, higher graduation rates, better wages later in life—are modest, if detectable at all. (Despite this, a private school may still be desired by white families for the cultural and spiritual values it imparts.) For black families, however, private schooling yields large educational gains—higher test scores, higher graduation rates, and long-term economic benefits. Similar results are obtained from studies of a number of school voucher programs.[34]

In chapter 7, Wolf attributes the larger benefits for African Americans to the fact that they have less choice within the U.S. public school system. Access to public schools in the United States is determined by the school district and neighborhood in which one lives. When choosing a neighborhood in which to live, Whites have a wide range of choice, Blacks a more restricted one. As a result, any new choice program, such as school vouchers, is likely to benefit African Americans disproportionately.

School vouchers also provide an opportunity to change the anti-learning culture of the high school. Currently, street culture penetrates many neighborhood high schools because these schools are shaped more by peer groups than adult educational objectives. Schools of choice can establish barriers that separate the school from the more perverse influences within the community. Just as the family chooses the school, so the school chooses the student. Since no student has a right to attend a particular school, the student is obligated to conform to the educational expectations and practices of the school the family has chosen. Otherwise, the student can be asked to leave. It does not take many such instances for a school to communicate its expectations to all students. A soft voice, backed by a big stick, is more effective discipline than explicit regulation, monitoring, and harassment. All of these considerations make the private setting an especially attractive haven for learning, especially among African Americans threatened by a seductive but pernicious peer group culture.

Given the differential impact of school choice on Blacks and Whites, the policy innovation holds great promise for closing the test-score gap. Currently, there are three types of government-sponsored school choice programs in the United States—public school choice, charter schools, and small school voucher programs. None are yet large enough to provide a range of options that black parents need, if achievement gains are to be realized. Public school choice is supposedly available to all parents attending schools deemed to be failing by NCLB, but school districts are sharply limiting parental choices—as well as information about those choices.[35] Charter schools—institutions that are privately operated under a government charter—are found in over thirty states, but less than a million (out of over 50 million) students are attending them. In only a few places are there enough charter schools to offer significant competition to public schools in the vicinity. And, finally, government-funded voucher schools can be found only in Milwaukee, Cleveland, Florida, and the District of Columbia. In all four places, the size of the program is small, and the impact on the larger educational environment incidental. Opposition to the formation of additional programs is intense. Unfortunately, school choice is currently too circumscribed to make much of a contribution to the closing of the education gap.

CONCLUSION: THE POLITICAL QUESTION

Ironically, the programs that hold the greatest promise to the closing of the education gap are the very ones that are politically most difficult to introduce. Some policies—greater expenditure, class size reduction, and school accountability—have won general acceptance. But none have shown much promise of closing the test-score gap among high school students. Educationally focused preschooling, school desegregation, student accountability, and parental choice, on the other hand, have much greater promise. Yet all four have encountered strong resistance from vested interests.

Appropriately designed preschool education is opposed by the social work community within which the Head Start program is embedded. Inter-district desegregation programs have little legal or public support. The opposition to student accountability is also intense, unless exam standards are low enough to enable nearly all students to pass. Finally, school vouchers and large-scale charter school interventions face the bitter resistance of teacher unions and school board associations.

In the end, one cannot be particularly optimistic about the chance of realizing the O'Connor vision of the future, a world in which affirmative action is no longer necessary because talent will be distributed without any particular connection to ethnic background. But the problem is neither heredity nor even environment, despite continuing differences in black and white family life. Nor is it a lack of knowledge. In chapter 8, Chester Finn, after reviewing the evidence previously set forth, provides a roadmap, which, if followed, would bring the country's educational and political leaders many miles down the path they need to travel.

In the end, the problem is political. To assemble the necessary political will is the task of the next generation. Perhaps that is the reason Justice O'Connor chose a time limit of twenty-five years.

NOTES

1. NAEP participation rates have been drifting downward in recent years. Also, since 1999, some students have been given special accommodations, which may enhance test scores. These changes could account for some of the recent rise in student test score performance. If so, then the trends described in the text could be more optimistic than the underlying reality.

NAEP tests have been administered in other subject areas as well, but not as frequently. Results from these tests are ignored here, both because these tests add little additional information concerning overall trends and, given the lesser experience with their construction, they may be less precise.

2. The standard deviation used to calculate the reported estimated gains for each ethnic group is the same—the average standard deviation for students of that age group in the subject for the testing period, 1970 to 1999. For specific information, see Paul E. Peterson, "Little Gain in Student Achievement," in *Our Schools and Our Future*, Paul E. Peterson, ed. (Stanford, CA: Hoover Institution Press, 2003), figures 3–5, pp. 50–53.

3. Sanders Korenman and Christopher Winship, "A Reanalysis of the Bell Curve: Intelligence, Family Background, and Schooling," in *Meritocracy and Economic Inequality*, Kenneth Arrow, Samuel Bowles, and Stephen Durlauf, eds. (Princeton, NJ: Princeton University Press, 1999), pp. 137–178. See also Christopher Winship and Sanders D. Korenman, "Economic Success and the Evolution of Schooling and Mental Ability," in *Earning and Learning, How Schools Matter*, Susan

Mayer and Paul E. Peterson, eds. (Washington, DC: Brookings Institution Press, 1999), pp. 49–78.

4. Christopher Jencks and Meredith Phillips, "The Black-White Test Score Gap: An Introduction," in *The Black-White Test Score Gap*, Christopher Jencks and Meredith Phillips, eds. (Washington, DC: Brookings Institution Press, 1998), pp. 1–52.

5. Jencks and Phillips, "The Black-White Test Score Gap," pp. 3–4.

6. Richard J. Herrnstein and Charles Murray, *The Bell Curve: Intelligence and Class Structure in American Life* (New York: Free Press, 1994).

7. Richard Rothstein, *Class and Schools: Using Social, Economic, and Educational Reform to Close the Black-White Achievement Gap* (Washington, DC: Economic Policy Institute, 2004).

8. The time periods are different, because NAEP math and reading tests were being administered in different years.

9. David Grissmer, Ann Flanagan, and Stephanie Williamson, "Why Did the Black-White Score Gap Narrow in the 1970s and 1980s?" in Jencks and Phillips, pp. 182–228.

10. James S. Coleman et al., *Equality of Educational Opportunity* (Washington, DC: Government Printing Office, 1966). See, for example, chapters in Jencks and Phillips, *The Black-White Test Score Gap*, and Karl R. White, "The Relation between Socioeconomic Status and Academic Achievement," *Psychological Bulletin* 91 (May 1982):461–481.

11. U.S. Bureau of the Census, *Statistical Abstract of the United States*, 2003, table 626.

12. Grissmer, Flanagan and Williamson, "Why Did the Black-White Score Gap Narrow," p. 203.

13. *Ibid.*

14. Caroline M. Hoxby, "What Has Changed and What Has Not," in Peterson, *Our Schools, Our Future*, figure 19, p. 102.

15. See chapter 4 by Fryer and Levitt.

16. Hoxby, "What Has Changed," figure 2.1, p. 105.

17. See chapter 2 by Neal and chapter 4 by Fryer and Levitt.

18. Grissmer, Flanagan, and Williamson, "Why Did the Black-White Score Gap Narrow," p. 216.

19. Alan B. Krueger, "Experimental Estimates of Education Production Functions," *Quarterly Journal of Economics* 114 no. 2 (May 1999): 497–532.

20. Eric Hanushek, "The Economics of Schooling: Production and Efficiency in Public Schools," *Journal of Economic Literature* 24, no. 3 (1986): 1141–1177; Caroline M. Hoxby, "The Effects of Class Size on Student Achievement: New Evidence from Population Variation," *Quarterly Journal of Economics* 115, no. 4 (2000):1239–1285. For a review of recent research see Eric A. Hanushek, "Publicly Provided Education," in *Handbook of Public Finance*, A. Auerbach and M. Feldstein, eds. (Amsterdam: North Holland, forthcoming). See also Eric A. Hanushek, "Comments," in *Inequality in America: What Role for Human Capital Policies?*, Benjamin M. Friedman, ed. (Cambridge, MA: MIT Press, 2003), pp. 260–265.

21. Brian M. Stecher, Daniel F. McCaffrey, and Delia Bugliari, "The Relationship between Exposure to Class Size Reduction and Student Achievement in California," *Education Policy Analysis Archives* 11, no. 40 (November 2003).

22. Susannah Loeb and John Bound, "The Effects of Measured School Input on Academic Achievement: Evidence from the 1920s, 1930s and 1940s Birth Cohorts," *Review of Economics and Statistics* 78, no. 4 (1996):653–654.

23. Hoxby, "What Has Changed," figures 17 and 18, pp. 96–100.

24. Caroline M. Hoxby and Andrew Leigh, "Wage Distortion: Why America's Top Women College Graduates Aren't Teaching," *Education Next* 2 (Spring 2005): 50–56.

25. John T. Yun and Sean F. Reardon, "Trends in Public School Segregation in the South 1987–2000," paper presented at the Resegregation of Southern Schools Conference (Chapel Hill: University of North Carolina), August 30, 2002.

26. Eric A. Hanushek et al., "Does Peer Ability Affect Student Achievement?" *Journal of Applied Econometrics* 18, no. 5 (September/October 2003):527–544. Desegregation appears to have reduced high school dropout rates. See Johann Guryan, "Desegregation and Black Dropout Rates," National Bureau of Economic Research Working Paper No. 8345, June 2001.

27. Charles T. Clotfelter, *After* Brown: *The Rise and Retreat of School Desegregation* (Princeton, NJ: Princeton University Press, 2004). Although the widely quoted study of the Harvard Civil Rights Project claims to find rising levels of segregation in the 1990s, its analysis leaves much to be desired. See Erica Frankenberg, Chungmei Lee, and Gary Orfield, "A Multiracial Society with Segregated Schools: Are We Losing the Dream?" The Civil Rights Project, Harvard University, Cambridge, MA, 2003. The study fails to consider that the U.S. schools have become increasingly multiethnic and that the white population is becoming a smaller proportion of the total. If one looks at the percentage of black Americans in schools with other ethnic groups, recent trends are upward, not downward.

28. Grissmer, Flanagan and Williamson, "Why Did the Black-White Score Gap Narrow," p. 211.

29. U.S. Department of Justice, "Homicide trends in the United States." www.ojp.usdoj.gov/bjs/homicide

30. Ronald F. Ferguson, "A Diagnostic Analysis of Black-White GPA Disparities in Shaker Heights, Ohio," in *Brookings Papers on Education Policy 2001*, Diane Ravitch, ed. (Washington, DC: Brookings Institution Press, 2001), pp. 347–414. Also, see John Ogbu, "Opportunity Structure, Cultural Boundaries, and Literacy," in *Language, Literacy and Culture: Issues of Society and Schooling*, Judith Langer, ed. (Norwood, NJ: Ablex, 1987), pp. 149–177.

31. Roland G. Fryer, Jr. and David Austen-Smith, "An Economic Analysis of 'Acting White,'" Department of Economics, Harvard University, February 28, 2005; Roland G. Fryer, Jr., "'Acting White,'" *Education Next* 5, no. 1 (Winter 2006); John Ogbu and Herbert D. Simons, "Voluntary and Involuntary Minorities: A Cultural-Ecological Theory of School Performance with Some Implications for Education," *Anthropology and Education Quarterly* 29 (1998):155–188; John Ogbu, "Differences in Cultural Frame of Reference," *International Journal of Behavioral Development* 16, no. 3 (1993):483–506.

32. Given data availability, it was not possible to estimate accountability impacts on reading scores.

33. Ludger Woessman, "Central Exit Exams and Student Achievement: Interna-

tional Evidence," in *No Child Left Behind?*, Paul E. Peterson and Martin R. West, eds. (Washington, DC: Brookings Institution Press, 2003), pp. 292–324; John H. Bishop, "Nerd Harassment, Incentives, School Priorities, and Learning," in *Earning and Learning: How Schools Matter*, Susan E. Mayer and Paul E. Peterson, eds. (Washington, DC: Brookings Institution Press, 1999), pp. 231–280; ACHIEVE, "Do Graduation Tests Measure Up? A Closer Look at State High School Exit Exams," Report of the American Diplomacy Project, 2004.

34. William G. Howell and Paul E. Peterson, with David E. Campbell and Patrick J. Wolf, *The Education Gap* (Washington, DC: Brookings Institution Press, 2002).

35. Paul E. Peterson, "A Conflict of Interest: District Regulation of School Choice and Supplemental Services," in *Within Our Reach: How America Can Educate Every Child*, John E. Chubb, ed. (Lanham, MD: Rowman and Littlefield, 2005).

2

How Families and Schools Shape the Achievement Gap

Derek Neal, University of Chicago and NBER

INTRODUCTION

The fiftieth anniversary of the *Brown* decision is an appropriate time for reflection on and analysis of the educational experiences of black Americans. However, the reasons to be engaged in such work go far beyond proper awareness of an important historical event or an associated desire to understand how this event shaped our country. Many statistics suggest that now, more than at any time since the *Brown* decision, there are reasons to worry that progress toward racial equality in educational outcomes is not inevitable.

During the late 1980s and early 1990s, an important period of convergence in black-white test scores came to a halt, and for more than a decade, black children have either gained no ground or fallen farther behind their white counterparts in reading and math. The NAEP Long Term Trend (NAEP-LTT) data track performance in several subjects using exams that provide comparable assessments of specific sets of knowledge and skills. Data are available for selected years from 1971 through 1999. In the first reading assessment in 1971, the black-white gap in reading scores was −1.04 standard deviations among nine-year-olds and −1.08 standard deviations among thirteen-year-olds. Reading scores for black youth improved notably from 1971 to 1988 both in levels and relative to white scores. Black score gains were particularly dramatic among thirteen-year-olds, and in 1988, the black-white reading gap among thirteen-year-olds was just over one half of a standard deviation in absolute value. Since 1988, reading scores for black children have fallen, while scores for white children have risen slightly. During the 1990s, the black-white gap in reading scores ranged from roughly −.7 to −.9.

The long-term trend data on math scores follow a similar pattern. Math scores among black youth improved dramatically between 1978 and 1986. During this period, the black-white gap in math scores among thirteen-year-olds shrank in size from −1.08 to −.79, and the corresponding gap among nine-year-olds shrank in size from −.88 to −.74. However, black-white gaps in math scores among nine- and thirteen-year-olds widened slightly after 1986. In the 1990s, the black-white gap in age nine math scores ranged from −.74 to −.82 standard deviations, and the black-white gap in age thirteen scores ranged from −.87 to −.98.[1]

Since 1990, black-white gaps in attainment among young adults have also remained constant at best and may have widened.[2] The U.S. Census began collecting data on individual educational attainment in 1940, and in every census year from 1940 to 1990, each new cohort of black adults came closer and closer to the attainment level of their white peers, but this trend came to a halt in 1990. In 1940, the black-white attainment gap among persons ages twenty-six to thirty was 3.5 years of schooling.[3] In 1990, the black-white gaps in years of completed schooling among adults ages twenty-six to thirty were −.45 among women and −.66 among men, but there has been no further closing of these gaps. In 2000, these gaps were −.62 among women and −.72 among men.

The recent stability or possible widening of measured black-white gaps in education and skills is striking because the parents, grandparents, and great grandparents of today's black children all acquired more education and skills, relative to Whites, than the generations before them. In 1990, social scientists could look back on more than fifty years of progress toward educational parity between black and white young adults. The possibility that this process may have stopped is noteworthy because less skilled workers generally, and less skilled black workers in particular, appear to face bleak prospects in today's labor market. Table 2.1 presents data from recent census files concerning the experiences of young adult men, ages twenty-one to thirty. Each cell contains two numbers. The top is the percentage of men who were working or enrolled in school at the time of their census interview. The bottom is the percentage of men who were institutionalized on their interview date. The vast majority of these institutionalized men were incarcerated. Total rates of idleness and incarceration increased dramatically among black men during the 1980–2000 period both in absolute terms and relative to Whites. However, the truly unprecedented outcomes reported in table 2.1 apply to men who are both black and less educated. In 2000, roughly one in four black men ages twenty-one to thirty did not have a high

Table 2.1. Percentage of Black and White Young Male Adults Working (or in School) and Institutionalized by Level of Education, 1980–2000

			1980	1990	2000
Less than High School	White	Working[a]	75.8%	76.6%	70.6%
		Institutionalized	3.6	4.3	5.4
	Black	Working[a]	56.6	48.3	41.3
		Institutionalized	10.6	19.1	27.6
High School	White	Working[a]	88.1%	88.5%	84.1%
		Institutionalized	0.8	1.6	2.6
	Black	Working[a]	75.8	73.0	62.7
		Institutionalized	3.8	7.5	10.9
Some College	White	Working[a]	94.4%	95.0%	93.7%
		Institutionalized	0.5	0.9	0.8
	Black	Working[a]	86.1	85.8	81.3
		Institutionalized	2.8	5.9	5.9
College	White	Working[a]	96.1%	96.6%	95.6%
		Institutionalized	0.2	0.1	0.2
	Black	Working[a]	90.9	94.1	90.6
		Institutionalized	0.7	0.9	1.1

[a] *Notes:* or in school.
Sources: Data are from the decennial census IPUMS 1980–2000. The table displays the fraction of men working or in school in the census reference week and the fraction of men institutionalized. Individuals with allocated age, sex or race have been dropped from the sample. Sample weights "perwt" are used for year 2000.

school credential. Among these men, only about four in ten were employed or attending school and over one in four were institutionalized.[4]

In my recent work, I compared the overall distributions of math and reading skills among black and white youth using several different data sets collected at different points in time. In all data sets that I examined, a significant fraction of black youth post reading and math scores that place them in the very bottom percentiles of the corresponding white test score distributions. Thus, one expects that black adult high school dropouts in the 2000 census possessed levels of basic math and reading skills that were quite low relative to population averages. The high degree of idleness and imprisonment among less skilled black males suggests that, over time, the interaction between the persistence of the black-white skill gap and the rising relative demand for skilled workers in our economy has created a crisis in the black community.

Before going further, let me state that I take as well established the proposition that both educational attainment and the cognitive skills measured by achievement tests are malleable among both black and white youth. The black-white gap in attainment closed dramatically during the past century, and the NAEP-LTT data clearly show that group differences in the distribution of cognitive test scores can change notably over a relatively short period. With respect to data on individual test scores, several recent studies show that schooling directly affects performance on cognitive tests, and the literature on early childhood interventions shows that high-quality programs can have large and lasting impacts on academic achievement among black youth.[5]

The experience of the past decade is the exception and not the rule. Most economic models of the intergenerational transmission of human capital predict that a given intragroup difference in human capital will diminish over successive generations. In 1900, centuries of slavery and oppression placed Blacks far behind Whites not only in terms of financial wealth but also in terms of human capital. Yet, throughout most of the twentieth century, Blacks made steady progress toward closing this human capital gap, and much of this progress occurred during periods when most Blacks still attended schools that were separate and far from equal in terms of per-pupil resources. In the 1980s, social scientists did not and could not have predicted the stability of black-white skill gaps during the 1990s.

In 2054, on the hundredth anniversary of the *Brown* decision, the 1990s may be viewed as only a temporary pause in the process of skill convergence between black and white Americans. Nonetheless, it is fitting at this time to evaluate what we know and do not know about black-white differences in how families invest in children and how these differences affect black-white skill gaps among adults.

In economics, three types of investment models dominate the literature that explores why a black child may acquire fewer skills than a white child with comparable intellectual capacities. The first I refer to as "self-fulfilling prophecy" models. In these models, Blacks do not invest in skills because employers are known to assume that all Blacks are generally less likely to be skilled. In equilibrium, employer stereotypes are confirmed precisely because black youth make their investment decisions with the expectation that employers will statistically discriminate against them based on their race. These models do not provide a compelling explanation for skill deficits among black youth because they miss an important feature of the data. They require that the actual gain from investing in skills must be lower for Blacks than Whites. However, there is no evidence that this is true in existing data on skills and labor market outcomes. Wage, employment, and earnings gaps between black and white workers are smallest among groups of workers who are highly skilled and well educated, and this has been true for decades.[6]

A second class of models highlights the fact that black families and other economically disadvantaged groups may invest less than is optimal in their children's human capital simply because their families are credit constrained. No market exists that allows economically disadvantaged families to take out loans to pay for tutoring, private schools, a house in a better school district, or other educational expenditures based on the promise that the children who benefit from these expenditures will repay these loans as adults. For wealthy families, this is not an issue because they can finance these investments out of their savings.[7]

A third and more troubling possibility is that, holding potential family income constant, there may exist black-white differences in norms that hinder investment in black children. Two-parent families are now the exception and not the rule in black communities, and this may harm black children. Weiss and Willis[8] describe a particular benefit of two-parent families. When both parents live with their children, they can more effectively coordinate investments in children. When parents live apart, each parent cannot determine whether or not the other parent is devoting time and money to his or her own private consumption that should be devoted to investments in children. This monitoring problem hinders effective coordination and resource sharing among parents and reduces levels of investment in children, regardless of the level of resources that each parent enjoys.

I present evidence below that black-white skill gaps are evident even among young children. Thus, I adopt the working hypothesis that black-white skill gaps result from different investment behavior by groups of parents who differ with respect to their wealth and their access to educational opportunities for their children. My goal here is to spell out the factors that shape black-white differences in human capital investments and discuss how public policy may affect the acquisition of skills among black youth. The next section describes resource levels in public schools and discusses differences in the school resources available to black students versus white students. The following section explores black-white differences in family resources. A final section discusses how various public policies may influence the black-white skill gap by affecting racial differences in investments in children.

PUBLIC SCHOOLS

The process of convergence in school quality between black and white children was well under way before 1954. Margo[9] provides a history of black schooling from 1880 through 1950. He shows that between 1890 and 1910 black schools in the South suffered considerable losses in relative funding compared to white schools. Thus, by 1910, class sizes in black schools were often 50 percent greater than class sizes in white schools in the same state, and on average, term lengths were significantly shorter in black schools. Margo notes that black schools did gain more resources after 1910, but he points to the 1930s as the decade when a process of gradual convergence in school quality between black and white children began.

Card and Krueger[10] focus on measured school quality in a sample of segregated states that contained the vast majority of black children during the first half of the twentieth century. They document a brief period of improvement in relative black school quality between 1915 and the early 1920s, but like Margo, they identify the 1930s as the beginning of permanent improvements in relative school quality for black children. Donohue, Heckman, and Todd[11] document how private philanthropy enhanced the absolute quality of black schools during the 1920s, but they also conclude that sustained improvement in the relative quality of black schools began in the 1930s.

Boozer, Krueger, and Wolkon[12] (BKW) explore changes in public school resources after the *Brown* decision. They draw several conclusions. The first is that there is no discernable break in the trend toward convergence between black and white pupil-teacher ratios in 1954. The decade prior to 1954 and the decade after 1954 saw the same rates of progress toward closing the black-white gap in pupil teacher ratios. Taking the evidence from the literature as a whole, it appears that, with respect to standard quality measures such as term length, per-pupil expenditure and class size, black children experienced steady school quality gains relative to white children from the mid-1930s until some point in the 1970s or early 1980s, when black children reached near parity with white children on these dimensions of school quality.

Grogger[13] reports that by 1980, black and white students attended schools that were quite similar with respect to measured dimensions of quality such as term length, pupil-teacher ratios, and the prevalence of teachers with advanced degrees. Using data from the 1989 Common Core data on public schools, BKW calculate pupil-teacher ratios that describe the average class size experienced by black and white children under the assumption that class sizes are constant within schools. They report average pupil teacher ratios of 18.3 for white students and 18.1 for black students. I repeated these calculations using data from the 2001–02 Common Core file. I found ratios of 17.2 for white students and 17.1 for black students.

BKW did note that black children in public schools in 1989 typically had much less access to computers than white children in public schools. However, the magnitude of the digital divide between black and white school children diminished in the 1990s. A recent National Center for Education Statistics (NCES) report indicates that access to computers is now universal in public elementary schools, and further that black-white differences in opportunities for computer-based learning are quite small.[14] Among first graders, the only noteworthy black-white difference in access to computer resources within public schools involves Internet access. An estimated 88 percent of white first graders in public school attend schools with Internet access. The corresponding figure for black children is 80 percent. This difference is small compared to the racial gaps in computer access reported a decade earlier by BKW, and it also falls just short of standard rules of thumb for statistical significance. However, this 8 percent point gap is identical to the entire estimated gap in school Internet access between high and low socioeconomic status children in public schools, where high and low are defined by membership in the top and bottom quintiles of a standard SES index.

Under the assumption that spending per student does not vary by race within a school district, the combination of school district data on per-pupil expenditure and school-level data on the racial composition of students provides information on average per pupil spending by public schools on black and white students. Given several different definitions of average expenditure, average spending per black student in public schools ranged from roughly $100 to $500 more than the corresponding figure for white students in 2001.[15] These data provide suggestive but not definitive evidence concerning racial differences in resources provided to public schools. Teacher pay greatly influences variation in expenditures among school districts, and this source of variation reflects many factors that have nothing to do directly with the quality of classroom instruction. These factors include: (1) how the age profile of the teaching force interacts with the salary schedule for the district; (2) whether or not the local teacher's union was successful in its last round of collective bargaining; and (3) geographic differences in costs of living. These are just a few examples of factors that may greatly influence school expenditures without affecting school quality.[16] Most are variations on the same theme. All schools do not pay the same prices for inputs. Due to geographic variation in price levels generally and also the political economy of school financing, some schools must spend more for the same quality inputs. In addition, some school systems are more efficient than others and manage to create better schools given the same effective resource budget.

It is difficult to definitively determine whether or not state and local governments systematically allocate more or less effective resources to schools that typically serve black children than do schools that typically serve their white peers, but existing data provide no indication that public schools systematically provide fewer resources for the education of black children than the education of white children. If one restricts attention to the most common school resource measures (e.g., per-pupil expenditures, term length, pupil-teacher ratios, and teacher qualifications), black and white children enjoyed roughly equal resource levels in public schools by the end of the twentieth century. This result is striking given the enormous black-white resource gaps that existed among public schools at the beginning of the same century.

FAMILY RESOURCES

The *Brown* decision is the most visible single event in a decades-long struggle by black Americans to knock down racial barriers that not only prevented them from attending certain public schools but also prevented adequate funding of public schools that did serve black communities. By the end of the past century, these barriers were broken, but more important obstacles may remain for black youth. Equal treatment under the law is not enough to eliminate the current resource deficit facing black children.[17] Even if governments allocated the exact same resources to all schools, one could not conclude that black and white students attend or even have the opportunity to attend public schools that, on average, receive equal resources. Public schools receive many resources that are never measured in any data set and that are not purchased directly with government funds. Although it is not possible to know for sure, one suspects that black children often attend schools with fewer real resources than predominately white schools in the same school district, even if both schools receive the same levels of government expenditures per pupil. The source of these resource differences is not race per se, but rather the correlation between race and family resources.

When parents volunteer to spend several hours per week in first-grade classrooms helping children learn to read, they change the effective pupil-teacher ratio in an important way. When parents engage teachers and work to reinforce lesson plans at home, they make teachers more effective. These activities and other ways that parents complement the work of teachers require time, and in some instances, a certain level of parental education. Given that white children are much more likely than black children to come from two-parent families with well-educated parents, it is not surprising that in a recent NCES report, Barton[18] documents higher rates of volunteer activity in schools among white parents than among black parents.

Parents who are wealthy and well educated are not only better able to complement the work of schools, they are also in a better position to build cognitive skills in their children during the preschool years. Several recent studies that use different data sets document large black-white test score gaps among children who are quite young. Phillips et al.[19] and Brooks-Gunn et al.[20] document large black-white differences in scores on the Peabody Picture Vocabulary Test-Revised (PPVT-R) and the Wechlser Preschool and Primary Scale of Intelligence (WPPSI). Philips et al. analyze PPVT-R scores for five- and six-year-olds in the Children of the National Longitudinal Survey of Youth (CNLSY) file. Both studies analyze PPVT-R and WPPSI scores for five-year-old children in the Infant Health and Development Program (IHDP). Neither the CNLSY nor the IHDP provide random samples of children. Children of young mothers are overrepresented in the CNLSY and all the children in the IHDP began life as low-birth-weight babies. Still, it is noteworthy that the baseline black-white test score gaps reported in these studies of young children are all over one standard deviation.

Fryer and Levitt[21] examine data from the Early Childhood Longitudinal Study (ECLS-K), an on-going panel study that began in 1998 and is following students from kindergarten through elementary school. This data set does provide a nationally representative sample of students entering kindergarten, and Fryer and Levitt report that black children begin kindergarten well behind white children in terms of basic reading and math skills. The black-white gap in reading scores among those beginning kindergarten is $-.4$ standard deviations and the corresponding gap in math scores is -.64 standard deviations. It is noteworthy that, in the 1999 NAEP-LTT data, black-white gaps in reading scores are $-.91$ standard deviations among nine-year-olds and $-.74$ standard deviations among thirteen-year-olds. The corresponding gaps in math scores are $-.82$ and $-.98$. Much of the black-white skill gap observed among elementary school children and young adolescents may reflect gaps in basic school readiness.[22]

Philips et al., Brooks-Gunn et al., and Fryer and Levitt all report that detailed measures of each child's family background and home environment help explain much if not all of the black-white test score gaps observed among young children. The CNLSY and IHDP data include observational measures of parenting styles that account for a significant portion of the black-white test score gap in these samples, even in analyses that contain controls for family resources and maternal human capital. In the ECLS-K data, low birth weight and an absence of books in the home are both signs of environmental deficits that are particularly common among black children and also correlated with low test scores in kindergarten.

Table 2.2 presents a compilation of statistics from recent government reports concerning racial differences in home environment and early life outcomes. Low birth weight and infant mortality are more than twice as common among black children as among white children. Less than half as many black children as white children live in two-parent homes, and half of all black kindergarten students have twenty-five or fewer children's books in their home, while less than one in ten white children have so few books in their homes. Note that even if a particular kindergarten student is the oldest child in her family, twenty-five books represents an average of only five new books per year between birth and her fifth birthday.

Census data suggest that levels of family resources available to black children as they prepare for and begin school have not improved in recent dec-

Table 2.2. Black-White Differences in Early Home Environments

	White (percentage)	Black (percentage)
3–5-Year-Olds Read to Every Day in Past Week, 2001[a]	64	48
Kindergartners with fewer than 26 Children's Books in the Home, 1998[b]	9	50
Kindergartners with at least 101 Children's Books in the Home, 1998[b]	25	4
Children Under 18 in 2-Parent Home, 2000[c]	78	37
Infants Born with Low Birthweight, 2000[c]	6.6	13.1
Children Under 18 With no Health Insurance, 2000[c]	7	13
Children 19–35 Months Without 4:3:1:3 Vaccination Series, 2000[c]	21	28
Infant Mortality Rate, 1999[c]	0.58	1.41

Sources a: Paul E. Barton. "Parsing the Achievement Gap," Educational Testing Service, Oct. 2003. b: U.S. Department of Education, National Center for Education Statistics, Early Childhood Longitudinal Study, Public-Use Base-Year File. c: "Status and Trends in the Education of Hispanics," by Llagas and Snyder, NCES, April 2003.

ades and are likely declining. Tables 2.3–2.5 provide descriptive statistics concerning the families of children ages zero–seven in various census years. Table 2.3 shows that between 1960 and 1980 there was a dramatic improvement in education levels among the parents of black children who were just reaching school age and a dramatic narrowing of the black-white gap in parental education. Since 1980, there has been little progress toward closing the black-white gap in parental education. In fact, the gaps in maternal education for 1980 are slightly smaller than the corresponding gaps for 2000.

Table 2.4 presents the fractions of children ages zero–seven who live with both, one, or neither of their parents. Many have noted the decline in two-parent families over the past several decades, but table 2.4 also illustrates a significant rise in the number of black children who live in a home with neither of their parents. In 2000, over one in ten black children under seven lived apart from both their parents. The comparable number among white children is less than one in twenty-five. The census data do not permit a concrete determination of the custodial arrangements for these children, but few of these children are in group homes or other institutions. Most are likely in the care of relatives or a foster parent.

Table 2.5 presents data on the total household income. The unit of observation is a child under age eight. Household incomes for black children actually fell during the 1980s, and although black incomes rose during the 1990s,

Table 2.3.   Parents' Education (children ages 0–7)

Panel A: Mother's Average Years of Schooling

Year	Whites	Blacks
1960	10.63	8.49
1970	11.38	10.02
1980	11.98	11.39
1990	12.78	12.19
2000	13.30	12.33

Panel B: Father's Average Years of Schooling

Year	Whites	Blacks
1960	10.85	7.64
1970	11.79	9.51
1980	12.58	11.57
1990	13.18	12.55
2000	13.41	12.68

Notes: Data are from the decennial census IPUMS 1960–2000. The IPUMS variables used for constructing years of schooling are "higraded" for 1960, 1970, and 1980 and "educ99" for 1990 and 2000, and the variables used for identifying parents are "momloc" and "poploc." Education is topcoded at 18 years of schooling. Individuals with allocated age, sex or race have been dropped from the sample. Sample weights "perwt" are used for year 2000.

Table 2.4.   Percentage of Children by Number of Parents in the Household (children ages 0–7)

Number of Parents in the Household	1960	1970	1980	1990	2000
White (Panel A)					
0	1%	1%	1%	2%	3%
1	6	9	13	18	19
2	93	90	86	80	78
Black (Panel B)					
0	8%	6%	6%	7%	11%
1	24	35	48	58	56
2	68	58	46	35	33

Notes: Data are from the decennial census IPUMS 1960–2000. The ipums variables used for defining the number of parents are "momloc" and "poploc". Individuals with allocated age, sex or race have been dropped from the sample. Sample weights "perwt" are used for year 2000.

Table 2.5.   Household Income (children ages 0–7)

Panel A: Average Household Income (1999 dollars)

Year	Whites	Blacks
1960	35,459	18,335
1970	47,019	28,167
1980	46,386	31,309
1990	53,340	31,164
2000	64,846	36,153

Panel B: Average Household Income by Number of Parents in the Household (1999 dollars)

Whites

Parents	1960	1970	1980	1990	2000
0	23,622	33,570	41,268	43,002	45,680
1	20,744	26,968	27,645	31,868	37,520
2	36,539	49,152	49,325	58,442	72,192

Blacks

Parents	1960	1970	1980	1990	2000
0	15,589	22,647	29,403	29,297	35,285
1	13,167	18,832	21,940	22,555	25,479
2	20,492	34,402	41,489	45,928	54,462

Notes: Data are from the decennial census IPUMS, 1960–2000. The IPUMS variable used for constructing total household income is "inctot." Total household income is the sum of "inctot" across individuals who live in the same household. Negative values of "inctot" have been recoded to zeros. Values are expressed in 1999 USD. Current monetary values have been adjusted using the CPI-U. The variables used for defining the number of parents are "momloc" and "poploc." Individuals with allocated sex, age, or race have been dropped from the sample. Comparable results that exclude allocated income imply slightly larger black-white family income gaps in recent decades. Sample weights "perwt" are used for year 2000.

white household incomes rose much faster. Panel B shows that the rapid decline in black two-parent families contributed to the actual decline in real household income during the 1980s as well as the slow overall growth between 1980 and 2000. However, holding family structure constant, black incomes have still risen less than white incomes.

The existing literature indicates that children from two-parent families do better in school and that educational attainment and achievement vary positively with maternal education and family income.[23] The estimated effects of income per se on educational outcomes among children are not large, but declines in black family income during the 1980s are coincident with significant worker displacement and structural changes in the labor market that placed stress on black families and communities. It may or may not be a coincidence that black children born during this period made no progress toward closing black-white test score gaps in reading and math.

Fryer et al.[24] point to another shock to the black community that may help explain black test score performance among children born in the 1980s and tested in the 1990s. The crack epidemic began to ravage black communities in large cities around 1985, and problems associated with crack spread through various cities until well into the 1990s. In my recent work, I point out that data on individual NAEP scores suggest that achievement among black youth in large central cities fell dramatically between 1982 and the mid-1990s, especially among boys.

POLICY OPTIONS

In modern economies, knowledge and cognitive skills are important determinants of individual earnings capacities, and it is inconceivable that Blacks will achieve economic parity with Whites during the coming century if black children continue to lag well behind white children in terms of basic skills and eventual educational attainment. Thus, it is appropriate to consider what public policy choices are most likely to enhance human capital formation among black children.

Krueger discusses gains in achievement that might come from large-scale programs to reduce class sizes. There is a large literature on this topic,[25] but regardless of one's position on the overall merit of such a policy, it is clearly not the first option that comes to mind when considering ways to address the black-white skill gap. Class size reductions combined with efforts to hold teacher quality constant as the number of teachers rises would prove quite costly, and there is limited evidence that black children, in particular, would benefit from smaller classes.[26]

Among policies designed to help disadvantaged children, the approach that is currently attracting the most attention involves accountability systems built around high-stakes testing. The No Child Left Behind Act has created an environment in which many public school teachers and administrators face great pressure to raise test scores, and this pressure is often intense in schools where students are predominately black and economically disadvantaged. Proponents of this approach argue that it is important to hold public schools accountable for performance and to provide incentives for effort and innovation.

I agree with critics who argue that too often teachers and principals in traditional public schools have little incentive to perform well, but I am still not a fan of accountability systems built around high-stakes testing. Economists understand clearly now that simple incentive systems based on one-dimensional performance measures can have serious negative consequences when employees are expected to perform many tasks simultaneously. Workers tend to game such incentive systems by allocating too much effort to activities that increase the simple performance measure without enhancing the value of total output. The output that schools desire from teachers is multidimensional. Thus, accountability systems based on test scores will provide incentives for teachers to divert effort toward raising scores on a particular test and away from other important parental objectives. Parents want children to develop true understanding of the material in a given subject and not simply a mastery of the material that will be on the next assessment. Further, parents want teachers to assist them in building important noncognitive skills in their children. Children are not born with good habits. They are not inherently persistent, honest, intellectually curious, or able to work well with others. These traits must be developed, and parents expect teachers to help them foster such development.

I am concerned that test-based accountability systems may be distorting teacher effort away from activities that have high long-term value for students but low returns with respect to the next standardized assessment. Because black students may be overrepresented in schools where principals and teachers fear negative consequences from poor student performance on standardized tests, the unintended consequences of accountability systems among black children are a pressing concern. We do not have direct evidence on the hidden costs of high-stakes testing because we have no measures of the noncognitive skills that are compromised by test-based accountability systems. Further, it is conceivable that high-stakes testing fosters important noncognitive skills. It is possible that the activity of preparing for the test as a group helps create good work habits and character among students. However, some evidence that we do have concerning effort distortion in response to high-stakes testing is not encouraging. A recent paper by Koretz[27] demonstrates clearly that test score gains induced by high stakes testing may not generalize at all to tests of the same material that are developed by a different testing company. Further, Jacob and Levitt[28] show that, in Chicago, high-powered incentives linked to student test performance created considerable amounts of cheating, which took the form of teachers or principals simply changing student answer sheets.

Voucher programs are often discussed as a potential solution to the problem of poorly performing schools in disadvantaged urban communities. These communities often have large minority populations, and my own work on the effects of Catholic schooling,[29] taken together with work by Howell and Peterson,[30] suggests that economically disadvantaged black youth in inner-city public schools may indeed have the most to gain from access to private schools. This makes sense to me because families with low incomes, little education, and meager political clout are not likely to get good service from large public bureaucracies, and vouchers could give many disadvantaged families the type of consumer sovereignty that more affluent families already enjoy when choosing schools for their children. The most important ingredient in any voucher plan is that the budget of both government operated and privately operated schools should be solely determined by enrollment. Teachers and principals should know that, regardless of year to year variation in test scores, regardless of their income or political power, parents can vote with their feet and reduce the school's budget if they feel the school is not serving their children well.

This arrangement makes for real accountability, and it gives the principals of schools the same incentives that the principals of law firms, accounting firms, and other professional partnerships face. Principals in these firms must identify, hire, and retain other talented professionals, or they will not make money. Although we cannot boil things down to simple measured traits, existing research shows that teachers differ greatly in their ability to foster learning. Vouchers may help create a labor market for teachers where principals face strong incentives to hire and reward the teachers who are best able to serve the students in a particular community.

I have written elsewhere[31] that voucher systems involve risks. We cannot predict exactly what would happen if large urban school districts adopted large-scale voucher programs, and details concerning targeting, financing, and regulation of admissions rules would surely matter for many outcomes. However, vouchers targeted to economically disadvantaged students in large central city school districts would provide new options for black families in communities where black children most often fail to learn and public schools most often appear inept and corrupt.[32] My recent work demonstrates that over the 1980s and early 1990s, black children in large urban school districts lost significant ground in reading and math relative to white children. Further, Flanagan and Grissmer[33] show that black students in large northern cities actually lag well behind black students from the rural southeast in reading and math.

Regardless of one's views on the relative merits of vouchers versus other reform proposals, it is hard to imagine that any feasible reforms of K–12 education could truly close the black-white skill gap in the near future.[34] Scholars have known since the 1966 Coleman report that black children begin school well behind their white peers in terms of basic skills, and in a 1972 volume devoted to analyses of the Equality of Education Opportunity (EEO) data Coleman collected, David Armor wrote, "Since blacks are just about as disadvantaged in first grade as they are in later grades, . . . it is clear that special programs will have to concentrate on the early years, possibly even the infancy period."[35] My recent work compares results from the ECLS-K and EEO data and concludes that black children are likely better prepared for school now than they were in 1965, but large black-white skill gaps remain among preschool children, and it may be ill-advised to expect K–12 schools to bear the entire burden of closing this gap.

A recent book by James Heckman and Alan Krueger[36] contains a spirited debate between the two concerning various options for improving public policies that promote human capital growth. One of the areas of agreement between the two involves the importance of early childhood interventions. Both agree that existing studies suggest that intensive interventions in the early years of life can significantly enhance both cognitive and noncognitive skill development in ways that foster improved outcomes among adults.[37] Economically disadvantaged families, especially disadvantaged black families, are now quite likely to have only one parent in the home, and relatively recent reforms to welfare, as well as the expansion of the Earned Income Tax Credit, provide increased incentives for these single parents, usually single mothers, to work outside the home.

It is not possible to know a priori what the best options are for providing enriched preschool environments for disadvantaged children. However, state and federal subsidies to higher education dwarf government spending on preschool education, and this funding strategy may be a form of putting the cart before the horse. Economically disadvantaged students who are well prepared for college at the end of their high school years enjoy many financial aid options that make college attendance feasible. The problem is that many disadvantaged students, especially in black communities, are so poorly prepared for the beginning of first grade that they have little chance of becoming prepared for college by the end of high school. Learning is a process that builds on itself. Children who know the alphabet can then learn the sounds associated with letters. Children who have mastered the sounds associated with letters are in a better position to learn how to read. Numerate children who read well are best prepared for all kinds of learning experiences, and the ability to learn is not only vital for further success in school but also vital for success in modern labor markets. Thus, as long as black children enter kindergarten with much weaker preparation for school than their white peers, they are likely to fare poorly as adults in the economy of the twenty-first century.

CONCLUSION

In the late 1980s, there were many reasons to believe that each successive generation of black Americans would continue to close black-white gaps in education, wealth, and incomes. Test score gaps between black and white children were at historic minimums as were attainment gaps between black and white adults. However, much went wrong for Blacks in the 1990s. Black-white gaps in achievement and attainment among youth and young adults remained constant at best. Further, employment rates among black men continued to fall while incarceration rates among black men rose to alarming levels, and rates of never-married motherhood continued to rise.

Recent results from the national fourth- and eighth-grade NAEP assessments in reading and math offer some suggestion that the 1990s may have been only a temporary pause in the process of black-white skill convergence. Reading scores for black fourth graders increased dramatically between 2000 and 2002, and math scores for black fourth and eighth graders rose sharply between 2000 and 2003. In all three instances, these gains are both large in terms of educational significance and larger than contemporaneous gains among Whites. Nonetheless, one should not draw too much from these results. The NAEP National Assessments are not designed to measure trends, and the program changed sampling procedures between 2000 and 2002.[38] The pending release of the 2003 NAEP-LTT results will shed more light on the most recent changes in black achievement levels.

My recent work points out that black-white convergence in human capital is expected as long as there are no permanent barriers to investment in black children. Most models of the intergenerational transmission of human capital imply that the black-white human capital gap should become smaller in each successive generation. This result holds because there are diminishing returns to investments in a child. Diminishing returns implies that if one group of parents is, on average, twice as skilled as another group, then the former group will have to invest more than twice as much in their children to maintain the same intergroup skill difference in the next generation.[39] Viewed through the lens of standard economic models of families, the fact that black-white skill gaps shrank during much of the twentieth century is not a surprise.

However, as Smith and Welch were using data from the 1940–1980 census files to form the core results in their influential 1986 monograph, *Closing the Gap: Forty Years of Economic Progress for Blacks*,[40] no one could have predicted the employment and incarceration outcomes for black men in table 2.1. Although we do not completely understand all the links between adult earnings opportunities, family structure, and outcomes for children, the problems of adults do impact the lives of their children. As part of efforts to understand human capital development among today's black youth, we must strive to understand why the current generation of young adult black men experience rates of idleness and incarceration that would have been unthinkable in 1954. Then, great attention was rightly devoted to the fact that segregated school systems had historically provided significantly fewer resources for black children than for their white peers. But in 2004, the family resource deficits that harm many black children are much more acute than any resource deficits attributable to the funding decisions of state and local school boards.

NOTES

I thank Nathaniel Baum-Snow, Marisa Jackson, Mario Macis, and Marie Tomarelli for research assistance. I thank the D&D foundation for research support. I thank James Heckman and Steven Levitt for useful conversations.

1. I provide a detailed accounting of trends in black-white test scores gaps from the 1970s forward. The NAEP-LTT sample sizes were smaller in the 1990s, and the differences between black-white test score gaps in the 1990s and the late 1980s tend not to be statistically significant. See Derek Neal, "Why Has Black-White Skill Convergence Stopped?" in *The Handbook of Economics of Education*, Eric Hanushek and Finis Welch, eds. (Amsterdam: Elsevier, Forthcoming), NBER Working Paper 11090.

2. Here, I present results based on census data. Neal (*ibid.*) contains a comparison on changes in the black-white attainment gap after 1990 among several data sets.

3. See Williams J. Collins and Robert A. Margo, "Historical Perspectives on Racial Differences in Schooling in the United States," in *The Handbook of Economics of Education*, Eric Hanushek and Finis Welch, eds. (Amsterdam: Elsevier, Forthcoming), NBER Working Paper 9770.

4. See Becky Pettit and Bruce Western, "Mass Imprisonment and the Life Course: Race and Class Inequality in U.S. Incarceration," *American Sociological Review* 69 (2004):151–169 for more details on incarceration rates among black men.

5. See Karsten T. Hansen, James Heckman, and Kathleen J. Mullen, "The Effect of Schooling and Ability of Achievement Test Scores," *Journal of Econometrics* 121, no. 1 (2004):39–98; Derek Neal and William Johnson, "The Role of Pre-Market Factors in Black-White Wage Differences," *Journal of Political Economy* 104 (1996):869–895; and C. Winship and S. Korenman, "Does Staying in School Make You Smarter? The Effect of Education on IQ in the Bell Curve," in *Intelligence, Genes, and Success: Scientists Respond to The Bell Curve*, B. Devlin et al., eds. (New York: Copernicus Press, 1997), pp. 215–234, for work on the effect of schooling on test scores. See Stephen J. Ceci, "How Much Does Schooling Influence General Intelligence and Its Cognitive Components?: A Reassessment of the Evidence," *Developmental Psychology* 27, no. 5 (1991):703–722 and Richard Nisbett, "Race, IQ, and Scientism," in *The Bell Curve Wars*, Steven Fraser, ed. (New York: Basic Books, 1995), for overviews of the literature on race and intelligence tests. See David Blau and Janet Currie,"Pre-School, Day Care, and After School Care: Who's Minding the Kids?" in *The Handbook of Economics of Education*, Eric Hanushek and Finis Welch, eds. (Amsterdam: Elsevier, Forthcoming), for a survey of results from early childhood intervention programs.

6. Stephen Coate and Glenn C. Loury, "Will Affirmative-Action Policies Eliminate Negative Stereotypes?" *The American Economic Review* 83, no. 5 (1993):1220–1240, is the most well-known model of this type. Neal, "Why Has Black-White Skill Convergence Stopped?" provides a detailed analysis of returns to skill and education by race.

7. See Casey B. Mulligan, *Parental Priorities and Economic Inequality* (Chicago: University of Chicago Press, 1997) and Gary Becker, *A Treatise on the Family* (Cambridge, MA: Harvard University Press, 1991).

8. Yoram Weiss and Robert J. Willis, "Children as Collective Goods and Divorce Settlements," *Journal of Labor Economics* 3, no. 3 (July 1985):268–292.

9. Robert A. Margo, *Race and Schooling in the South, 1880–1950: An Economic History* (Chicago: University of Chicago Press, 1990).

10. David Card and Alan B. Kreuger, "School Quality and Black-White Relative

Earnings: A Direct Assessment," *Quarterly Journal of Economics* 107, no. 1 (1992):151–200 and "School Resources and Student Outcomes: An Overview of the Literature and New Evidence from North and South Carolina," *The Journal of Economic Perspectives* 10, no. 4 (1996):31–50.

11. John J. Donohue, III, James Heckman, and Petra Todd, "The Schooling of Southern Blacks: The Roles of Legal Activism and Private Philanthropy, 1910–1960," 2000, PIER Working Paper No. 01–036.

12. Michael A. Boozer, Alan B. Krueger, and Shari Wolkon, "Race and School Quality since Brown Versus the Board of Education," *Brookings Papers on Economic Activity: Microeconomics* (1992):269–338.

13. Jeffrey Grogger, "Does School Quality Explain the Recent Black/White Wage Trend," *Journal of Labor Economics* 14, no. 2 (1996):231–253.

14. See Amy H. Rathburn, Jerry West, and Elvira Haisken, "Young Children's Access to Computers in the Home and at School in 1999 and 2000," NCES 2003–036 (Washington, DC: U.S. Department of Education, National Center for Education Statistics, 2003).

15. The data come from two Common Core of Data files: the Local (School District) Education Financial Survey and the Public Elementary/Secondary School Data. I calculated averages based on just educational expenditures as well as total expenditures. I also examined the sensitivity of results to the inclusion of allocated data.

16. Dale Ballou, "Do Public Schools Hire the Best Applicants?" *Quarterly Journal of Economics* 111, no. 1 (1996):97–133 and Dale Ballou and Michael Podgursky, "Seniority, Wages and Turnover among Public School Teachers," *Journal of Human Resources* 37, no. 4 (2002):892–912, analyze personnel policies in public schools. It is likely that victories at the bargaining table for teachers' unions do not translate into immediate increases in teacher quality for school systems.

17. Below, I present information about the current resource gap between black and white families. However, the basic point is not new. The 1966 Coleman Report created significant controversy by arguing that family background differences between black and white children were more important than black-white differences in school resources. Eric Hanushek also raised questions about the strength of the relationship between school resources and educational outcomes in Hanushek, "The Economics of Schooling: Production and Efficiency in Public Schools," *Journal of Economic Literature* 24, no. 3 (1986):1141–1177.

18. Paul Barton, *Parsing the Achievement Gap* (Princeton, NJ, Educational Testing Service, 2003).

19. Meredith Phillipse et al., "Family Background, Parenting Practices, and the Black-White Test Score Gap," in *The Black-White Test Score Gap*, Jencks and Phillips, eds., pp. 103–145.

20. Jeanne Brooks-Gunn, Greg Duncan, and Pamela Klebanov, "Ethnic Differences in Children's Intelligence Test Scores: Role of Economic Deprivation, Home Environment, and Maternal Characteristics," *Child Development* 67, no. 2 (1996):396–408.

21. Roland Fryer and Steven Levitt, "Understanding the Black-White Test Score Gap in the First Two Years of School," *Review of Economics and Statistics* 86, no. 2 (2004):447–464.

22. These comparisons are only suggestive. We will not have NAEP-LTT scores for the ECLS-K birth cohorts until the 2003 NAEP-LTT is released. Further, it is far from clear that standard deviation gaps provide meaningful measures of distance that can be compared across different tests taken at different ages. One can imagine changes in the shape of test score distributions that could alter test score gaps between groups measured in standard deviation units even if these changes in shape had no effect on the percentile rankings of individuals.

23. Brooks-Gunn et al., "Ethnic Differences in Children's Intelligence Test Scores"; Fryer and Levitt, "Understanding the Black-White Test Score Gap"; and Meredith Phillips et al., "Family Background, Parenting Practices, and the Black-White Test Score Gap," provide related results and discussions of the literature. See also David Blau, "The Effect of Income on Child Development," *Review of Economics and Statistics* 81, no. 2 (1999):261–276; Sarah McLanahan and Gary Sandefur, *Growing Up with a Single Parent, What Hurts, What Helps*. (Cambridge, MA: Harvard University Press, 1994); and Susan Mayer, *What Money Can't Buy: Family Income and Children's Life Chances* (Cambridge, MA: Harvard University Press, 1997).

24. Roland Fryer, Paul S. Heaton, Steven D. Levitt, and Kevin M. Murphy, "The Impact of Crack Cocaine," 2004, mimeo, University of Chicago.

25. See Eric Hanushek, "Publicly Provided Education," in *Handbook of Public Finance*, A. Auerbach and M. Feldstein, eds. (Amsterdam: North Holland, 2002), pp. 2045–2141 for a survey.

26. Alan B. Krueger and Diane Whitmore, "Would Smaller Classes Help Close the Black-White Achievement Gap?" in *Bridging the Achievement Gap*, John E. Chubb and Tom Loveless, eds. (Washington, DC: Brookings Institution Press, 2002), do argue based on results from the Tennessee STAR experiment that black students would benefit more than white students from smaller classes.

27. Daniel Koretz, "Limitations in the Use of Achievement Tests as Measures of Educators' Productivity," *Journal of Human Resources* 37, no. 4 (2002):752–811.

28. Brian A. Jacob and Steven D. Levitt, "Rotten Apples: An Investigation of the Prevalence and Predictors of Teacher Cheating," *Quarterly Journal of Economics* 188, no. 3 (2003):843–877.

29. See Derek Neal, "The Effects of Catholic Secondary Schooling on Educational Achievement," *Journal of Labor Economics* 15, no.1 (1997):98–123 and J. Grogger and Derek Neal, "Further Evidence on the Effects of Catholic Secondary Schooling," in *Papers on Urban Affairs*, William G. Gale and Janet Rotheberg Park, eds. (Washington, DC: Brookings Institution Press, 2000), pp. 151–202.

30. William G. Howell and Paul E. Peterson, *The Education Gap* (Washington, DC: Brookings Institution Press, 2002).

31. Derek Neal, "How Vouchers Could Change the Market for Education." *Journal of Economics Perspectives* 16, no. 4 (2002):25–44.

32. See Neal, "How Vouchers Could Change the Market for Education," for a discussion of corruption in urban public school systems.

33. Ann Flanagan and David Grissmer, "The Role of Federal Resources in Closing the Achievement Gap," in *Bridging the Achievement Gap*, John E. Chubb and Tom Loveless, eds. (Washington, DC: Brookings Institution Press, 2002).

34. See Chubb and Loveless, *Bridging the Achievement Gap* (Washington, DC: Brookings Institution Press, 2002) for a collection of papers that evaluate the potential relative gains in achievement among black youth that might result from various policy reforms.

35. See David Armor, "School and Family Effects on Black and White Achievement: A Reexamination of the USOE Data," in *On Equality of Educational Opportunity*, Frank Mosteller, ed. (New York, Random House, 1972), pp. 168–229, esp. p. 225.

36. James J. Heckman and Alan B. Krueger, *Inequality in America: What Role for Human Capital Policies?* Benjamin M. Friedman, ed. (Cambridge, MA: MIT Press, 2004).

37. See Alan Krueger, "Inequality: Too Much of a Good Thing," in *Inequality in America*, James Heckman and Alan Krueger, eds. (Cambridge, MA: MIT Press, 2004), pp. 1–76 and Pedro Carneiro and James Heckman, "Human Capital Policy," in *Inequality in America*, James Heckman and Alan Krueger, eds. (Cambridge, MA, MIT Press, 2004), pp. 1–76. See Blau and Currie, "Pre-School, Day Care, and After School Care," for a complete description of results from the literature on early childhood interventions. Neal, "Why Has Black-White Skill Convergence Stopped?" provides a detailed discussion of results from the Carolina Abecedarian Project.

38. Sample sizes for the national NAEP now include the state-level NAEP samples. Thus, the sample sizes in 2002 and 2003 are more than ten times greater than the corresponding sample sizes in 2000 or earlier.

39. Here, the initial skill difference between groups reflects previous group differences in human capital investments. There are no studies that document a direct link between black-white genetic differences and black-white differences in cognitive skills.

40. James P. Smith and Finis R. Welch, *Closing the Gap: Forty Years of Economic Progress for Blacks* (Santa Monica, CA: RAND, 1986).

3

Putting Education into Preschools

*Ron Haskins, Brookings Institution and
Annie E. Casey Foundation*

AMERICA'S COMMITMENT TO
EDUCATIONAL EQUALITY

From his perch as an assistant secretary in the Department of Labor, in 1965 Daniel Patrick Moynihan wrote a report, intended primarily as an internal administration document, that rocked the civil rights community and drove the scholarly world to apoplexy.[1] Moynihan argued that the explosion of female-headed families, especially those created by nonmarital births, was the major reason black Americans were not making greater social and economic progress. The reaction to Moynihan's paper was swift and predictable. As Rainwater and Yancey show in their volume on the report and its aftermath, many in the civil rights and scholarly worlds utterly rejected Moynihan's thesis as a virulent form of blaming the victim.[2]

As Moynihan's report was causing a firestorm in the academic world and even being reported in the popular press in somewhat breathless tones, his stature within the Johnson administration was rising. He was asked by the White House to draft a speech for President Johnson to deliver at Howard University's June 5, 1965, commencement. The speech was every bit as shocking as the Moynihan report. For in this address, the president told the nation that the civil rights movement had reached a new, more important, and more difficult stage. Paraphrasing Churchill, President Johnson told a surprised audience of graduating students, nearly all of whom were black, that the voting rights bill that Congress was in midst of enacting was "not the end . . . not even the beginning of the end . . . perhaps the end of the beginning."[3]

47

Johnson was preparing to commit his presidency and the full force and authority of the federal government to a new stage of civil rights. Congress had already enacted and was in the midst of expanding civil rights laws that would require generations to fully implement and that a considerable fraction of Americans—the George Wallaces, Byron de la Beckwiths, and Lester Maddoxes of our nation—would oppose with every resource at their command, including violence. And yet here was their president announcing to the nation that these achievements were not nearly enough and that he would do more, much more. His language in describing the next stage of the civil rights movement was sinewy, muscular: "We seek not just freedom but opportunity—not just legal equity but human ability—not just equality as a right and a theory, but equality as a fact and as a result."

Let the phrase "equality as a fact and as a result" be planted firmly in the mind of every person who wants to understand our current predicament. For as a nation we are still trying to achieve "equality as a fact and as a result." All the more reason we should attend to how Johnson planned to achieve it.

First, the problem as Johnson saw it:

> You do not take a person who for years has been hobbled by chains and liberate him, bring him up to the starting line of a race and say "you are free to compete with all the others," and still justly believe that you have been completely fair. Thus, it is not enough just to open the gates of opportunity. All citizens must have the ability to walk through those gates.

At which point Johnson turned to the infamous thesis of the Moynihan report:

> The family is the cornerstone of our society. More than any other force it shapes the attitude, the hopes, the ambitions, and the values of the child. When the family collapses it is the children that are usually damaged. When it happens on a massive scale the community itself is crippled. So, unless we work to strengthen the family, to create conditions under which most parents will stay together—all the rest: schools and playgrounds, public assistance and private concern, will never be enough to cut completely the circle of despair and deprivation.

Let us fervently hope that Johnson and Moynihan were wrong. The conditions they deplored have gotten much worse. Then, about 25 percent of black children were born outside marriage; now the figure is 70 percent. Then, about half of black children spent part of their childhood in a single-parent family; today the figure is over 85 percent. Today, Whites have nonmarital birth rates above the 25 percent for Blacks that so alarmed Moynihan in

1965, and the rate for Hispanics is 45 percent. Amazingly, 33 percent of all babies born in America have unmarried parents.[4]

The Moynihan report and Johnson's Howard University address called attention to the importance of two-parent families for children's development. Although the harsh reaction to Moynihan's report served to temporarily squelch attention to the importance of two-parent families for children, it was only a matter of time before the force of Moynihan's thesis, and the gradual accretion of evidence to support it,[5] would bring the scholarly and policy worlds to the understanding that an increase in the proportion of children being reared by married parents would be a boon to the nation—and would help in the battle to achieve equality as a fact and as a result. Moynihan was right—if early.

Although Moynihan's recommendations emphasized government action on behalf of the poor, his diagnosis of the problem clearly implicated the behavior of the poor themselves. Indeed, calling the poor to account is precisely what caused all the furor. How outrageous to assert that people might be poor because they make bad decisions like quitting school, having babies outside marriage, and applying for welfare rather than jobs. Moynihan's diagnosis of the problem leads inevitably to programs that require improved behavior by the poor. But major reforms of this type would have to wait for three decades until Congress and President Clinton enacted the welfare reform law of 1996—passed, ironically, over the strong, highly public, and even vituperative objections of Moynihan, who deeply opposed major parts of the legislation such as ending guaranteed benefits and placing young mothers and their children at risk by cutting their welfare benefits if they didn't work.[6]

Johnson didn't just pluck Moynihan out of the Labor Department because the Moynihan report convinced him that poverty was important. Johnson came to the presidency believing that poverty was important and that the federal government should do something about it. Indeed, Johnson intended to follow a theme established by the Kennedy administration by making an attack on poverty the central domestic thrust of his administration.[7] To emphasize the importance of poverty, he declared war on it—and became the most important elected official in the nation's history to both call public attention to poverty and fight for and actually implement programs to fight it. As his leading general in the war on poverty, he selected Sargent Shriver, the director of the Peace Corps in the Kennedy administration, and, by virtue of marriage, a member of the Kennedy clan.

Over the next four decades, the nation launched scores of programs and spent $9 trillion helping poor and low-income individuals and families.[8] Federal and state spending on these programs increased from around $50 billion in 1965 to around $450 billion in 2002 in constant dollars. Eight major types of benefits were provided, including medical, cash, food, housing, education, jobs and training, social services, and energy aid.[9]

Despite this level of expenditure of Johnsonian proportions, the goals of the Moynihan report and President Johnson's Howard University address have not been achieved. Blacks and Hispanics, who taken together constitute a quarter of the nation's population, still have less education, lower income, and more unemployment than Whites. Although the teen pregnancy rate has fallen and the nonmarital birth rate has been more or less level for several years, most minority children still spend a major portion of their childhood in a female-headed family. Black and Hispanic families live in poorer neighborhoods with higher crime victimization rates and worse schools. Because of these inequalities, government has resorted to affirmative action programs that are highly controversial, favor one race or ethnic group over another, and are based on the conclusion that some groups need special help. Justice Sandra Day O'Connor, however, writing for the majority in the 2003 *Grutter v. Bollinger* affirmative action case, predicted that "25 years from now the use of racial preferences will no longer be necessary."[10] How, then, will equality as "a fact and a result" be achieved?

As always, education is the biggest door through which children walk in their journey to the land of economic and social success. And yet, far too many poor and minority children are failing in school, which in turn greatly depresses their life chances. By President Johnson's analogy of a foot race, there is every reason to believe that too many children are still coming to the starting line unequal and unable to compete effectively. Great economic and social inequalities flow from this lack of educational achievement by poor and minority children.[11] The question now is whether the nation can fulfill the commitment to equality as a fact and a result in educational achievement.[12]

THE CASE FOR PRESCHOOL EDUCATION

We have learned a lot about educating poor and minority children since President Johnson's Howard University address forty years ago.[13] There seems to be widespread agreement on three points. The first is that school-age black and Hispanic students are far behind white students on every test of achievement for which data exist.[14] Although the test score gap has closed somewhat since the 1960s, it is still large. Second, reflecting the values of scholars, politicians, and the public, there is considerable agreement that the long-standing commitment to equality of opportunity is an appropriate target of government spending, and that education is the leading strategy in promoting equality. As Jencks and Phillips put it in a recent volume: "Reducing the black-white test score gap would probably do more to promote [full racial equality] than any other strategy that commands broad political support" (p. 4).[15] Third, all the available data show clearly that the achievement gap opens before children enter the schools at age five. Thus, closing the gap may well require intervention during the preschool years.

The Gap at School Entry

The evidence showing that poor and minority children enter the public schools already behind other children is abundant. A study initiated by the U.S. Department of Education in 1998, the Early Childhood Education Longitudinal Study, Kindergarten Cohort (ECLS-K), is a source of reliable and recent data on the abilities of children entering kindergarten. Investigators selected a sample of about 1,000 nationally representative public and private schools and then randomly selected twenty-five kindergartners from each school. Children were individually tested in reading and math near the beginning of the kindergarten year and their parents completed a survey that provided extensive background information on the child and the child's family.

Results from the ECLS-K have been extensively analyzed by Lee and Burkam of the University of Michigan. Figure 3.1 shows the scaled scores on two achievement subtests for white, black, and Hispanic children entering

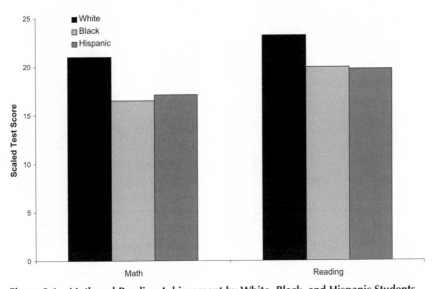

Figure 3.1   Math and Reading Achievement by White, Black, and Hispanic Students

Source: Lee and Burkham, "Inequality at the Starting Gate: Social Background Differences in Achievement as Children Begin Kindergarten," 2002.

kindergarten. Relative to white children, black and Hispanic children are about .6 and .55 standard deviation units behind, in math and reading respectively, when they enter school. Both differences are well over twice the .25 standard deviation units widely considered to be "educationally meaningful."[16] Figure 3.2 shows the entering children's scaled scores by socioeconomic status. Both math and reading achievement show a perfectly orderly relationship in which rising socioeconomic status is associated with rising achievement test scores. Students from minority families and families of low socioeconomic status are already far behind more advantaged students when school begins.

Nor is kindergarten entry at approximately age five the earliest age at which these striking differences make their appearance. Investigators conducting the Family and Child Experiences Survey (FACES) sponsored by the U.S. Department of Health and Human Services tested samples of three- and four-year-old children entering Head Start, at the end of the first and second year in the program (in the case of students who attended for two years), and at the end of the kindergarten year.[17] Although there is no comparison group of children not attending Head Start, several of the tests administered to entering students had national norms. Figure 3.3 presents

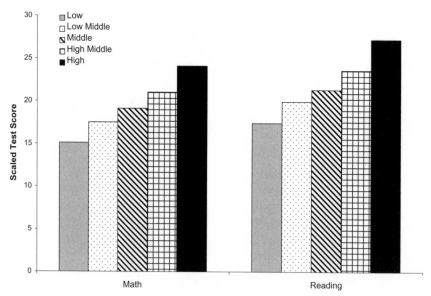

Figure 3.2   Math and Reading Achievement by Students of Differing Socioeconomic Status

Source: Lee and Burkham, "Inequality at the Starting Gate: Social Background Differences in Achievement as Children Begin Kindergarten," 2002.

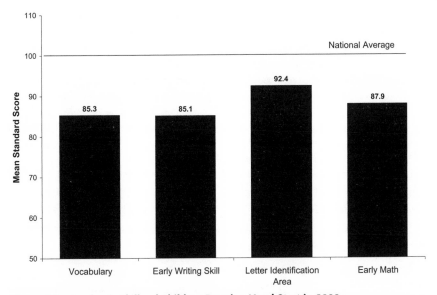

Figure 3.3   Academic Skills of Children Entering Head Start in 2000

Source: Zill et al., "Head Start FACES 2000: A Whole-Child Perspective on Program Performance," 2003.

standard scores from four subtests of the Peabody Picture Vocabulary Test
and the Woodcock-Johnson achievement test. The average Head Start child
at age three or four is about one standard deviation (15 points on many IQ
and achievement tests) below national norms on vocabulary, early writing,
and early math, and a little more than half a standard deviation below
national norms on letter identification. Since Head Start is composed almost
exclusively of poor or minority children, once again we see, this time as early
as ages three and four, that the nation's poor and minority children are at a
serious disadvantage in educational achievement long before they reach public school age.

This conclusion is confirmed by nationally representative data from the
National Longitudinal Survey of Youth Child Data. Jencks and Phillips
obtained vocabulary scores from the Peabody Picture Vocabulary Test-
Revised that was administered to 1,134 black and 2,071 white three- and
four-year-olds in the National Longitudinal Survey of Youth Child Data.[18]
In this case, black children are more than one standard deviation below the
national average and somewhat more than a standard deviation below white
children. Around 85 percent of the black children in this sample perform
below the average white child.

These three independent national data sets provide a consistent message:
poor and minority children are behind when they enter the school years—or

even earlier.[19] President Johnson's call for equality at the "starting gate" is far from being realized. The children's home, neighborhood, and child care or preschool environments are implicated as failing to provide the types of preschool experiences that prepare children for the rigors of schooling. If we believe that equality as a fact and a result is important, and if we believe education provides a strategy for increasing opportunity, then there are at least two types of interventions that could bring poor and minority children to the starting line better prepared to achieve. Society can intervene to change parents and society can intervene directly with the children to provide them with experiences during the preschool years that are designed to better prepare them for school.[20] My goal here is to explore how successful the nation might be in closing the education gap through direct intervention with children by providing them with high-quality preschool programs.[21]

Preschool Programs: The Evidence

Advocates long ago concluded that preschool programs boost school achievement and, in the long run, save money. But their claims have often been overblown and in any case leave out the nuances that are vital for those planning to spend additional public dollars. A more judicious approach may prove useful to policymakers, the primary audience of my concern.

The literature on preschool programs is vast, but several reviews simplify the task of extracting the important findings and conclusions.[22] The literature falls logically into several categories extending from model programs implemented under ideal circumstances to broad-scale programs implemented in many locations that roughly mimic the circumstances under which a universal program would be implemented. Since the studies vary in quality, they should not be given equal weight. Instead, the following criteria are used to evaluate the evidence:

- Random Assignment. Random assignment is the gold standard of evaluation.[23] Studies of preschool programs are especially subject to selection bias, meaning that children enrolled in preschool programs, as compared with children not enrolled, might differ systematically in ways that would confound comparison. For example, children in good preschool programs might be there because their parents were diligent in seeking a good program. Such parents may differ from parents who do not seek quality programs in many other ways that also promote better development in their children[24];
- Broad Measures of Performance and Life Success. The program should collect measures of intellectual performance and social behavior as well as extensive information about children's family background. Once children enter the schools, programs should collect information on

school performance and classroom behavior, as well as grade retention, special education placement, and graduation. In later adolescence and early adulthood, information on teen pregnancy, delinquent or criminal behavior, college attendance, employment, marriage, childbearing, and use of welfare and social services should be collected;

- Longitudinal Follow-Up. Children should be followed beyond preschool into the elementary grades, high school, and, if possible, into adulthood to determine whether children who participate in the preschool program and children who do not (control children) differ and whether differences in preschool performance translate to the types of broad measures suggested previously;
- Replication. Even with random assignment, the threats to generalizability of findings are greatly reduced if the treatment can be implemented under different conditions with different children, different teachers, different facilities, and so forth and still produce similar impacts;
- Field Conditions. The major limitation of many of the most important studies of preschool programs is that they were small scale and implemented under ideal conditions. Results are more generalizable if they are based on programs that are large scale and involve the types of children, teachers, and facilities that would be likely to participate in a national program.

The preschool literature is organized into three categories: studies of small-scale model programs that feature strong designs but often small sample sizes and little or no replication; studies of Head Start; and studies of state-sponsored preschool programs.

Model Programs

The studies of model programs provide strong evidence that high-quality preschool programs can produce immediate impacts as well as long-lasting gains. This latter category includes school achievement measures, special education placements, and grade retention. In a limited number of cases, high school graduation rates were increased and arrest rates were reduced. All in all, it is difficult to survey the model program literature without concluding that preschool programs can move poor and minority children toward better educational performance as well as performance on a wide array of measures of life success.

Perhaps the two best-known and widely admired model programs are the Abecedarian program conducted at the University of North Carolina starting in 1972 and the Perry Preschool program conducted in Ypsilanti, Michigan, starting in 1962. Model programs, and especially these two, set a kind of upper bound on what could be achieved by a national preschool program.

Abecedarian

This study featured the random assignment of children in Chapel Hill, North Carolina, to an elaborate infant and preschool program or a control group.[25] All children were judged to be at high risk for poor development based on their family's income, educational background, and other factors. The intervention consisted chiefly of quality care beginning early in the first year of life and then quality preschool education until children reached kindergarten age. The preschool curriculum was designed to develop gross-motor, fine-motor, language, and social-emotional skills with age-appropriate activities.[26] Children also received health care at their child-care facility and were offered free transportation. A total of 111 children from 109 families, fifty-seven of whom were randomly assigned to the program group, participated in the study. Nearly all the children were black. Extensive data from participants have been collected during the preschool, school age, and young-adult periods. At most measurement points through age twenty-one, data were obtained on 90 percent or more of the sample.

The pattern of results on intellectual measures during the preschool and elementary school years is impressive. Throughout the preschool years, beginning as early as age three, program children were significantly ahead of control children in IQ scores, often by as much as one standard deviation (15 IQ points). Even more impressive, the program children's IQ scores were normal during the preschool period, slightly over 100. Scores on the Peabody Individual Achievement Test (PIAT) in the spring of the kindergarten year were more than half a standard deviation higher than those of control children. Scores on the Woodcock-Johnson Psychoeducational Battery reveal differences favoring program children of between five and eight points at years three, seven, and ten after school entry. Although program children performed significantly better than control children on both tests, their performance was below average on both tests at school entry and all three testing occasions after school entry. On the Woodcock-Johnson, program children consistently performed in the low nineties as compared with the mid-eighties for control children. Thus, on at least one school achievement test, Abecedarian children cut the one standard deviation deficit of control children—which, as shown above, is quite comparable to the average performance of black children in the nation as a whole—by about one-half.

But that's not all. Program children consistently outperformed control children on a wide range of school performance measures. Program children were less likely to be retained in grade or placed in special education. Although about 70 percent of both groups graduated high school, nearly three times as many adolescents from the program group enrolled in college. At age twenty-one, young adults who had attended preschool were more likely to have a good job, about half as likely to have been teen parents, half as likely to have used marijuana in the last month, and much less likely to smoke. In short, children in the Abecedarian program not only came to the starting line performing at a level equal to the average for all children on IQ tests, but were able to translate this preparation into life successes on a wide variety of educational, social, and economic measures. It should be noted that, beginning shortly after birth and extending until school entry, the Abecedarian program provided the longest-lasting intervention of all preschool programs.

Perry Preschool

In the early 1960s, Perry investigators identified 128 black children in Ypsilanti, Michigan, who were "living in poverty and assessed to be at high risk of school failure."[27] To qualify for selection into the study, children had to live in families with parents who had little schooling and were either employed in a low status job or had no job. In addition, the family had to live in inferior housing. Children were randomly assigned to a program group that attended a high-quality preschool program or a control group that did not. Four children did not complete the preschool program and one died, leaving 123 children who were still in the study at the end of preschool and whom investigators have been following for more than three decades.

Findings for the preschool period and the early school years are roughly consistent with the Abecedarian program. At entry to preschool (at ages three or four), children in the program group and in the control group had Stanford-Binet IQs of a little below 80, confirming that the two groups were equivalent in IQ at the beginning. After the first preschool year, however, the groups had diverged sharply, with program children rising all the way to IQ 95 and control children rising only modestly to 84. This IQ difference remained at age six, although it had been cut in half. But all subsequent testing through age ten failed to show a continuing difference between the IQ scores of the two groups. Worse, both groups had scores of only slightly over 85, with program children typically higher by only one or two IQ points. A Wechsler full-scale IQ test administered at age fourteen showed both groups at IQ 81, more than a standard deviation below average.

On the Peabody Picture Vocabulary Test, which approximates school readiness for language ability, significant differences between program and control children were evident at the end of one and two years of preschool. However, in this case program children achieved scores of only 74 and 81 after one and two years respectively (control children scored 64 and 63 on the two occasions), which placed them considerably more than a standard deviation below the average score of 100, even after two years of preschool.[28]

By contrast, differences in school achievement were found at every follow-up point through age nineteen.[29] At age fourteen, for example, program chil-

dren completed 8 percent more items correctly on the California Achievement Test. There were also several differences in student and parent ratings
of school performance favoring program children. At the end of schooling,
28 percent of the years for control children had been spent in special education as compared with only 16 percent for children who had attended the
preschool.[30]

These results follow the typical pattern for the impact of preschool programs on IQ. Within a year of attending preschool, program children show
their superiority to control children on a wide range of tests of intellectual
skills, including both IQ and tests of language skills and, when the tests are
administered, school readiness. But these differences tend to fade within a
year or two after the intervention ends, typically because program children
decline somewhat and control children increase somewhat. In addition, even
when superior to control children on test scores, program children seldom
reach average scores. Children participating in model programs also often
experience less placement in special education classes and fewer grade reten-
tions. School achievement tests are intermediate between IQ tests that almost
always fail to show program-control differences within a few years after the
end of intervention, and special education placement and grade retention
that tend to persist during the school years. The finding of superior performance on standardized tests of school achievement by Perry program children
is relatively rare in the preschool literature. Perry program children were also
significantly more likely to graduate from high school, 67 percent as compared with 49 percent for control children.[31] The follow-up at age twenty-
seven found many other impacts on the lives of children who had participated in the Perry program. These include higher monthly earnings, higher
likelihood of home ownership, lower percentage of receiving social services
in the previous ten years, and fewer arrests, including fewer arrests for drug-
related offenses.[32]

The results of the Perry program are broadly similar to those of the Abecedarian program, especially on school performance measures and measures
of success in adapting to the educational, social, and economic requirements
of late adolescence and young adulthood. A major difference between these
two exemplary programs is that students from the Perry program lost their
IQ advantage quickly on entering the schools and often performed far below
average on achievement tests. However, on other important measures of
school performance, including grade retention and special education placement, program students were superior in both programs. In addition, again
like Abecedarian, on many important measures of success as young adults,
including earnings, home ownership, and receipt of social services, program
children are more successful than controls. Both the Abecedarian and Perry
programs were successful in changing the life trajectory of poor and minor-

ity students—exactly what Lyndon Johnson and Sargent Shriver had in mind.

It is appropriate to interpret these two fine programs as showing that preschool intervention can make a dramatic difference in the lives of poor and minority children that can last at least into early adulthood. If we return to the criteria by which preschool evaluations should be assessed, both programs get high marks for random assignment, broad measures, and longitudinal follow-up. The fact that two completely separate projects conducted in different sections of the country both produced such impressive results increases confidence that the findings are generalizable. On the other hand, experience shows that it is unwise to base predictions about the success of broad-scale intervention on results from only two small programs. Moreover, the greatest limitation of these two studies is that they were not implemented under field conditions. Both were very intense programs implemented by motivated staff supervised by highly motivated researchers.

Other Model Programs

The Consortium for Longitudinal Studies organized nearly three decades ago by Irving Lazar of Cornell University is yet another exceptional study of preschool programs.[33] Lazar and his colleagues identified eleven early childhood education programs, located in nine states in New England, the mid-Atlantic, the South, and the Midwest, that had been initiated during the late 1950s or early 1960s. All the programs had comparison groups, but only four of the eleven were randomized. In 1976 and 1977, Lazar contacted the original investigators from these projects and offered financial assistance to help each of them locate and retest as many of the original program and comparison children as possible.[34] Children were between the ages of nine and nineteen at the time of the follow-up study.

This study produced several notable results. Perhaps of greatest importance, based on pooled data across the programs, children who attended the model preschool programs were significantly less likely to be enrolled in special education (based on the six projects that reported these data) or to be retained in grade (based on eight projects) during their school careers by the time of the follow-up. Both effects were robust in that the pooled program-comparison group difference remained statistically significant even after the single program with the greatest program-comparison difference had been removed from the analysis.

Turning to school achievement data, after extensive review of the data collected by the various projects, investigators found that they had roughly comparable achievement data from six of the projects, including both mathematics and reading scores in fourth grade. Pooled analysis of these scores showed that program children had significantly higher math but not reading achievement than control children in the fourth grade.

Building on results from the Consortium for Longitudinal Studies, Steven Barnett of Rutgers University identified fifteen programs (the eleven in the Lazar consortium and four additional programs) that met four criteria: (1) children entered before age five; (2) the program served disadvantaged children; (3) at least one measure of intellectual ability or social behavior was collected at or beyond age eight or third grade; and (4) the research design was random-assignment or had a no-treatment comparison group that was similar to the program group.[35]

Table 3.1 summarizes the results of Barnett's review for IQ scores and school performance measures at grade three or later for fourteen of the fifteen programs that met his selection criteria (one program is dropped from this analysis because the entire intervention consisted of home visits; that is, there was no preschool program). As shown in the IQ score column of table 3.1, only three of the eleven projects (Abecedarian, Milwaukee, and Philadelphia) that reported IQ scores at grade three or later found that children who had attended the preschool program had significantly higher scores. Thus, the evidence that model preschool programs produce lasting impacts on IQ scores is not persuasive.

The last two columns in table 3.1 summarize, respectively, achievement test scores and other measures of school performance. Of the ten programs that obtained achievement test data, three (Abecedarian, Florida, Perry) reported that program children had significantly higher scores on either (but not necessarily both) reading or math subtests, one (Harlem) reported that program children did better than comparison children on one subtest (math), while comparison children did better on one subtest (reading), and six (Houston, Milwaukee, Yale, Early Training, Experimental Head Start, and Philadelphia) reported that the scores of program and comparison children did not differ on achievement test performance. These results constitute at best modest evidence that model programs can produce long-lasting effects on school achievement, although the fact that more than half the programs failed to show differences beyond third grade makes even this claim a little shaky. Eleven of the fourteen projects reported information on special education placement and grade retention. Of the eleven reports of special education placement, three (Abecedarian, Florida, Early Training) projects reported that program children were significantly less likely to be placed in special education, while two (Abecedarian, Harlem) of the projects reported that program children were significantly less likely to be retained in grade. These findings, however, are somewhat misleading because the Lazar consortium reviewed above showed that when results for special education placement and grade retention are pooled across many of these same projects, both measures show superior performance by children who attended the preschool programs.

A final model program that deserves especially careful scrutiny is the Chi-

Table 3.1. Follow-Up I.Q. and Achievement Test Results for Fourteen Model Preschool Programs

Program	Year Began	Evaluation Design	Sample Size	I.Q.	School Outcomes — Achievement Tests	Other Measures
Carolina Abecedarian	1972	Randomized	111	P>C (ages 3–21)	P>C (ages 15 and 21)	Special ed: P<C Grade retention: P<C
Houston Parent/Child Development Center	1970	Randomized	216	—	P=C	Special ed: P=C Grade retention: P=C
Florida Education Center	1966	Initially randomized but additional control group added at 24 months. Randomization lost when new "controls" added	397	P=C (grades 4–7)	Reading: P=C Math: P>C (grades 4–7)	Special ed: P<C Grade retention: P=C
Milwaukee Project	1968	Groups of 3–4 children assigned alternately to P and C groups	40	P>C (grade 8)	P=C (grades 4 and 8)	Special ed: P=C Grade retention: P=C
Syracuse Family Research Program	1969	Matched comparison group selected at 36 months. Not randomized	154	P=C (age 5)	—	—
Yale Child Welfare Research Program	1968	Two comparison groups from same neighborhood for first follow-up. Matched comparison group for follow-up at 30 months. Not randomized	36	P=C (age 10)	P=C (age 10)	Special ed: P=C
Early Training Project	1962	Randomized	65	P=C (age 17)	P=C	Special ed: P<C Grade retention: P=C *(continues)*

Table 3.1. Continued

Program	Year Began	Evaluation Design	Sample Size	I.Q.	School Outcomes Achievement Tests	Other Measures
Experimental Variation of Head Start	1968	Post hoc comparison group from same communities. Not randomized	140	P<C (age 13)	P=C	Special ed: P=C, Grade retention: P=C
Harlem Training Project	1966	Comparison group recruited from children from 1–2 months later. Not randomized	312	P=C (age 12)	Reading: P<C, Math: P>C (grade 7)	Grade retention: P<C
Perry Preschool Project	1962	Randomized	123	P=C (age 14)	P>C (age 14)	Special ed: P=C, Grade retention: P=C
Howard University Project	1964	Comparison group from neighboring tracts. Not randomized	107	—	—	Grade retention: P=C
Institute for Developmental Studies	1963	Randomized	503	—	—	Special ed: P=C, Grade retention: P=C
Philadelphia Project	1963	Matched comparison group from same kindergarten classes. Not randomized	113	P>C (age 10)	P=C	Special ed: P=C, Grade retention: P=C
Curriculum Comparison Study	1965	Post hoc comparison group from original pool. Not randomized	312	—	—	Special ed: P=C, Grade retention: P=C

Note: P = Program group; C = Comparison group
Source: Barnett, "Long-Term Effects of Early Childhood Programs on Cognitive and School Outcomes," 1995; and Barnett, "Long-Term Effects on Cognitive Development and School Success," 1998.

cago Longitudinal Study.[36] Initiated in 1967 in Chicago, the program is designed to provide a stable learning environment for children beginning at age three and extending until age nine (two years of preschool and four years of school-age intervention). The program is based on a set of predetermined learning activities administered in classrooms with low child-to-teacher ratios in both preschool (seventeen to two) and kindergarten (twenty-five to two). Instruction emphasizes language and math. A parent-resource teacher coordinates the family support component of the program, which consists of home visits and needed services. Parents are required to participate for a half day each week.

To examine the effectiveness of the preschool and school-age programs, Reynolds and his colleagues followed an entire cohort consisting of 1,539 low-income, minority children (93 percent black; 7 percent Hispanic) who lived in inner-city neighborhoods in Chicago; 989 of these children participated in the Chicago preschool program, called Chicago Child-Parent Centers (CPC), while 550 participated in alternative programs. All the children were born in 1980 and attended early childhood programs in twenty-five sites in 1985–86. Of the total group of 1,539 children, 850 also attended at least one year of the school-age program, while 689 did not attend at all. Children were not randomly assigned to the CPC and comparison groups. Rather, samples of convenience were employed as comparison groups. Of the preschool comparison group of 550 children, 374 attended kindergarten in five randomly selected schools plus two additional schools. The remaining 176 children in the comparison group attended kindergarten in six of the CPC schools but had not attended preschool. All children in all groups were from poor neighborhoods and the income of their families was below 130 percent of the federal poverty level (equal to about $24,000 for a family of four in today's dollars).

At the end of intervention at age nine, program children had higher reading and math achievement scores and lower rates of grade retention than comparison children. By age fourteen, program children also had lower rates of special education placement.

Reynolds and his colleagues also conducted a follow-up study when the children were between fifteen and twenty years of age. These data showed that, even when adjusted for covariates (including sex, race/ethnicity, risk index), children who had attended preschool had a significantly higher rate of high school graduation (50 percent vs. 38 percent) as well as more years of education (10.6 vs. 10.2). As in the Abecedarian project, participation in the school-age program did not show effects on any measure of educational performance. However, children who had received at least a combined total of four years of preschool and school-age intervention showed the strongest effects on measures of academic achievement, thereby indicating that the school-age program may have had some effects when provided in combination with preschool. The follow-up study also showed that children who received the preschool intervention had fewer total arrests, fewer multiple arrests, and fewer arrests for violent crime.

The Reynolds study is important because it occupies a kind of mid-point between the small-scale model evaluations and a national program. The study was conducted in ordinary schools in one of the nation's largest inner cities, had long-term follow-up, and enjoyed modest attrition rates. Because a program with these strong methodological characteristics produced substantial differences on standardized achievement measures, special education and grade retention, and even juvenile arrests, confidence that large-scale programs can produce lasting impacts is increased. And yet, the fact that the program did not use random assignment is reason for concern.

Head Start

As we have seen, Head Start was founded before much was known about the efficacy of preschool education. Perhaps for this reason, optimism abounded. Even so, President Johnson seemed to understand that it might take many years to overcome the educational disadvantages of the nation's poor and minority children. In his 1967 message to Congress, he said: "I believe that our people do not want to quit—though the task is great, the work hard, often frustrating, and success is a matter not of days or months, but of years—and sometimes it may be even decades."[37]

But how to know if "success" has been achieved? It may seem obvious now, but an important part of the federal government's way of conducting social programs is often by subjecting them to evaluations, usually at considerable cost, to find out whether the programs are producing their intended effects. Peter Rossi, an evaluation expert who is now an emeritus professor at Amherst, concluded in a famous 1987 article that the expected impact of any social intervention is zero.[38] His conclusion was based on years of careful study of what might be called the first wave of evaluations of large-scale social intervention programs. However, Rossi's point should not be interpreted to mean that impacts are impossible, only that they are difficult and therefore usually not achieved.[39]

Thus, it should come as no surprise that in 1969 the first major evaluation of Head Start, conducted by the Westinghouse Learning Corporation, found that the effects of Head Start on test performance quickly faded. Although the study was strongly criticized by scholars,[40] the Westinghouse evaluation was the first in a long line of Head Start evaluations that reported modest effects. "Modest effects" could also have been the title of a massive review of the Head Start literature through 1985 conducted by Ruth McKey, now with Xtria of Richardson, Texas, for the Department of Health and Human Services.[41]

Given this background, two points serve as cautions to those wanting to draw conclusions from the Head Start literature. First, the early and heady expectations of massive impacts from a half-day, nine-month preschool program such as Head Start have been considerably tempered. Second, despite the fact that Head Start has been in operation since 1965 and has served around 23 million children, there has not been a random-assignment national study of the program that could provide a solid answer to the question of whether the typical Head Start program actually helps poor children increase their school readiness and subsequent school achievement. Primarily for this reason, the Government Accountability Office (formerly the General Accounting Office) has informed Congress that the body of Head Start research "is inadequate for use in drawing conclusions about the impact of the national program in any area in which Head Start provides services such as school-readiness or health-related service."[42] Fortunately, a national random-assignment study is now being conducted, by order of Congress, but the first results will not be available until 2005.

Evaluations of Head Start Programs

Even so, enough information is available to reach tentative conclusions about the effects of Head Start on academic performance. A comprehensive review of Head Start evaluations that met at least minimum scientific standards has been published by Steven Barnett.[43] The major findings of Barnett's review regarding effects of Head Start on children's school achievement are summarized in table 3.2. All fourteen of the Head Start programs in Barnett's review provide school achievement data for at least one grade and eight programs provide achievement data for more than one grade. Of the fourteen projects, six (Detroit 1969–1970; Detroit 1972–1973; ETS Longitudinal; New Haven, Connecticut; Westinghouse; and Rome, Georgia) report significant differences in school achievement and half of these are at grade one (ETS Longitudinal, New Haven, and Westinghouse). All three of the projects reporting results at grade one found that that program children had higher scores than comparison children. By contrast, only three (Detroit 1969–1970, Detroit 1972–1973, and Rome, Georgia) of the fourteen programs that tested achievement above grade one found any significant differences. Thus, the evidence of Head Start producing a significant boost in achievement at grade one is consistent, although only based on three projects. The evidence of effects above grade one is preponderantly negative.

Five of the projects also reported information on special education placement, grade retention, or both. Of the three reports on special education placement, one (Rome, Georgia) found that program children were less likely to have been in special education while two (Hartford, Connecticut, and Washington, DC) showed no difference between program and comparison

Table 3.2.   Follow-Up Achievement Test Results for Selected Head Start Programs

Program	Number of children	School Outcomes	
		Achievement Tests	*Other*
Cincinnati Head Start, 1968–69	Initial: Unknown Follow-up: Unknown	P = C (grade 3)	—
Detroit Head Start, 1969–70	Initial: Unknown Follow-up: Unknown	P>C (grade 4)	—
ETS Longitudinal Study of Head Start, 1969–71	Initial: 1,875 Follow-up: 852	P>C (grade 1) P = C (grades 2–3)	—
Hartford Head Start, 1965–66	Initial: 293 Follow-up: 198	P = C (grade 6)	Special ed: P = C Grade retention: P<C
Kanawha County, West Virginia, 1973–74	Initial: Unknown Follow-up: Unknown	P = C (grade 3)	—
Montgomery County, Maryland, 1970–79, Selected Years	Initial: 2,534 Follow-up: 298	P = C (various grades)	—
New Haven Head Start 1968–69	Initial: 109 Follow-up: 61	P>C (grade 1) P = C (grade 3)	Grade retention: P<C
Pennsylvania Head Start, 1986–87	Initial: Unknown Follow-up: 72	P = C (grades 2–3)	—
Westinghouse National Evaluation 1965–66	Initial: Unknown Follow-up: 3,980	P>C (grade 1) P = C (grades 2–3)	—
Rome, Georgia Head Start 1966	Initial: 218 Follow-up: 154	P>C (grade 5) P = C (grades 6 and up)	Special ed: P<C Grade retention: P = C
Detroit Head Start and Title I, 1972–73	Initial: Unknown Follow-up: Unknown	P>C (grade 4)	—
D.C. Public Schools and Head Start, 1986–87	Initial: 461 Follow up: Varies	P = C (grades 3–5)	Special ed: P = C Grade retention: P = C
Philadelphia School District Get Set and Head Start, 1969–71	Initial: 2,697 Follow-up: 1,212	P = C (grades 4–8)	Grade retention: P>C
Seattle Distar And Head Start, 1970–71	Initial: Unknown Follow-up: 64	P = C (grades 6, 8)	—

Note: P = Program group; C = Comparison group
Source: Barnett, "Long-Term Effects of Early Childhood Programs on Cognitive and School Outcomes,"
1995; and Barnett, "Long-Term Effects on Cognitive Development and School Success," 1998.

children. On grade retention, two (Hartford and New Haven) of the five programs found that program children were less likely to be retained, one (Philadelphia) found that program children were more likely to be retained, and two (Rome, Georgia, and Washington, DC) found no difference. Thus, the studies provide inconsistent evidence that Head Start is associated with reduced placement in special education but somewhat stronger evidence that Head Start is associated with reduced likelihood of grade retention.

The effects shown by the Head Start evaluations, however, are suspect because most of the studies are of low quality. Although all the studies had comparison groups, none of the studies were randomized experiments. This fact alone renders any conclusions drawn from the studies dubious. Another problem is that the studies were not always well reported. As a result, for eight of the fourteen programs the number of children participating at the beginning of the study, at the time of follow-up, or both was not known. Even worse, for the six projects in which the number of subjects is known, attrition is a major issue. Attrition rates ranged from 29 percent to 88 percent with an average of over 50 percent. Attrition rates of this magnitude make already dubious conclusions even less dependable. Of course, poor-quality studies are as likely to report effects that are underestimates as well as overestimates of the true effects. No results from a bad study are dependable.

High/Scope Long-Term Benefits of Head Start Study

One of the most interesting studies of Head Start is a retrospective study conducted by the High/Scope Foundation of Ypsilanti, Michigan, the same organization that conducted the Perry Preschool program.[44] As part of a complex study called Head Start Planned Variation, sponsored by the U.S. Department of Education from 1969 to 1972, High/Scope had conducted a study of the effect of the preschool curriculum it developed for the Perry Preschool project. The curriculum had been tested at two sites, one in northwestern Florida and one in northern Colorado. In both sites, High/Scope used random assignment to compare a regular Head Start classroom with a special Head Start classroom that used the High/Scope curriculum. Seventeen years after the conclusion of the Planned Variation study, High/Scope investigators returned to the Florida and Colorado sites to identify a retrospective comparison group of children from the same neighborhoods as children who had participated in the earlier study, and to test both the original children and the comparison group to determine if the two types of Head Start programs conducted in 1970–71 had produced lasting effects. Children for the comparison groups met the criterion of living in the same or similar neighborhoods as children in the original study. Only a few significant differences between children who attended Head Start and the retrospective comparison group were found at either the Colorado or Florida sites. There were two significant effects for the Florida site; namely, that a higher proportion of girls who attended Head Start finished high school and a smaller proportion of these girls were arrested. There were also indications, based on statistical modeling, of a few additional differences between the Head Start groups and the comparison group. Unfortunately, differences between the two groups may have been suppressed by a lack of comparability between the Head Start groups and the comparison group. In any case, at most this study provides very modest evidence for long-term impacts of Head Start on school performance and delinquent and criminal behavior of females and virtually no evidence of impact on males.

The Head Start FACES Study

The FACES study, described previously, provides information on test performance of nationally representative samples of children in Head Start at the beginning and end of the Head Start year (or two years in the case of children who entered at age three). The average child entering Head Start was about a standard deviation behind national norms on four achievement subtests. Given that the FACES study retested these same children at the end of their Head Start year, it is possible to use this information to arrive at tentative judgments about how much children attending Head Start learned during the year. Of course, without a control group of similar children not attending Head Start, we cannot be certain that the changes in performance are due to Head Start itself.

As shown in figure 3.4, children's scores on all four subtests improved during the course of the Head Start year. The gains in vocabulary and early writing, 3.8 and 2.0 points respectively, were statistically significant. The slight improvements in letter identification and early math were not statistically significant. Of course, even with these improvements during the course of the Head Start year, children were still about 11 points or nearly three-quarters of a standard deviation below national norms on the average subtest. The FACES study shows that the typical child leaving Head Start is far below average in academic preparedness entering the school years.

The Currie Studies Using National Data Sets

Janet Currie and her colleagues at UCLA have written several papers about the long-term effects of Head Start using data from the National Longitudinal Survey of Mothers and Children and from the Panel Study of Income Dynamics.[45] In the former study, Currie and Thomas control for many of the differences between Head Start and comparison children by using data on siblings, one of whom did and one of whom did not attend Head Start. Like most studies of Head Start, the analysis revealed immediate gains in test scores for siblings who attended Head Start. These gains, how-

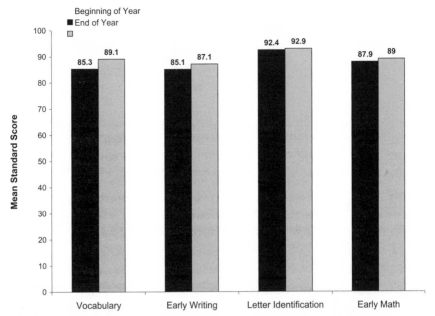

Figure 3.4   Head Start Students Show Small Gains in Vocabulary and Early Writing Skills

Source: Zill et al., "Head Start FACES 2000: A Whole-Child Perspective on Program Performance," 2003.

ever, fade for black siblings as they grow older, but not for white siblings who not only maintain their superior performance on an achievement test but who also repeat fewer grades. The Garces, Thomas, and Currie study reported somewhat similar findings from the Panel Study of Income Dynamics, again using a sibling comparison design. In this study, Whites who attended Head Start showed an increased probability of finishing high school and attending college as well as slightly higher earnings in their early twenties. Black children were less likely to have been charged with or convicted of committing a crime.

The Currie studies, although employing a clever design, are not based on random assignment and are therefore somewhat questionable. In addition, neither study found impacts on the academic performance of black children. Given that about one-third of the children attending Head Start are black, and that these are precisely the children who have the greatest difficulty in achieving average educational performance, Currie's no-difference finding for academic performance by Blacks raises serious questions about the program's effectiveness. In addition, Barnett has criticized the Currie and Thomas study on methodological grounds, especially because their methods result in selection of a biased sample and because the achievement test they report has technical limitations.[46] These are important qualifications on Currie's conclusions, but, at least in my view, not enough to completely discount the possibility that Head Start is producing more longer-term impacts than previously thought.

Head Start Summary

The evidence on Head Start's effects is not as strong as the evidence on model programs, a conclusion similar to that drawn by previous reviews of Head Start.[47] In explaining this result, Barnett points out that "model programs began at earlier ages, lasted longer, were more intense, and were better implemented"—all of which have been shown to contribute to the effectiveness of preschool programs.[48] Thus, it seems wise to maintain some humility about the extent to which a universal program like Head Start could contribute substantially to closing the preschool achievement gap.

State-Sponsored Preschool Programs

There has been a steady increase since 1960 in the number of states that offer their own preschool programs for at least some three- and four-year-olds.[49] By 2002, forty states sponsored preschool programs that enrolled about 700,000 children, mostly four-year-olds. Like Head Start, the programs tended to follow the nine-month school year and to provide half-day classes.[50] Total state spending on these programs was around $2.4 billion in 2002, although just ten states spent nearly $2 billion of this amount, indicating that most of the state programs are very small. Not only are most of the programs small, but most states do not spend enough money per student to maintain high quality. The average state spends about $3,500 less per student than Head Start. For our purposes, the major question is whether these state programs provide evidence that they can increase the school readiness of poor and minority children. Through 1998, thirteen of the states with preschool programs had conducted evaluations. Like the evaluations of model programs and Head Start reviewed above, the evaluations of state preschool programs suffer from a wide variety of flaws. Walter Gilliam of Yale has conducted two thorough analyses of these thirteen evaluations.[51] Most of the information summarized here is taken from these reviews.

None of the evaluations were based on random assignment. Thus, their conclusions are open to question. Three of the thirteen evaluations did not enlist any kind of comparison group and are therefore ignored here. Of the ten remaining evaluations, nine reported achievement test results at the end of preschool or for at least one occasion between kindergarten and third grade (table 3.3). The results of these tests can be summarized in three gener-

Table 3.3. Achievement Test Results for Nine State-Funded Preschool Programs

Program	End of Preschool	K	1	2	3
		Year of Testing			
District of Columbia	yes	mixed	mixed	—	—
Florida	yes	yes	—	—	—
Georgia	—	—	no	—	—
Kentucky	yes	mixed	mixed	no	—
Maryland	—	yes	—	—	—
Michigan	—	yes	—	—	—
New York	yes	mixed	—	—	no
South Carolina	—	—	yes	—	—
Washington	yes	—	—	—	—

Note: "Yes" means that significant effects were found for all cohorts studied; "no" means no significant effects were found; "mixed" means at least one but not all cohorts studied revealed a significant effect.

Source: Gilliam and Ripple, "What Can Be Learned from State-Funded Prekindergarten Initiatives? A Data-Based Approach to the Head Start Devolution Debate," in The Head Start Debates by E. Zigler & S.J. Styfco, Eds. 2005.

alizations. First, of the five projects that obtained achievement test results at the end of the preschool year, all found significant differences between program children who attended the state preschool and comparison children who did not. Second, all but one of the nine states (Georgia) found at least one significant achievement test difference between program and comparison children at some point between the end of preschool and the first grade. Third, only two programs tested children beyond the first grade and neither found that earlier gains were maintained.

Like most of the preschool programs reviewed here, the state preschool programs produce an immediate boost in children's learning. In this sense, they may be increasing school readiness. But Gilliam finds little evidence that state preschool programs produce lasting benefits. In his most recent assessment of the evidence, he concluded that some of the state programs are roughly on par with Head Start, but most are below Head Start in overall effectiveness.

Many scholars of state preschool programs believe that Oklahoma sponsors one of the nation's best programs. A recent study of the short-term effects of the Tulsa, Oklahoma program, based on a stronger research design than is typical of evaluations of state preschool programs, yields evidence of substantial impacts on school readiness. In September 2001, the Tulsa Public Schools administered a test that included items on social-emotional development, general knowledge, motor skills, and language skills to children just beginning the preschool program and children just beginning kindergarten. Gormley and Gayer used an analytic technique called regression discontinuity to, in effect, compare the scores of children who barely made the age cutoff in 2000 and received the preschool intervention program to children who barely missed the age cutoff in 2000 and therefore had to enroll in the pre-school program in 2001.[52] Thus, this study closely approximates random assignment. Gormley and Gayer present numerous comparisons of charac-teristics of the two groups of children to show that they are nearly identical in composition.

This clever design demonstrated substantial differences between children who attended the preschool program and those, of approximately the same age, just entering the program. Specifically, program children had knowledge scores and language scores that were nearly .4 standard deviation units and motor skills scores .24 standard deviation units higher than comparison chil-dren. Moreover, program impacts were greater for Blacks and Hispanics as well as for children qualifying for free lunches. Thus, it appeared that the boost in school readiness occurred primarily among minority children and children from poor or low-income families, precisely the group that most needs the help.

The Gormley and Gayer study is an important contribution to the litera-ture on state preschool programs. It is almost as good as a random assign-ment evaluation; it took place under field conditions; it tested children from almost an entire city; and it collected measures of school achievement. How-ever, the most that can be said for the study is that it strengthens the conclu-sion that state preschool programs can produce immediate impacts on school readiness. This is an important outcome because it is the necessary—but not sufficient—condition for establishing the basis for subsequent school achievement. Whether, in fact, subsequent school success will be realized must await follow-up studies with these youngsters.

WHAT TO DO NOW: EXPANDING PRESCHOOL EDUCATION WHILE IMPROVING QUALITY

Factors that Should Shape Federal Policy on Preschool Programs

Recommendations for public policy on preschool programs should be shaped by three factors. First, of course, is the body of evidence on the effects of preschool programs. There is strong evidence of immediate impacts from model programs, Head Start, state preschool programs, and even good-quality center-based child care.[53] Good studies and bad show clearly that even moderately high-quality programs have immediate impacts on children's performance as measured by test scores. But there is only a modest amount of evidence, from the best Head Start programs and from the Reynolds Chicago study, that it is possible to implement large-scale pro-grams and still maintain enough quality that the program produces lasting impacts on school performance. Most of the studies fail to meet most of the criteria for persuasive evaluations; even the Chicago study, despite its impressive long-term impacts and its large scale, is not based on random assignment. Reviewing studies of broader programs cannot fail to leave the impression that, in accord with Rossi's Iron Law of program evaluation,[54] creating long-term impacts in a large-scale program is a difficult undertaking.

Preschool education is the little train that could, not the little train that will. The field of early childhood education is not in a position to tell policymakers that if they just spend the money, the evidence allows a confident prediction that the school readiness gap will be closed or even substantially reduced. If the expansion of preschool programs is to contribute materially to correcting the education gap, the new programs must be implemented in such a way that quality is improved. Here is the most troubling consideration: if new programs were to achieve no more than the quality of the average state preschool program, lasting effects would not be forthcoming. And there is good reason to believe that new programs that achieved the quality of the average Head Start program would not produce much either. Thus, policymakers and program designers not only face the inevitable hazards of program expansion, but programs must be expanded while improving and maintaining quality.[55]

The second consideration in formulating policy recommendations is that preschool policy cannot start afresh. The environment for preschool policymaking is exceptionally complex. Federal policy on preschool programs falls roughly into two legislative traditions; namely, legislation on quality programs designed to promote child development and legislation on day care programs in which the major purpose is to provide a decent place for children to stay while parents (often single mothers) work.[56] As we will see, it would be a mistake to ignore either of these distinct sets of policies in the attempt to expand quality preschool programs.

The third major factor that should shape recommendations for preschool policy is the sheer importance of closing the educational gap between poor and minority children and their more advantaged peers. This is a consideration that is often lost in academic debates about public policy. Yes, it would be a good thing for policymakers to follow the economists' injunction to spend the last dollar where it will do the most good—and a long list of distinguished social scientists, including Nobel Laureate James Heckman, have argued that investing in preschool is cost effective.[57] But to supplement this rule, I pose a second that should have at least modest claim on policy decisions: some problems are so important that we should take our best shot. There are few domestic problems that are more important than closing the education gap. President Johnson committed the vast influence and resources of the federal government to achieving equality as a fact and a result. And

choosing education—along with improved civil rights—as his primary strategy was consistent with the American tradition of education as the route to
success. Now that four decades of research have shown how difficult it is to
overcome the family and neighborhood backgrounds of poor and minority
children through improved education, federal policy should respond by—
what? Giving up? The notorious level of American impatience aside, the fact
is that we are just beginning to find out what preschool can achieve. Now we
need a plan for capitalizing on what we know and, of major importance, for
more effectively using the resources at hand while gradually adding new
resources—and new knowledge.

The Federal Policy Environment

As we have seen, two strands of federal policymaking must be considered
in moving the nation toward expanded high-quality preschool programs for
four-year-olds. The first is the line of policy that began with Head Start in
1965. This tradition now includes preschool programs sponsored under Title
I of the No Child Left Behind Act and the various programs authorized
under the Individuals with Disabilities Education Act as well as state-funded
preschool programs (see table 3.4). The essence of this tradition is high-quality and relatively expensive programs designed to boost child development.

The second tradition, established as part of both the tax code and welfare
reform legislation with roots as far back as the Kennedy administration in
the early 1960s, is support of day care. The major purpose of day care programs is to provide a decent place for children to stay while their parents
work or prepare for work. One of the most colorful chapters in the history
of legislation on federal preschool programs was the attempt by child advocates and others to establish federal regulations that would require that federal dollars be spent only in facilities that provide high-quality care. In effect,
advocates hoped to use federal regulations to convert day care programs into
high-quality child development programs. Going by the unlikely name of
FIDCR (Federal Interagency Day Care Requirements), there were numerous
attempts during the 1970s and early 1980s to revise the requirements so that
they could pass Congress and thereby improve the quality of all day care
paid for with federal funds.[58] All failed.

The primary reason they failed is even more important today than it was
in the 1970s. Working parents, especially poor and low-income working parents, need inexpensive day care. Since the welfare reform legislation of 1996,
more low-income single mothers are employed than at any time in the past.[59]
These mothers typically earn around $11,000 or $12,000 per year, which is
typically supplemented by over $1,000 in food stamps and up to $4,300 in
cash payments from the Earned Income Tax Credit.[60] If these mothers, and
other low-income families, were to pay the full cost of high-quality child

Table 3.4. Spending on Preschool and Child Care Programs in 2003

Program	Spending (millions)
Title I Grants	$ 284
Early Reading First	75
Individuals with Disabilities Education Act	
Infants and Families	437
Preschool Grants	390
Grants to States	512
Discretionary Child Care and Development Fund (CCDF)	2,100
Mandatory CCDF	2,717
Transfers from Temporary Assistance for Needy Families (TANF)	
Block Grant to CCDF	2,000
TANF Direct Expenditures on Child Care	1,580
State CCDF Match and Maintenance Effort Payments	2,247
TANF MOE in Excess of CCDF MOE	750
Head Start	6,668
Social Services Block Grant (Title XX)	160
Child and Adult Care Food Program	1,940
Total	$21,860

Source: Personal Communication with Matthew McKearn, Program Examiner, Office of Management and Budget, July 2002.

care that, I will argue below, is around $7,000 per year (and a few thousand additional for infant care), it would take nearly half of their income. Unless low-income families receive large subsidies, most of them will vote with their feet and select inexpensive day care.

A major part of the welfare reform debate in 1995 and 1996 was how much money the federal government and the states should spend on day care. Although a few Democrats and many child advocates—reminiscent of the days of the FIDCR battles—inserted quality of care into the debate (and actually won some small victories), the major consideration driving policy was offering subsidies for day care to as many families as possible. The calculus here was straightforward: cheaper care means more coverage. In the end, the welfare reform law terminated numerous categorical day care programs, put all the money from these programs into one program called the Child Care and Development Block Grant, and added an additional $4 billion over seven years to spending that would have occurred under the terminated programs. The legislation left in place a provision, enacted in the 1990 child-care reforms, that required every state to offer parents a voucher so they could select their own care. When left to their own devices, parents often choose care of indifferent quality but of moderate price, thereby maximizing both parental choice and the number of families that could receive support from the child care block grant.[61]

In addition to the reformed Child Care and Development Block Grant, the 1996 reform law ended the Aid to Families with Dependent Children entitlement program and put a block grant with fixed funding in its place. The legislation also placed a five-year time limit on the receipt of welfare and required states to meet work standards that specified that half of their welfare caseload be employed or in welfare-to-work programs. As states began to emphasize work programs in the early 1990s, and especially after the 1996 federal reform law, the welfare rolls declined dramatically for the first time in history. By 1999, the rolls were less than half of the peak of 5.2 million families reached in 1994.[62] Thus, as the welfare rolls declined and the block grant remained flat at $16.5 billion, states had enormous surpluses because their cash welfare payments were falling so rapidly. In some years, states used as much as $4 billion of their surpluses to pay for day care.[63]

The 1996 reforms, abetted by a strong economy and other policy changes such as dramatic expansions of the Earned Income Tax Credit in 1990 and 1993 and a series of expansions of health care coverage for children, have led, not simply to a decline in the welfare rolls, but to historic increases in employment among single mothers, to large increases in both earnings and total income among female-headed families, and to the first sustained decline in child poverty since the early 1970s.[64] Even the recession of 2001 made only a modest dent in employment of single mothers,[65] and the increase in child poverty in the three years following the onset of the recession was dramatically lower than the increases of the previous three recessions. At least part of this success is due to the widespread availability of day care subsidies—and the dollars are going further because parents are purchasing care that is relatively inexpensive.

In short, there is a tradeoff between inexpensive day care, lots of day care coverage, and low-income parents entering the labor force on the one hand and more expensive high-quality programs, less coverage, and difficulty entering the labor force by low-income parents on the other hand. Republicans in Washington, much to the consternation of child advocates and most developmental researchers, have long been intent on ensuring that federal regulations or other requirements do not force a large share of market child care to meet high standards and thereby drive up prices.[66] The route of trying to use federal law to upgrade all day care facilities is bound to fail—especially now that welfare reform has demonstrated the central role of inexpensive day care in promoting work and reducing poverty.

Of course, if the federal government is willing and able to spend more money on high-quality child care, both child advocates who want quality care and those focused on increasing work as a way to reduce welfare dependency could get their way. The problem is that the additional billions of dollars needed to fund universal high-quality care are not likely to be forthcoming, given the current fiscal problems at both the federal and state levels. Thus, recommendations for providing a high-quality preschool program to poor and minority children should not disrupt the child-care arrangements now being made by millions of low-income parents. The best way to achieve this goal is to ensure that government funds pay all or nearly all of the cost of any new program as it affects low-income families.

The combination of moderate evidence on the potential impact of high-quality preschool programs and the importance of continuing and expanding the national commitment to better educational outcomes for poor and minority children leads me to make recommendations that are compatible with the state of knowledge about preschool education, the traditions of federal legislation on preschool issues, and the fiscal austerity and spending priorities that are likely to afflict Congress in the next several years.[67]

Child advocates, scholars,[68] and others[69] frequently recommend that Congress adopt a universal program of high-quality preschool programs. As a means of addressing the education gap between poor and minority students and their more advantaged peers, I disagree with this recommendation for two reasons. First, my review of the research leads to the conclusion that high-quality preschool programs hold promise for improving the school readiness of poor and minority children. But there is still a major question: could a national program be implemented that maintained quality in all or the large majority of sites? Existing research suggests that maintaining quality would be a formidable challenge. Second, the cost estimates for a national program are huge (see below), a point that should be carefully considered by anyone who wants to make recommendations that are feasible and could be enacted by Congress now. Given the federal deficit, and the likelihood that Congress will be in a budget cutting rather than expansionist mode for the next several years,[70] modest proposals are more practical than grandiose proposals. Besides, the research does not justify either major claims or major new spending.

Clearly, a formidable obstacle to proposing a national program of high quality preschool programs is cost. A recent and very sophisticated proposal by David Blau of the University of North Carolina at Chapel Hill would provide parents with vouchers that vary in value depending on family income and the quality of care they select. The annual cost of the Blau voucher program for children zero to five would be $56 billion.[71] But the Blau estimate is for a universal program covering all children birth to age five. We can greatly increase the financial attractiveness of a proposal for expanding preschool programs by limiting the program in two ways. First, the program can be confined to four-year-olds. Second, the program can be confined to children from families with incomes below some cutoff, say 125 percent of the poverty level (about $18,500 for a family of four in 2002).

How much would a high-quality program meeting these specifications cost? The answer, of course, depends on the per-child cost of a high quality program. Wolfe and Scrivner, in proposing a universal, high-quality program for all four-year-olds, estimate the annual cost of a program at $6,700 per child or around $27 billion total.[72] To arrive at their estimate, Wolfe and Scrivner use data on actual market rates of child care, inflated to 2001 dollars, from the Cost, Quality, and Outcomes study.[73] This innovative and careful survey estimated costs for care of five levels of quality; Wolfe and Scrivner used the cost estimate for care of the highest quality, reasoning that this level of quality would produce impacts on children's development (as in fact it did in the Cost, Quality, and Outcomes study). Interestingly, the per-child cost of both Head Start (not counting the local contribution, which is usually in-kind) and the Chicago Child-Parent Center program is about $7,000 (my computation for Head Start costs, Wolfe and Scrivner's for the Chicago program).[74]

If we assume a per-child cost of $7,000 for a high quality program, the next step in computing a cost estimate is to obtain data on the number of four-year-olds in families with incomes under 125 percent of poverty. Census Bureau data show that there were 3.84 million four-year-olds in 2002.[75] About 24 percent of these children are from families with incomes below 125 percent of poverty.[76] Thus, a high-quality program for poor children that meets our income cutoff would cost $7,000 × (.24 × 3.84 million), or about $6.4 billion per year. Although this cost is considerably less than the nearly $27 billion a universal program for four-year-olds would cost, it is still very high.

There are ways to reduce this estimate, though. Head Start already provides a program with costs that are comparable to our estimate of $7,000 per child. In 2002, there were about 490,000 four-year-olds in Head Start. If the Head Start program itself or Head Start funding could be coordinated with the new preschool program, about $3.4 billion of the $6.4 billion cost would be covered by funds currently spent on four-year-olds in Head Start, reducing the money needed for the program to a much more manageable $3 billion. But not all of this $3 billion would have to come from new spending. In addition to the four-year-olds enrolled in Head Start, a large fraction of four-year-olds receive assistance from other programs listed in table 3.4, especially the Child Care and Development Block Grant and Title I. Wolfe and Scrivner estimate that about $1 billion of the Child Care and Development Block Grant is now being spent on four-year-olds.[77] Capturing this money for the new program would reduce needed funds to around $2 billion. Nor does this accounting include any of the $.28 billion federal funds that states spend on Title I preschool programs (table 3.4) or the over $2 billion that states spend on their own preschool programs.[78] Thus, with proper coordination between existing programs and any new money that might be appropriated, it should be possible to provide one year of high-quality preschool to all low-income four-year-olds for around $1 billion per year in new funds.

Given these cost calculations, here are the outlines of a national demonstration program of preschool projects, characterized by manageable costs, that could move the nation a major step toward offering a high-quality preschool program for all four-year-olds in families with incomes below 125 percent of poverty. Congress should enact a program of competitive grants to states or cities that submit a proposal meeting several conditions[79]:

- A plan for providing a high-quality preschool program for all four-year-olds from families with incomes below 125 percent of the federal poverty level that live within the jurisdiction covered by the program;
- Evidence that the preschool program is coordinated with the public school kindergarten program and includes activities to help children meet the academic and behavioral expectations of kindergarten teachers;
- A plan for maintaining a high level of professional development;
- A plan for ensuring that the preschool programs meet several criteria; these include lead teachers with college degrees and at least one year of training in child development, child to teacher (and assistant teacher) ratios of 12:1, and curriculum activities that emphasize math and literacy and the social behaviors such as cooperation and following instructions that are required for school success;
- An evaluation plan that provides for standardized testing at the beginning and end of the preschool year, continuous monitoring and testing of students as they enter the schools, and integration of the testing plan with the testing plan for the No Child Left Behind Act;
- Some mechanism for parent choice in selecting the preschool program their child will attend;
- An explanation of provisions for allowing centers operated under private (nonprofit or for-profit) auspices to participate in the program;
- Evidence of consultation about the plan with Head Start programs in the state;
- A plan for coordinating, either at the city or state level, funds for Head Start, Title I preschool, and funds from the Child Care and Development Block grant (the legislation would give the secretary the authority to allow states or cities to assume control of all Head Start programs within their jurisdiction; if this option is taken, the state or city must present evidence that they have made reasonable efforts to conduct mutual planning with the Head Start programs affected by the grant proposal).

This program should be funded at $1 billion per year for ten years, although it may be necessary to increase funding in the out years if enough states rise to the challenge of mounting programs. In addition, the secretary should have the authority to waive some of these criteria under special circumstances and to allow at least one state to enroll children in a two-year preschool program beginning at age three.

CONCLUDING COMMENT

The momentous 1954 *Brown v. Board of Education* decision set the nation on a path that many thought would lead to equality of educational opportunity and thence to equality of social and economic outcome. This goal was reinvigorated by President Lyndon Johnson in the mid-1960s when he placed the full faith and credit of the federal government behind the goals of bringing children to the starting line equal and achieving equality as a fact and a result, largely through improved education. Yes, the nation has made great progress in reducing poverty, increasing family income, and bringing millions of minority families into the middle class and beyond. But too many are still left behind. We are not achieving perhaps the most basic and most reasonable and most truly American goal set by President Johnson—equality of educational outcome across income and ethnic groups. Worse, we are not making much progress.

Many Americans believe that affirmative action is a stopgap measure intended to carry us over until the time when equality as a fact and a result has been achieved. But affirmative action violates the American value of individual achievement, is guaranteed to continue causing controversy, and shows little sign of contributing to equality as a fact and a result. As old-fashioned parents used to say—and some still do—there is no substitute for hard work and individual achievement. But no matter what one thinks of affirmative action as a major tool in the nation's approach to achieving equality as a fact and a result, Justice O'Connor's recent majority decision in the *Grutter v. Bollinger et al.* case may well have given it a death sentence.[80] On the basis of unknown evidence, she declared that: "25 years from now, the use of racial preferences will no longer be necessary." Her statement may well mean that in twenty-five years, the Supreme Court will declare that affirmative action has fulfilled its purpose and eliminate or severely modify it as a strategy for pursuing equality. A time limit appears to be in place.

Those committed to achieving equality had better redouble their efforts to fill the achievement gap in education. The plans for preschool programs outlined here could play an important role in reducing the gap. At the very least, they will yield useful information for intensifying our efforts if it proves necessary to do so. And well it might.

NOTES

1. Daniel P. Moynihan, *The Negro Family: The Case for National Action* (Washington, DC: U.S. Department of Labor, 1965).

2. Lee Rainwater and William L. Yancey, *The Moynihan Report and the Politics of Controversy* (Cambridge, MA: MIT Press, 1967).

3. Lyndon B. Johnson, *Public Papers of the Presidents of the United States: Lyndon B. Johnson, 1965*, Vol. II, entry 301 (Washington, DC: U.S. Government Printing Office, 1966), pp. 635–640; Daniel P. Moynihan, "The President and the Negro: The Moment Lost," *Commentary* 1 (February 1967):31–45.

4. Stephanie J. Ventura et al., "Nonmarital Childbearing in the United States, 1940–99," *National Vital Statistics Reports* 48, no. 16 (Washington, DC: National Center for Health Statistics, 2000).

5. Sarah McLanahan and Gary Sandefur, *Growing Up with a Single Parent: What Hurts, What Helps* (Cambridge, MA: Harvard University Press, 1994); Paul R. Amato, "The Impact of Family Formation Change on the Cognitive, Social, and Emotional Well-Being of the Next Generation," *Future of Children* 15, no. 2(Fall 2005):75–96.

6. *Congressional Record*, 104th Congress, 1st session, September 16, 1995, 141, no. 137: S12681.

7. Maris A. Vinovskis, *The Birth of Head Start: Preschool Education Policies in the Kennedy and Johnson Administrations* (Chicago: University of Chicago Press, 2005).

8. Both Vee Burke of the Congressional Research Service and Robert Rector of the Heritage Foundation have made estimates of spending on means-tested programs (those that give benefits to an individual or family with income below some criterion) since the mid-1960s. Because their definitions vary somewhat, their estimates differ, but only slightly. The $9 trillion figure comes from Burke's latest volume updated through 2004 with figures from the U.S. Budget. See Vee Burke, *Cash and Noncash Benefits for Persons with Limited Income: Eligibility, Rules, Recipient and Expenditure Data, FY 2000–2002* (RL 32233) (Washington, DC: Congressional Research Service, 2003), pp. 4–5 and Robert Rector and William F. Lauber, *America's Failed $5.4 Trillion War on Poverty* (Washington, DC: Heritage Foundation, 1995).

9. Burke, *Cash and Noncash Benefits*.

10. *Grutter v. Bollinger et al.*, 539 U.S. 31 (2003).

11. Christopher Jencks and Meredith Phillips, eds., *The Black-White Test Score Gap* (Washington, DC: Brookings Institution Press, 1998).

12. In a review arguing that preschool programs can boost academic achievement, leaping into the perilous field of genetic influences on behavior is not necessary. It is impossible to read the relevant literature without concluding that interventions can have substantial impacts on ability and achievement. An impressive recent example is provided by a French adoption study by Duyme and his colleagues on children with IQs of less than 86 who had been abused or neglected and then adopted by age six into families of high socioeconomic status. Their IQs increased by nearly twenty points by adolescence. Thus, whatever one's views on the impact of genetic influences—and for most behaviors they are considerable—there is plenty of room left

for environmental impacts. See Michel Duyme et al., "How Can We Boost IQs of 'Dull Children'?: A Late Adoption Study," *Proceedings of the National Academy of Sciences* 96 (1999):8790–8794.

13. Much of what is known is captured in two superb edited volumes: Jencks and Phillips, *The Black-White Test Score Gap* and John E. Chubb and Tom Loveless, eds., *Bridging the Achievement Gap* (Washington, DC: Brookings Institution Press, 2002), as well as a volume devoted exclusively to the educational achievement of black students, Abigail Thernstrom and Stephan Thernstrom, *No Excuses: Closing the Racial Gap in Learning* (New York: Simon & Schuster, 2003).

14. Larry V. Hedges and Amy Nowell, "Black-White Test Score Convergence since 1965," in *The Black-White Test Score Gap*, Jencks and Phillips, eds., 149–181.

15. Christopher Jencks and Meredith Phillips, "The Black-White Test Score Gap: An Introduction," in *The Black-White Test Score Gap*, Jencks and Phillips, eds., 1–54.

16. Valerie E. Lee and David T. Burkham, *Inequality at the Starting Gate: Social Background Differences in Achievement as Children Begin Kindergarten* (Washington, DC: Economic Policy Institute, 2002), p. 14; Ruth H. McKey et al., *The Impact of Head Start on Children, Families, and Communities* (Washington, DC: U.S. Government Printing Office, 1985), DHHS Publication No. 85–31193, p. 5.

17. Nicholas Zill et al., *Head Start FACES 2000: A Whole-Child Perspective on Program Performance* (Washington, DC: U.S. Department of Health and Human Services, 2003), Fourth Progress Report.

18. Jencks and Phillips, "The Black-White Test Score Gap: An Introduction," 2.

19. A recent paper by Fryer and Levitt finds that, unlike previous research, a modest number of covariates (age, birth weight, socioeconomic status, WIC participation, mother's age at first birth, number of children's books in the home) statistically eliminates the black-white test score gap in math and reading for children entering school. Even if these covariates explain the gap, however, black and white children entering school still actually differ in the characteristics measured by these covariates. Without experimental evidence, it is not even certain that changing the covariates would reduce the gap. Fryer and Levitt also find that after two years of schooling, black students lose .2 standard deviation units in achievement relative to white children. As the authors point out, the implication is that black children attend lower quality schools. There is no question that even if preschool programs could bring minority children to the starting line performing at an average level, bad schools could easily cause them to fall behind. The success of the No Child Left Behind Act is crucial to any strategy of achieving equality as a fact and a result. See Roland G. Fryer, Jr., and Steven D. Levitt, "Understanding the Black-White Test Score Gap in the First Two Years of School," *Review of Economics and Statistics* 86, no. 2 (May 2001):447–464.

20. Society could also intervene in the environment beyond the individual and family. There is evidence, for example, that neighborhoods influence child development and evidence that the social environment provided by peers in school influences school performance. In the interest of space, the possibility that these broader environments could be used to boost school achievement of poor and minority children is ignored here. See Susan E. Mayer and Christopher Jencks, "Growing Up in Poor Neighborhoods: How Much Does It Matter?" *Science* 243, no. 4897 (March 17, 1989):1441–1445; Joshua D. Angrist and Kevin Lang, "Does School Integration Gen-

erate Peer Effects? Evidence from Boston's Metco Program," 2002, Working Paper 9263 (Cambridge, MA: National Bureau of Economic Research); and James Coleman et al., *Equality of Educational Opportunity* (Washington, DC: U.S. Government Printing Office, 1966).

21. There is a strong and consistent literature, beginning with the Coleman Report in 1996, that family characteristics and behaviors are correlated with child outcomes. There is also a strong literature showing that there are major differences in parenting behaviors of children from families of differing socioeconomic status and that parent behaviors such as the frequency and complexity of language directed to the child, discipline practices, expressions of warmth, and intellectual stimulation, all of which favor children from higher socioeconomic status families, are correlated with development and school performance. Thus, it is no surprise that a few parent-training programs have shown impacts on parent behavior and children's development. Perhaps the best known of these programs was designed by David Olds. His research, which shows long-term impacts on parents and children, is based on random-assignment and large samples. It is entirely possible that widespread implementation of the Olds program or a similar program could contribute to closing the education gap. It would be consistent with the approach to policy taken in this chapter to recommend that Congress allocate a few hundred million per year for states that are willing to put up matching funds to implement an Olds-type program with low-income families. Federal dollars should be contingent on state programs that meet several conditions, including scientific evaluations. See Coleman, *Equality of Educational Opportunity*; Jeanne Brooks-Gunn, Lisa J. Berlin, and Allison Sidle Fuligni, "Early Childhood Intervention Programs: What About the Family?" in *Handbook of Early Childhood Intervention*, 2d ed. (New York: Cambridge, 2000), pp. 549–577; David L. Olds et al., "Long-Term Effects of Home Visitation on Maternal Life Course and Child Abuse and Neglect: Fifteen Year Follow-up of a Randomized Trial," *JAMA* 278, no. 8 (1997):637–643; Olds et al., "Home Visiting by Paraprofessionals and by Nurses: A Randomized, Controlled Trial," *Pediatrics* 110, no. 3 (2002):486–496; and Olds et al., "Prenatal and Infancy Home Visiting by Nurses: From Randomized Trials to Community Replication," *Prevention Science* 3, no. 3 (2002):153–172.

22. W. Steven Barnett, "Long-Term Effects of Early Childhood Programs on Cognitive and School Outcomes," *Future of Children* 5, no. 3 (1995):25–50; W. Steven Barnett, "Long-Term Effects on Cognitive Development and School Success," in *Early Care and Education for Children in Poverty*, W. Steven Barnett and Sarane Spence Boocock, eds. (Albany: State University of New York Press, 1998), pp. 11–44; W. Steven Barnett, "Does Head Start Have Lasting Cognitive Effects? The Myth of Fade-Out," in *The Head Start Debates*, Edward Zigler and Sally J. Styfco, eds. (Baltimore, MD: Brooks Publishing Company, May 2004), pp. 221–250; Janet Currie, "Early Childhood Intervention Programs: What Do We Know?" Children's Roundtable Working Paper Series (Washington, DC: Brookings Institution Press, April 2000); Dale C. Farran, "Another Decade of Intervention for Children Who Are Low Income or Disabled: What Do We Know Now?" in *Handbook of Early Childhood Intervention*, 2d ed., Jack P. Shonkoff and Samuel J. Meisels, eds. (New York: Cambridge University Press, 2000), pp. 510–548; Kevin M. Gorey, "Early Childhood Education: A Meta-Analytic Affirmation of the Short- and Long-Term Benefits of

Educational Opportunity," *School Psychology Quarterly* 16, no. 1 (2001):9–30; Ron Haskins, "Beyond Metaphor: The Efficacy of Early Childhood Education," *American Psychologist* 44, no. 2 (1989):274–282; Lynn A. Karoly et al., *Investing in Our Children: What We Know and Don't Know about the Costs and Benefits of Early Childhood Interventions* (Santa Monica, CA: RAND, 1998); McKey et al., *The Impact of Head Start*; Geoffrey Nelson, Anne Westhaus, and Jennifer MacLeod, "A Meta-Analysis of Longitudinal Research on Preschool Prevention Programs for Children," *Prevention and Treatment* 6, Article 31 (2003); U.S. Department of Health and Human Services, *Strengthening Head Start: What the Evidence Shows* (Washington, DC: Author, 2003); Karl White and Glendon Castro, "An Integrative Review of Early Intervention Efficacy Studies with At-Risk Children: Implications for the Handicapped," *Analysis and Intervention in Developmental Disabilities* 5, no. 1 (1985):7–31.

23. Larry L. Orr, *Social Experiments: Evaluating Public Programs with Experimental Methods* (Thousand Oaks, CA: Sage, 1998).

24. Greg J. Duncan and Christina Gibson, "Childcare Quality and Child Outcomes: Drawing Policy Lessons from Nonexperimental Data," *Journal of Policy Analysis and Management* (Forthcoming).

25. Frances A. Campbell et al., "Early-Childhood Programs and Success in School: The Abecedarian Study," in *Early Care and Education for Children in Poverty*, W. Steven Barnett and Sarane Spence Boocock, eds. (Albany: State University of New York Press, 1998), pp. 145–166; Frances A. Campbell et al., "The Development of Cognitive and Academic Abilities: Growth Curves from an Early Childhood Educational Experiment," *Developmental Psychology* 37, no. 2 (2001):231–242; Frances A. Campbell et al., "Early Childhood Education: Young Adult Outcomes from the Abecedarian Project," *Applied Developmental Science* 6, no. 1 (2002):42–57. Note: For the sake of full disclosure, I worked on the Abecedarian program for nearly a decade, beginning in the mid-1970s.

26. Joseph Sparling and Isabelle Lewis, *Learningames for the First Three Years: A Guide to Parent-Child Play* (New York: Walker, 1979).

27. Lawrence J. Schweinhart, Helen V. Barnes, and David P. Weikart, *Significant Benefits: The High/Scope Perry Preschool Study through Age 27* (Ypsilanti, MI: High/Scope Press, 1993).

28. Schweinhart, Barnes, and Weikart, *Significant Benefits*, table 14, p. 70.

29. John R. Berrueta-Clement et al., *Changed Lives: The Effects of the Perry Preschool Program on Youths through Age 19* (Ypsilanti, MI: High/Scope Press, 1984); Lawrence J. Schweinhart and David P. Weikart, *Young Children Grow Up: The Effects of Perry Preschool Program on Youths through Age 15* (Ypsilanti, MI: High/Scope Press, 1980); Schweinhart, Barnes, and Weikart, *Significant Benefits*.

30. Berrueta-Clement et al., *Changed Lives*, 26.

31. *Ibid.*, 27.

32. Schweinhart, Barnes, and Weikart, *Significant Benefits*, xv.

33. Irving Lazar et al., "Lasting Effects of Early Education: A Report from the Consortium for Longitudinal Studies," *Monographs of the Society for Research in Child Development* 47(2–3), Serial No. 195, 1982.

34. I use the term "comparison group" for groups that were not created by ran-

dom assignment, reserving the term "control group" for groups that were created by random assignment.

35. Barnett, "Long-Term Effects of Early Childhood Programs"; Barnett, "Long-Term Effects on Cognitive Development"; Barnett, "Does Head Start Have Lasting Cognitive Effects?"

36. Arthur J. Reynolds, *Success in Early Intervention: The Chicago Child-Parent Centers* (Lincoln: University of Nebraska Press, 2000); and Arthur J. Reynolds et al., "Long-Term Effects of an Early Childhood Intervention on Educational Achievement and Juvenile Arrest," *JAMA* 285, no. 18 (May 2001):2339–2346.

37. Lyndon B. Johnson, *Public Papers of the Presidents of the United States*, 1967, Vol. I, entry 3 (Washington: U.S. Government Printing Office, 1968), pp. 2–14.

38. Peter H. Rossi, "The Iron Law of Evaluation and Other Metallic Rules," in *Research in Social Problems and Public Policy*, Vol. 4, J. Miller and M. Lewis, eds. (Greenwich, CT: JAI, 1987), pp. 3–20.

39. Peter H. Rossi, "The 'Iron Law of Evaluation' Reconsidered." Paper presented at the 2003 conference of American Association of Public Policy Analysis and Management, October.

40. Edward Zigler and Suan Muenchow, *Head Start: The Inside Story of America's Most Successful Educational Experiment* (New York: Basic Books, 1992).

41. McKey et al., *Impact of Head Start*.

42. General Accounting Office, *Head Start: Research Provides Little Information on Impact of Current Program*, GAO/HEHS-97-95 (Washington, DC: Author, 1997), p. 2.

43. Barnett, "Long-Term Effects of Early Childhood Programs" and "Long-Term Effects on Cognitive Development."

44. Sherri Oden, Lawrence J. Schweinhart, and David P. Weikart, *Into Adulthood: A Study of the Effects of Head Start* (Ypsilanti, MI: High/Scope Press, 2000).

45. Janet Currie and Duncan Thomas, "Does Head Start Make a Difference," *American Economic Review* 85, no. 3 (June 1995):341–364, and Eliana Garces, Duncan Thomas, and Janet Currie, "Longer Term Effects of Head Start," 2000, Working Paper 8054 (Cambridge, MA: National Bureau of Economic Research).

46. Barnett, "Long-Term Effects on Cognitive Development," 28.

47. *Ibid.*; Haskins, "Beyond Metaphor"; McKey et al., *Impact of Head Start*.

48. Barnett, "Long-Term Effects on Cognitive Development," 38.

49. W. Steven Barnett et al., *The State of Preschool: 2003 State Preschool Yearbook* (New Brunswick, NJ: National Institute for Early Education Research, Rutgers University, 2003).

50. Walter S. Gilliam and Edward F. Zigler, "A Critical Meta-analysis of All Evaluations of State-Funded Preschool from 1977 to 1998; Implications for Policy, Service Delivery and Program Evaluation," *Early Childhood Research Quarterly* 15, no. 4 (2000):441–473.

51. *Ibid.*; Carol H. Ripple and Walter S. Gilliam, "What Can Be Learned from State-Funded Prekindergarten Initiatives? A Data-Based Approach to the Head Start Devolution Debate," in *The Head Start Debates*, Zigler and Styfco, eds., 477–498.

52. William T. Gormley and Ted Gayer, "Promoting School Readiness in Oklahoma: An Evaluation of Tulsa's Pre-K Program." Unpublished manuscript (Georgetown University, October 2003).

53. Cost, Quality, and Child Outcomes Study Team, *Cost, Quality, and Child Outcomes in Child Care Centers: Technical Report* (Denver: University of Colorado Press, 1995); Katherine A. Magnuson et al., "Inequality in Preschool Education and School Readiness," *American Educational Research Journal* 41, no. 1 (2004):115–157.

54. Rossi, "The Iron Law."

55. It is worth noting that it is unclear exactly what activities or characteristics of successful preschool programs actually produce long-term impacts. Prereading and other academic activities might reasonably be supposed to have impacts on measures of school performance, but what about effects on crime, teen pregnancy, welfare use, and employment? The antecedents of these more general effects are not apparent.

56. Ron Haskins, "Child Development and Child Care Policy: Modest Impacts," in *Developmental Psychology and Social Change*, David B. Pillemer and Sheldon H. White, eds. (New York: Cambridge, 2005).

57. James J. Heckman and Alan D. Krueger, *Inequality in America: What Role for Human Capital Policies?* (Cambridge: MIT Press, 2003); James J. Heckman, "Policies to Foster Human Capital," *Research in Economics* 54 (2003):3–56.

58. John R. Nelson, "The Politics of Federal Child Care Regulation," in *Day Care: Scientific and Social Policy Issues*, Edward F. Zigler and Edmund W. Gordon, eds. (Boston: Auburn Press, 1982), pp. 267–306.

59. Gary Burtless, "The Labor Force Status of Mothers Who Are Most Likely to Receive Welfare: Changes Following Reform." Unpublished manuscript (Washington, DC: Brookings Institution, March 30, 2004); Ron Haskins, "Effects of Welfare Reform on Family Income and Poverty," in *The New World of Welfare*, Rebecca Blank and Ron Haskins, eds. (Washington, DC: Brookings Institution Press, 2001), pp. 103–136; Ron Haskins, "Welfare Reform: The Biggest Accomplishment of the Revolution" in *Republican Revolution Ten Years Later*, Chris Edwards and John Curtis Samples, eds. (Washington, DC: CATO Institute, 2005).

60. Committee on Ways and Means, U.S. House of Representatives, *2004 Green Book* (Washington: U.S. Government Printing Office, 2004), Section 13, pp. 35–41.

61. Ron Haskins, "Is Anything More Important than Day Care Quality?" in *Child Care in the 1990s: Trends and Consequences*, Alan Booth, eds. (Hillsdale, NJ: Lawrence Erlbaum Associates, 1992), pp. 101–115.

62. U.S. Department of Health and Human Services, *Temporary Assistance for Needy Families (TANF) Program*, Third Annual Report to Congress (Washington, DC: Author, 2000).

63. Rachel Schumacher, Mark Greenberg, and Janellen Duffy, *The Impact of TANF Funding on State Child Care Subsidy Programs* (CLASP Policy Brief) (Washington, DC: Center for Law and Social Policy, 2001).

64. Haskins, "Effects of Welfare Reform."

65. Burtless, *The Labor Force Status of Mothers.*

66. Haskins, "Is Anything More Important than Day Care Quality?"

67. Alice Rivlin and Isabel Sawhill, eds., *Restoring Fiscal Sanity: How to Balance the Budget* (Washington, DC: Brookings Institution Press, 2004).

68. David M. Blau, *The Child Care Problem: An Economic Analysis* (New York: Russell Sage, 2001).

69. Committee for Economic Development, *Preschool for All: Investing in a Productive and Just Society* (New York: Author, 2002).

70. Rivlin and Sawhill, *Restoring Fiscal Sanity*.

71. Blau, *The Child Care Problem*, 225.

72. Some scholars of preschool education think a good program would cost $8,000 per year. If so, the total cost would rise by about $1 billion to $7.4 billion. This amount would, of course, be more difficult to reach than $6.4 billion. Even so, especially in states that have created their own preschool program, if all current federal and state spending on preschool were coordinated, the new expenditures necessary to pay $8,000 per child would be fairly modest. See Barbara Wolfe and Scott Scrivner, "Providing Universal Preschool for Four-Year-Olds," in *One Percent for the Kids: New Policies, Brighter Futures for America's Children*, Isabel Sawhill, ed. (Washington, DC: Brookings Institution Press, 2003), p. 129.

73. Cost, Quality, and Child Outcomes Study Team, *Cost, Quality, and Child Outcomes*.

74. Wolfe and Scrivner, "Providing Universal Preschool," 116.

75. U.S. Census Bureau, *Statistical Abstract of the United States, 2003*, 123rd ed. (Washington, DC: U.S. Government Printing Office, 2003), p. 16.

76. Personal communication from Don Winstead, assistant secretary for Program Planning and Evaluation, Department of Health and Human Services, April 13, 2004.

77. Wolfe and Scrivner, "Providing Universal Preschool," 119.

78. Barnett, *The State of Preschool*, 5.

79. Office of the President of the United States, *Strengthening Head Start* (Washington, DC: Author, February 2003); Rachel Schumacher, Mark Greenberg, and Joan Lombardi, *State Initiatives to Promote Early Learning: Next Steps in Coordinating Subsidized Child Care, Head Start, and State Prekindergarten* (Washington, DC: Center for Law and Social Policy, 2001).

80. *Grutter v. Bollinger et al.*, 539 U.S. 31 (2003).

4

Losing Ground at School

Roland G. Fryer, Jr., Harvard Society of Fellows and National Bureau of Economic Research and Steven D. Levitt, American Bar Foundation and University of Chicago

The black-white test score gap is a robust empirical regularity. A simple comparison of mean test scores typically finds black students scoring roughly one standard deviation below white students on standardized tests. Even after controlling for a wide range of covariates including family structure, socioeconomic status, measures of school quality, and neighborhood characteristics, a substantial racial gap in test scores persists.[1]

Gaining a better understanding of the underlying causes of the test-score gap is a question of great importance. Neal and Johnson and O'Neill find that most of the observed black-white wage differentials among adults disappears once lower eighth-grade test scores among Blacks are taken into account.[2] Thus, eliminating the test-score gap that arises by the end of junior high school may be a critical component of reducing racial wage inequality.[3]

A wide variety of possible explanations for the test-score gap have been put forth. These explanations include differences in genetic make-up (see Hernstein and Murray and Jensen), differences in family structure and poverty (see Armor; Brooks-Gunn and Duncan; Mayer; and Phillips, Crouse, and Ralph), differences in school quality (see Cook and Evans), racial bias in testing or teachers' perceptions (see Delpit, Ferguson, and Rodgers and Spriggs), and differences in culture, socialization, or behavior (see Cook and Ludwig, Fordham and Ogbu, Fryer, and Steele and Aronson).[4] The appropriate public policy choice (if any) to address the test-score gap depends critically on the underlying source of the gap.

In this paper, we use the Early Childhood Longitudinal Study Kindergarten Cohort (ECLS-K) to shed new light on the test-score gap. ECLS-K is a new data set administered by the Department of Education. The survey covers a sample of more than 20,000 children entering kindergarten in the fall of 1998. An enormous amount of information is gathered for each individual including family background, school and neighborhood characteristics, teacher and parent assessments, and test scores. The original sample of students has subsequently been reinterviewed in the spring of kindergarten and first grade.

The results we obtain using these new data are informative and in some cases quite surprising. As in previous data sets, we observe substantial racial differences in test scores in the raw data: black kindergartners score on average .64 standard deviations worse than Whites. In stark contrast to earlier studies (including those looking at kindergartners), however, after controlling for a small number of other observable characteristics (children's age, child's birth weight, a socioeconomic status measure, WIC participation, mother's age at first birth, and number of children's books in the home), we essentially eliminate the black-white test score gap in math and reading for students entering kindergarten.[5] Controlling for a much larger set of characteristics yields the same conclusion. This same set of covariates accounts for much but not all of the Hispanic-white difference in test scores, but cannot explain the high test-scores of Asians.

There are three leading explanations for why our results differ so sharply from earlier research such as Phillips, Crouse, and Ralph (1998): (1) nonrandom sampling in the data sets used in earlier studies, (2) real gains by recent cohorts of Blacks, and (3) better covariates in ECLS. Based on our analysis of the Children of the National Longitudinal Survey of Youth (CNLSY) data used by Phillips, Crouse, and Ralph, we conclude that real gains by recent cohorts of Blacks are an important part of the explanation. The raw black-white test-score gap for recent cohorts in CNLSY are comparable to those in ECLS, in sharp contrast to earlier cohorts in CNLSY. Real gains by Blacks born in recent years would appear to be the leading explanation. We cannot, however, fully eliminate the racial test score gap among recent CLNSY cohorts. This is due in part to better covariates in ECLS. Even when nearly identical covariates are included, differences persist between ECLS and CNLSY.

Despite the fact that we see no difference in initial test scores for observationally equivalent black and white children when they enter kindergarten, their paths diverge once they are in school. Between the beginning of kindergarten and the end of first grade, black students lose .20 standard deviations (approximately .10 standard deviation each year) relative to white students with similar characteristics.[6] If the gap in test scores for these children continues to grow at the same rate, by fifth grade the black students will be .50 standard deviations behind their white counterparts—a gap similar in magnitude to that found in previous analyses (see Jones et al.; Phillips; and Phillips, Crouse, and Ralph).[7]

The leading explanation for the worse trajectory of black students in our sample is that they attend lower quality schools. When we compare the change in test scores over time for Blacks and Whites attending the same school, black students lose only a third as much ground as they do relative to Whites in the overall sample. This result suggests that differences in quality across schools attended by Whites and Blacks is likely to be an important part of the story. Interestingly, along "traditional" dimensions of school quality (class size, teacher education, computer:student ratio, etc.), Blacks and Whites attend schools that are similar. On a wide range of nonstandard school inputs (e.g., gang problems in school, percent of students on free lunch, amount of loitering in front of school by nonstudents, amount of litter around the school, whether or not students need hall passes, and PTA funding), Blacks do appear to be attending much worse schools even after controlling for individual characteristics.[8] Our story is incomplete, however, because the observable differences across schools do little to explain the widening black-white gap. This could be due to the coarseness of the school quality variables available in the ECLS.

We explore a range of other explanations as to why black children are losing ground, but find very little empirical support for these alternative theories. Black students do not appear to suffer bigger "summer setbacks" when school is not in session. The lower trajectories of black students are not simply an artifact of standardized testing. Subjective teacher assessments of student performance yield patterns similar to the test-score data. Having a black teacher provides no benefit to black students compared to their white classmates, calling into question the possible role of either overt discrimination or low expectations for black children on the part of white teachers. Finally, adding proxies for behavioral problems does not alter our findings.

The structure of the paper is as follows. The first section provides a brief review of the literature. The second section describes and summarizes the data set. Then we present the basic results for incoming kindergartners, demonstrating that the black-white test score gap disappears once other confounding factors are accounted for. In the next section we document the fact that a racial test-score gap emerges during the school-age years, and the following section analyzes the reasons for this divergence. We present our conclusions in the final section.

BACKGROUND AND PREVIOUS LITERATURE

The Coleman Report (Coleman et al.) was the first national study to describe ethnic differences in academic achievement among children at various stages of schooling. It documented that substantial differences in educational achievement between Blacks and Whites not only existed at every grade level, but increased with student age. Since then, substantial effort has been devoted to understanding what variables account for the gap, as well as how and why the magnitude of the gap has changed over time.[9] A number of stylized facts have emerged. Socioeconomic status and the effects of poverty are important factors in explaining racial differences in educational achievement (see Brooks-Gunn and Duncan, Mayer, Brooks-Gunn et al.).[10] Even after controlling for socioeconomic status in conventional regression analysis, a substantial gap still remains. That gap has generally been declining over time, although for high school students today, the gap is slightly larger than it was in the late 1980s (see Grissmer et al., Hedges and Nowell, and Humphreys).[11] Finally, the gap in test scores between Blacks and Whites historically emerges before children enter kindergarten and tends to widen over time (see Carneiro and Heckman and Phillips, Crouse, and Ralph).

THE DATA

The Early Childhood Longitudinal Study Kindergarten Cohort (ECLS-K) is a nationally representative sample of over 20,000 children entering kindergarten in 1998. Thus far, information on these children has been gathered at four separate points in time. The full sample was interviewed in the fall and spring of kindergarten and spring of first grade. A random sample of one-fourth of the respondents were also interviewed in the fall of first grade. The sample will eventually be followed through fifth grade.[12] Roughly 1,000 schools are included in the sample, with an average of more than twenty children per school in the study. As a consequence, it is possible to conduct within-school analyses.

ESTIMATING RACIAL TEST SCORE GAPS FOR INCOMING KINDERGARTNERS

Table 4.1 presents a series of estimates of the racial test score gap for the tests taken in the fall of kindergarten. The specifications estimated are of the form

$$TESTSCORE_i = RACE_i'G + X_i'T + e_i \quad (1)$$

where i indexes students. A full set of race dummies are included in the regression, with White as the omitted category. Consequently, the coefficients on race capture the gap between the named racial category and Whites. Our primary emphasis is on the black-white test score gap. The vector of other covariates included in the specification, denoted X_i, varies across columns in table 4.1. As one moves to the right in the table, the set of covariates steadily grows. In all instances, the estimation is done using weighted least

Table 4.1. The Estimated Black–White Test Score Gap in Fall of Kindergarten

Variables	Math					Reading				
	(1)	(2)	(3)	(4)	(5)	(6)	(7)	(8)	(9)	(10)
Black	-.638	-.368	-.238	-.094	-.102	-.401	-.134	-.006	.117	.093
	(.022)	(.022)	(.023)	(.023)	(.026)	(.024)	(.025)	(.026)	(.025)	(.030)
Hispanic	-.722	-.429	-.302	-.203	-.171	-.427	-.223	-.137	-.064	-.076
	(.022)	(.023)	(.024)	(.022)	(.028)	(.027)	(.026)	(.026)	(.025)	(.029)
Asian	.150	.070	.190	.265	.274	.335	.256	.371	.409	.375
	(.056)	(.051)	(.051)	(.048)	(.050)	(.064)	(.059)	(.059)	(.058)	(.060)
Other race	-.503	-.329	-.253	-.158	-.113	-.401	-.230	-.155	-.072	-.014
	(.041)	(.037)	(.036)	(.035)	(.035)	(.044)	(.040)	(.040)	(.038)	(.039)
Socioeconomic status composite measure		.456	.389	.302	.072		.451	.393	.299	.092
		(.014)	(.014)	(.014)	(.024)		(.014)	(.015)	(.015)	(.023)
Number of children's books			.007	.006	.005			.007	.006	.004
			(.001)	(.001)	(.001)			(.001)	(.001)	(.001)
(Number of children's books)^2 (*1,000)			-.023	-.020	-.027			-.025	-.021	-.017
			(.003)	(.002)	(.016)			(.003)	(.003)	(.017)
Female				.010	.000				.159	.153
				(.015)	(.015)				(.017)	(.016)

Table 4.1.   Continued

Variables	Math					Reading				
	(1)	(2)	(3)	(4)	(5)	(6)	(7)	(8)	(9)	(10)
Age at kindergarten fall (in months)				.056 (.002)	-2.680 (.542)				.041 (.002)	-2.409 (.483)
Birth weight (ounces) (*10)				.029 (.004)	.030 (.004)				.019 (.004)	.022 (.004)
Teenage mother at time of first birth				-.109 (.018)	-.029 (.021)				-.144 (.020)	-.069 (.022)
Mother at least thirty at time of first birth				.182 (.025)	.111 (.028)				.226 (.027)	.155 (.030)
WIC participant				-.211 (.019)	-.120 (.020)				-.184 (.021)	-.104 (.021)
R-squared	0.108	0.223	0.239	0.317	0.354	0.045	0.16	0.175	0.233	0.279
Number of observations			13290					12601		
Full set of covariates included in regression?	N	N	N	N	Y	N	N	N	N	Y

Notes: The dependent variable is the math or reading test score in the fall of kindergarten. Test scores are IRT scores, normalized to have a mean of zero and a standard deviation of one in the full, unweighted sample. Non-Hispanic Whites are the omitted race category, so all of the race coefficients are gaps relative to that group. The unit of observation is a student. Standard errors are in parentheses. Estimation is done using weighted least squares, using sample weights provided in the data set. In addition to the variables included in the table, indicator variables for students with missing values on each covariate are also included in the regressions. In addition, columns 5 and 10 report only a subset of the coefficients from regressions with ninety-eight covariates included in the specification. The full results for columns 5 and 10 are reported in Fryer and Levitt. Note that the specifications in columns 5 and 10 include age and age squared; that is why the coefficient on age changes so dramatically relative to other columns in the table.

squares, with weights corresponding to the sampling weights provided in the data set.

The first and sixth columns of table 4.1 presents the differences in means, not including any covariates. These results simply reflect the raw test score gaps. The next specification adds the composite indicator of socioeconomic status constructed by the ECLS survey administrators. Socioeconomic status is an important predictor of incoming test scores, carrying a t-statistic over forty. A one-standard deviation increase in the SES variable is associated with a .41 increase in both math and reading test scores. Controlling for socioeconomic status substantially reduces the estimated racial gaps in test scores (see also Coley). The black-white gap in math falls by more than 40 percent; the reading gap is reduced by more than two-thirds. The changes in the other race coefficients are not as large, but in every instance the estimated gaps shrink, and R-squared increases substantially.

The next set of specifications adds the number of children's books in the child's home, the square of that variable, and an indicator variable equal to one if the number of books takes on a missing value for that student. The number of books is strongly positively associated with high kindergarten test scores on both math and reading.[13] Evaluated at the mean, a one-standard deviation increase in the number of books (from 72 to 137) is associated with an increase of .143 (.115) in math and reading respectively. This variable seems to serve as a useful proxy for capturing the conduciveness of the home environment to academic success. Including number of books reduces the black-white gap on math to less than one-fourth of a standard deviation and completely eliminates the gap in reading. The gap for Hispanics also shrinks. The Asian-white gap, however, becomes even larger than the raw gap when number of books is added to the regression.

Columns 4 and 9 add controls for gender, age, birth weight, indicator variables for having a mother whose first birth came when she was a teenager or over 30 (the omitted category is having a first birth in one's twenties), and WIC participation. These covariates generally enter with the expected sign. Older children, those with higher birth weights, those with older mothers at the time of first birth all score better. Children on WIC do worse on the tests, suggesting that this variable is not capturing any real benefits the program might provide, but rather, the fact that eligibility for WIC is a proxy for growing up poor that the SES variable is not adequately capturing. Adding these variables to the specification further improves the test scores of Blacks and Hispanics. In fact, the estimates suggest that, controlling for other factors, black children actually score slightly better than Whites in reading, and only slightly worse in math. We do not have a compelling explanation as to why there is a difference between reading and math achievement.

Only a small gap persists for Hispanics. The advantage enjoyed by Asians becomes even greater. R-squared increases substantially relative to the previous specification.

The final specifications in table 4.1 (columns 5 and 10) include an exhaustive set of roughly 100 covariates capturing city size, neighborhood characteristics, region of the country, parental education, parental income, parental occupational status, family size and structure, whether the mother worked, type of preschool program participation, whether English is spoken at home, and the extent of parental involvement in a child's life and school. We report only a subset of the covariates in table 4.1; full results can be seen in Fryer and Levitt.[14] Almost all of the controls enter in the predicted direction and with coefficients of plausible magnitude. Interestingly, none of the coefficients on race change appreciably. Only a few of the parameters on the controls included in the parsimonious specifications are greatly affected either, and these are easily explained. The socioeconomic status coefficient shrinks because the full set of covariates includes variables that go into the construction of the composite indicator such as parent's income and occupational status. The coefficient on age becomes highly negative because an age-squared term (which is positive and significant) is included in the full specification. The inclusion of these additional variables does little to improve the fit of the model.

Table 4.2 explores the sensitivity of the estimated racial gaps in test scores across a wide variety of alternative specifications and subsamples of the data. We report only the race coefficients and associated standard errors in the table. The top row of the table presents the baseline results using a full sample and our parsimonious set of controls (corresponding to columns 4 and 9 of table 4.1).

Weighting all of the observations equally in the regressions leaves the black-white gap in math and reading virtually unchanged. Using an alternative test-score measure (T-scores, which are norm-referenced measurements of achievement) has very little impact on the results.

One might be concerned that restricting all the coefficient estimates to be identical across the entire sample may yield misleading results. Regressions on a common support (e.g., only on single mothers, region of the country, or only in rural areas) provide one means of addressing this concern. Almost every subset of the data examined yields results roughly similar to those for the overall sample. There is some slight evidence that black females do better relative to Whites than do black males. The results appear to be quite consistent across quintiles of the socioeconomic status distribution. Due in part to relatively imprecise estimates, the equality of black and white test scores on math and reading tests can rarely be rejected for any of the quintiles. Rural Blacks do somewhat worse relative to Whites than those in central cities.

Table 4.2. Sensitivity Analysis/Extensions of the Basic Model for Fall Kindergarten Test Scores

Specification	Coefficient on Black for:		Coefficient on Hispanic for:		Coefficient on Asian for:	
	Math	Reading	Math	Reading	Math	Reading
Baseline	−.094 (.023)	.117 (.025)	−.203 (.022)	−.064 (.025)	.265 (.048)	.409 (.058)
Unweighted	−.100 (.023)	.092 (.024)	−.206 (.021)	−.057 (.024)	.285 (.034)	.387 (.035)
Other test score measures						
T-scores	−.050 (.024)	.141 (.030)	−.057 (.022)	.065 (.028)	.176 (.040)	.298 (.048)
By Gender						
Males	−.126 (.034)	.093 (.037)	−.224 (.032)	−.095 (.035)	.338 (.078)	.385 (.087)
Females	−.058 (.030)	.147 (.035)	−.181 (.031)	−.035 (.036)	.203 (.059)	.433 (.077)
By SES Quintile:						
Bottom	−.092 (.044)	−.005 (.041)	−.202 (.044)	−.133 (.045)	.328 (.143)	.043 (.111)
Second	−.088 (.045)	.091 (.049)	−.179 (.046)	−.090 (.047)	.044 (.106)	−.001 (.090)
Third	−.097 (.049)	.068 (.045)	−.242 (.046)	−.106 (.051)	.249 (.121)	.351 (.167)
Fourth	−.082 (.058)	.292 (.077)	−.100 (.056)	.030 (.057)	.207 (.088)	.396 (.115)
Top	−.169 (.080)	.068 (.085)	−.323 (.078)	−.113 (.094)	.404 (.087)	.724 (.102)
By family structure:						
Single mother	−.087 (.043)	.070 (.043)	−.197 (.048)	−.119 (.047)	.086 (.149)	.114 (.144)
Two biological parents	−.127 (.034)	.141 (.042)	−.176 (.029)	−.033 (.033)	.291 (.054)	.456 (.064)
Teen mother at 1st birth	−.101(.036)	.014 (.033)	−.199 (.036)	−.127 (.038)	.170 (.105)	.251 (.114)
Teen mother at child's birth	−.062 (.046)	−.021 (.043)	−.196 (.045)	−.105 (.052)	.279 (.141)	.281 (.135)

(continues)

Table 4.2. Continued

Specification	Coefficient on Black for:		Coefficient on Hispanic for:		Coefficient on Asian for:	
	Math	Reading	Math	Reading	Math	Reading
By region:						
Northeast	−.087 (.060)	.129 (.076)	−.159 (.054)	−.030 (.060)	.305 (.124)	.483 (.156)
Midwest	.004 (.053)	.093 (.057)	−.140 (.064)	−.031 (.061)	.337 (.119)	.562 (.133)
South	−.153 (.032)	.051 (.033)	−.217 (.040)	−.119 (.048)	.154 (.104)	.368 (.111)
West	.098 (.077)	.362 (.095)	−.200 (.044)	−.001 (.048)	.269 (.071)	.353 (.088)
By location type:						
Central city	−.110 (.035)	.147 (.040)	−.235 (.033)	−.073 (.037)	.271 (.061)	.439 (.075)
Suburban	−.135 (.039)	.030 (.041)	−.261 (.041)	−.145 (.042)	.146 (.102)	.310 (.119)
Rural	−.184 (.048)	−.032 (.050)	−.253 (.062)	−.124 (.072)	.255 (.130)	.126 (.102)
By school type:						
Public	−.106 (.024)	.098 (.027)	−.214 (.024)	−.081 (.027)	.260 (.051)	.392 (.064)
Private	.022 (.070)	.281 (.074)	−.152 (.058)	.015 (.066)	.296 (.135)	.479 (.137)
School >80% Black	.053 (.269)	−.016 (.215)	−.084 (.298)	.057 (.273)	.285 (.382)	.788 (.641)
School >80% White	−.105 (.047)	.059 (.053)	−.186 (.025)	−.061 (.028)	.288 (.054)	.436 (.065)

Notes: Specifications in this table are variations on those reported in columns 4 and 9 of table 4.1. Only the race coefficients are reported in this table. The top row of the table simply reproduces the baseline results in columns 4 and 9 of table 4.1. The remaining rows of the table correspond to different weights, test score measures, or particular subsets of the data. For further details of the baseline specification, see the notes to table 4.1.

Blacks in private schools appear to do especially well, consistent with Neal and Grogger and Neal.[15]

The fact that the black-white test score gap essentially disappears with the inclusion of sufficient controls in ECLS is a very striking result given that in past research a substantial gap has persisted, regardless of the age of the individuals, the particular tests, or the covariates included (e.g., Hernstein and Murray; Neal and Johnson; Phillips, Crouse, and Ralph).[16] The most direct comparison to our research among previous studies is Phillips, Crouse, and Ralph, which looks at test outcomes for kindergartners in the early cohorts of CNLSY. Although Phillips, Crouse, and Ralph have the greatest success among earlier studies in explaining the racial differences in reading (they reduce the gap by two-thirds with their covariates), their raw gap is so large compared to ECLS that the *residual* gap in that paper is almost as large as the *raw* gap in ECLS.

Why our results differ so sharply from previous research, and Phillips, Crouse, and Ralph in particular, is a question of critical importance. There are three leading explanations for the divergence: (1) the sample of births included in CNLSY, especially in the early years, may be nonrepresentative; (2) better covariates are available in ECLS; and (3) Blacks born into recent cohorts have made real gains relative to Blacks born a decade earlier. The first two explanations appear to play only a small role empirically. While it is true that the sample of births in early cohorts of CNLSY analyzed by Phillips, Crouse, and Ralph is heavily skewed toward teenage mothers, because of the way the sample is generated (i.e., by births to those included in CNLSY), the nonrandom sampling, does not seem to provide the explanation for the differing results. When we restrict our ECLS sample to only include children born to teen mothers, our results are virtually unchanged.[17] When we try to estimate specifications in ECLS using only variables that are available in CNLSY, Blacks do somewhat worse than in our baseline sample (a gap of $-.183$ on math and $.034$ on reading), but this is nothing like the residual gap of $-.67$ on reading in Phillips, Crouse, and Ralph.

Real gains by Blacks in recent cohorts, in contrast, does appear to be an important part of the divergence between our results and past research. Limiting the CNLSY to cohorts born in the same years as the ECLS sample, the raw test score gaps in the CNLSY are nearly half as large as in earlier cohorts of CNLSY used by Phillips, Crouse, and Ralph and are remarkably close to those found in the ECLS. On the math skills test, the raw gaps are .638 and .665 respectively in ECLS and CNLSY. For reading, the gap is .401 in ECLS and .540 in the CNLSY. Real gains by Blacks in recent years could explain this result. Interestingly, however, using the same set of controls that yield math and reading gaps in ECLS of $-.183$ and $.034$ respectively, in recent cohorts of the CNLSY the estimated black-white residual gaps are $-.500$ and $-.41$ on math and reading. Thus, although the raw gaps are similar in

ECLS and recent cohorts of CNLSY, larger residual gaps remain in CNLSY for reasons we cannot explain.

THE EVOLUTION OF THE RACIAL TEST SCORE GAPS AS CHILDREN AGE

The results of the previous section demonstrate that although black test scores lag behind Whites by a large margin, the inclusion of a small number of covariates eliminates any systematic differences in the math and reading performances of Whites and Blacks entering kindergarten. Hispanics somewhat lag Whites, and Asians exceed all of the other races. In this section, we explore how those racial gaps change over time.

In terms of raw test scores, black students lose some ground relative to Whites between the fall of kindergarten and the spring of first grade: .090 standard deviations on math and .128 standard deviations on reading. Table 4.3 presents regression results for those two time periods. We report results only from our "parsimonious" regression specification; similar racial gaps emerge when the exhaustive set of covariates is included. Controlling for other factors in the regressions, black students appear to lose much more ground than they do in the raw means: −.156 standard deviations on math and −.188 standard deviations on reading.[18] If black students in the sample continue to lose ground through ninth grade at the rate experienced in the first two years of school, they will lag white students on average by a full standard deviation in raw math and reading scores and over two-thirds of a standard deviation in math even after controlling for observable characteristics (substantially smaller for reading). Raw gaps of that magnitude would be similar to those found in previous studies of high school age children (see Grissmer, Flanagan, and Williamson; Hedges and Nowell; Humphreys; Phillips; and Phillips, Crouse, and Ralph).

In striking contrast to the black-white gap, Hispanics show gains relative to Whites between the beginning of kindergarten and the end of first grade. Asians lose roughly as much ground as Blacks on math (although they start ahead of Whites) and also fall slightly on reading. Thus, black students are not only losing ground relative to Whites, but even more so relative to Hispanics, and somewhat less compared to Asians.

WHY ARE BLACK STUDENTS LOSING GROUND IN THE FIRST TWO YEARS OF SCHOOL?

Understanding why black students fare worse in the first two years of school is a question of paramount importance for two reasons. First, knowing the

Table 4.3.   The Evolution of Test Score Gaps by Race as Children Age

Variables	Math			Reading		
	Fall kindergarten	Spring kindergarten	Spring first grade	Fall kindergarten	Spring kindergarten	Spring first grade
Black	−.094 (.023)	−.201 (.025)	−.250 (.028)	.117 (.025)	−.009 (.027)	−.071 (.029)
Hispanic	−.203 (.022)	−.187 (.024)	−.120 (.026)	−.064 (.025)	−.005 (.027)	.001 (.029)
Asian	.265 (.048)	.221 (.049)	.115 (.044)	.409 (.058)	.434 (.054)	.345 (.045)
Other race	−.158 (.035)	−.166 (.039)	−.195 (.042)	−.072 (.038)	−.099 (.039)	−.163 (.042)
SES composite measure	.302 (.014)	.284 (.014)	.263 (.014)	.299 (.015)	.280 (.015)	.284 (.014)
Number of Books	.006 (.001)	.006 (.001)	.005 (.001)	.006 (.001)	.005 (.001)	.006 (.001)
(Number of Books) (squared) (*1000)	.020 (.002)	−.019 (.003)	−.019 (.003)	−.021 (.003)	−.020 (.003)	−.022 (.003)
Female	.010 (.015)	.003 (.016)	−.033 (.017)	.159 (.017)	.195 (.017)	.216 (.017)
Age at kindergarten fall (in months)	.056 (.002)	.051 (.002)	.036 (.002)	.041 (.002)	.034 (.002)	.021 (.002)
Birth weight (ounces) (*10)	.029 (.004)	.003 (.000)	.029 (.004)	.019 (.004)	.002 (.000)	.024 (.005)
Teenage mother at time of first birth	−.109 (.018)	−.112 (.021)	−.111 (.022)	−.144 (.020)	−.138 (.021)	−.131 (.024)
Mother in 30s at time of first birth	.182 (.025)	.127 (.024)	.093 (.022)	.226 (.027)	.158 (.025)	.085 (.024)
WIC Participant	−.211 (.019)	−.195 (.020)	−.201 (.021)	−.184 (.021)	−.152 (.02)	−.182 (.022)
R-squared	0.317	.282	.240	0.233	0.197	.194
Number of Obs.	13290	13,290	13,290	12601	12601	12,601

Notes: The dependent variable is fall kindergarten test scores in columns 1 and 3 and spring first grade test scores in columns 2 and 4. All specifications include the parsimonious set of controls corresponding to columns 4 and 9 of table 4.1. Test scores are IRT scores, normalized to have a mean of zero and a standard deviation of one in the full, unweighted sample. Non-Hispanic Whites are the omitted race category, so all of the race coefficients are gaps relative to that group. The unit of observation is a student. Standard errors in parentheses. Estimation is done using weighted least squares, using sample weights provided in the data set. In addition to the variables included in the table, indicator variables for students with missing values on each covariate are also included in the regressions.

source of the divergence may aid in developing public policies to alleviate the problem. Second, determining the explanation for the widening gap will help to determine whether the simple linear extrapolation over the academic career is a plausible conjecture.

There are a number of plausible explanations as to why the racial gap in test scores grows as children age: (1) black children attend lower quality schools on average; (2) the importance of parental/environmental contributions may grow over time. Since black children are on average disadvantaged in this regard, they fall behind; and (3) because of worse home and neighborhood environments, black students suffer worse "summer setbacks" when school is not in session.[19] We address each of these hypotheses in turn.

Are Black Students Losing Ground Because They Attend Worse Schools?

There is substantial racial segregation in school attendance in the United States. Our data samples roughly twenty children each from approximately 1,000 schools. In 35 percent of those schools, there is not a single black child in the sample.[20] The mean black student in our sample attends a school that is 59 percent black and 8 percent Hispanic. In contrast, the typical white student goes to a school that is only 6 percent black and 5 percent Hispanic. Given that Blacks and Whites have relatively little overlap in the schools they attend, differences in school quality are plausible explanations for why black students are losing ground.[21]

Because our data set has many individuals from each school included in the sampling frame, school-fixed effects can be included in the estimation. With school-fixed effects, the estimated black-white test score gap is identified off of the relative performance of Blacks and Whites attending the same school, as opposed to across schools. To the extent that differential average school quality across races is the complete explanation for the widening racial test score gap, one would predict that the gap should not widen over time when comparing Blacks and Whites attending the same school. There are, of course, thorny issues of sample selection that potentially complicate the interpretation of these results: white students who elect to attend schools with black students may have differential test score trajectories than other white students, even if they had gone to all white schools. Nonetheless, looking within schools provides a first attempt at testing this hypothesis.

The comparison of changes in the black-white test score gap over time including and excluding school-fixed effects is presented in table 4.4. All of the specifications in the table include the parsimonious set of covariates, although only the coefficient on the black-white gap is shown in the table. The first three columns reflect the full sample of students. The remaining columns restrict the sample to schools that have both black and white chil-

Table 4.4. Does Differential School Quality Explain Black Students Losing Ground: A Comparison of Cross-school and Within-school Estimates of the Test Score Trajectory by Race (Values reported in table are the coefficient on the variable Black)

Subject	Full Sample of Students			Excluding Students Attending All-White Schools					
	(1) Fall kindergarten	(2) Spring first grade	(3) Difference (2) − (1)	(4) Fall kindergarten	(5) Spring first grade	(6) Difference (5) − (4)	(7) Fall kindergarten	(8) Spring first grade	(9) Difference (8) − (7)
Math	−.094 (.023)	−.250 (.028)	−.156 (.036)	−.136 (.028)	−.261 (.034)	−.125 (.044)	−.175 (.034)	−.222 (.040)	−.047 (.052)
Reading	.117 (.025)	−.071 (.029)	−.188 (.038)	.072 (.030)	−.084 (.035)	−.156 (.046)	−.007 (.038)	−.057 (.042)	−.05 (.057)
Include school-fixed effects in regression?	N	N	N	N	N	N	Y	Y	Y
Number of Obs.	13,290			6,532					

Notes: Entries in the table are estimates of the Black-White test score gap, controlling for the parsimonious set of regressors. Columns 3, 6, and 9 represent the estimated change in the gap between kindergarten fall and first grade spring. The first three columns include all students. The remaining columns restrict the data set to schools that had students of different races included in the ECLS-K sample. The final three columns include school-fixed effects. Estimation is done using weighted least squares, using sample weights provided in the data set.

dren in our sample. This set of students is relevant because only mixed-race schools provide useful variation to identify the racial test score gap when school-fixed effects are included.

Column 3 of the table shows the baseline results reflecting the fact that Blacks are losing ground in the full sample ($-.156$ standard deviations relative to Whites in math, $-.188$ standard deviations in reading). When we eliminate students attending all-white schools from the sample, but otherwise estimate identical specifications, the results are not greatly affected (nor are they affected by eliminating students attending all-black schools). Blacks continue to lose substantial ground by the end of first grade. When school-fixed effects are included in the regression (columns 7–9), the black-white test-score gap is identified off of differences between Blacks and Whites attending the same school. The estimates of ground lost by Blacks shrinks to less than one-third of the magnitude in the full sample, and is not statistically different from zero in these specifications.[22]

These findings are consistent with—but not definitive proof of—the argument that systematic differences in school quality for Blacks and Whites may explain the divergence in test scores. An alternative explanation is that Whites who choose to attend schools with Blacks are systematically worse than other Whites. Note, however, that a comparison of columns 1 and 4 show that in the fall of kindergarten black students actually fare somewhat worse relative to Whites who attend schools with Blacks than they do with the full sample of Whites. This finding suggests that the Whites who go to school with Blacks (controlling for observables) actually achieve at a slightly higher level than do those who attend all-white schools, which is consistent with previous research. Moreover, comparing columns 4 and 7, in kindergarten fall, Blacks do even worse relative to Whites attending the same school than they do compared to other Whites. Thus, a simple selection story in which low-achieving Whites are more likely to go to school with Blacks is not consistent with the data. On the other hand, we cannot rule out a priori the possibility that Whites who attend school with Blacks are on lower academic trajectories, despite the fact that they initially score better on tests than other Whites.

If Blacks attend worse schools than Whites on average, one might expect that this would be reflected in observable characteristics of the schools. Table 4.5 analyzes this issue. Each row of the table corresponds to a different measure of school quality. Column 1 presents means and standard deviations of each variable in the data, some of which are standard measures of school inputs (e.g., average class size, teacher education) and others that are nontraditional (e.g., measures of gang problems and loitering). Unfortunately, the nontraditional measures are subjective responses by the school principal, administrator, or other person in charge to questions of how seri-

Table 4.5. Differences across Races in Measurable School Inputs

School Input	Mean of School Input	Coefficient on Race in Predicting Level of School Input:			
		Black	Hispanic	Asian	Other
Average Class Size	20.673 (3.875)	.591 (.340)	.699 (.271)	.799 (.349)	−.259 (.343)
Teacher Has Master's Degree	.280 (.449)	.037 (.028)	.012 (.025)	−.001 (.032)	−.080 (.032)
Computer:Student Ratio	1.257 (2.050)	.003 (.156)	−.131 (.140)	.040 (.119)	.683 (.443)
Internet Hookup:Student Ratio	.344 (.627)	−.048 (.037)	−.032 (.038)	.020 (.035)	.377 (.186)
Percent of Students in School with Free Lunch	29.83 (27.98)	19.32 (2.64)	8.17 (2.00)	3.27 (2.08)	6.81 (2.78)
Gang Problems in School (1–3)	1.409 (.585)	.261 (.058)	.338 (.044)	.128 (.044)	.336 (.069)
Problems with Teacher Turnover (1–5)	1.811 (.943)	.263 (.083)	.227 (.064)	.062 (.078)	.132 (.092)
Litter Around School (0–3)	.741 (.759)	.492 (.065)	.369 (.053)	.240 (.063)	.412 (.087)
People Loitering Around School (0–3)	.524 (.747)	.497 (.079)	.331 (.064)	.171 (.063)	.368 (.088)
Receives PTA Funding	.733 (.442)	−.048 (.033)	−.050 (.026)	.000 (.029)	−.133 (.050)
Hall Pass Required	.425 (.494)	.194 (.037)	.100 (.034)	.010 (.041)	.059 (.046)

Notes: The values in the first column of the table are the means and standard deviations of the named school input. The entries in the remaining columns are estimated coefficients on race (with non-Hispanic Whites as the omitted categories) from regressions of the named school inputs on the race dummies and other covariates included in the parsimonious set of controls. The method of estimation is weighted least squares using sample weights provided by ECLS. The reported standard errors have been corrected to take into account within-school correlation in the school-level measures.

ous problems such as gangs are at the school. Consequently, these measures are likely to be of poor quality. Columns 2–5 report the race coefficients from regressions that are parallel to those elsewhere in the paper, except that school inputs are the dependent variable rather than test scores. Thus, the entries in columns 2–5 reflect the extent to which children of other races attend higher or lower quality schools on each of the measures, controlling for our parsimonious set of covariates. On traditional measures of school quality such as class size, teacher's education, computers in class, and Internet connections, differences between Blacks and Whites are small. On the other hand, the percentage of students eligible for free lunch, the degree of gang problems in school, the amount of loitering in front of the school by nonstudents, and the amount of litter around the schools are much higher for Blacks.

There are important weaknesses in the argument that differential school quality explains the divergent trajectories of Whites and Blacks. First, the observable measures of school inputs included in table 4.5 explain only a small fraction of the variation in student outcomes. For instance, adding the school input measures to our basic student-level test-score regressions only increases the R-squared of the regression by .05. Second, even after the school input measures are added to the test-score regressions, the gap between Blacks and Whites continues to widen. Third, both Hispanics and Asians also experience worse schools than Whites, but neither of those groups is losing ground. Because of these important weaknesses in the story—perhaps as a consequence of poor school quality measures in the data—the evidence linking school quality differences to the divergent trajectories of Blacks can be characterized as no more than suggestive. *Does the importance of parental/environmental inputs grow as children age?*

Black children tend to grow up in environments less conducive to high educational attainment. If the importance of parental/environmental inputs grows as children age, Black students would be expected to lose ground relative to Whites. The evidence in table 4.3, however, argues just the opposite. If that were true, than one would expect to observe the *raw* gaps widening between Blacks and Whites, but to the extent our control variables adequately capture a child's environment, the residual gap after including all the covariates would remain constant. In fact, however, the residual gap increases more than the raw gap contradicting this explanation.[23] Also, the magnitude of the coefficients on socioeconomic status, age at kindergarten entry, and mother's age at first birth are smaller in the first-grade test-score regressions. That suggests that the relative importance of nonschool factors decreases over time, presumably because schools become a critical input into educational gains once children enter school.[24] Interestingly, the importance of school safety measures (e.g., gang problems, metal detectors, etc.) seem to become more important as children age.

Do Black Children Suffer Worse Summer Setbacks When School Is Not in Session?

Entwisle and Alexander and Heyns[25] have argued that black students lose more ground over the summer than white students as a consequence of worse home and neighborhood environments, and they gain ground over the school year while in school. If this were the explanation for the falling performance of Blacks, then public policies should be aimed not at schools, but rather, summer interventions. Our data provide a unique opportunity to test this hypothesis because a subset of the sample is tested both in the spring of kindergarten and in the fall of first grade, shortly after students return to class, allowing us to isolate the relative summer setbacks for Blacks and Whites. The results are reported in table 4.6. For the randomly chosen subset of the sample that is tested in the fall of first grade (about one-fourth of the students), we report at each point in time both the raw test score gap and the residual gap controlling for our parsimonious set of covariates. For the regression results, only the coefficient reflecting the black-white test score gap is shown in the table, and each entry in the table is from a separate regression. The test score gaps in the fall of kindergarten (column 1) and spring of first grade (column 4) for this subset of the sample are similar to those for the sample as a whole, suggesting that the subsample is indeed representative. Of greater interest is a comparison of the test scores in the spring of kindergarten versus the fall of first grade, since most of the intervening

Table 4.6. Do Black Students Suffer a Greater Summer Setback When School Is Not in Session? Estimates of the Black-White Test Score Gap for the Subset of the Sample Tested in Fall of First Grade (Values in the table are coefficients on the variable Black)

Subject	Date test administered:			
	Fall kindergarten	Spring kindergarten	Fall first grade	Spring first grade
Raw Gaps				
Math	−.601 (.040)	−.640 (.044)	−.631 (.045)	−.696 (.048)
Reading	−.376 (.042)	−.421 (.044)	−.390 (.043)	−.548 (.048)
With Controls				
Math	−.052 (.040)	−.097 (.044)	−.134 (.045)	−.236 (.052)
Reading	.142 (.043)	.054 (.045)	.071 (.044)	−.081 (.051)

Notes: Table entries are estimated black-white test score gaps at different points in time for the subset of the sample that has all four test scores. Only a small fraction of the sample was tested in fall of first grade. The total number of observations in the subsample is 5,223. The top panel of the table reflects raw test score gaps; the bottom panel is the residual test score gap, controlling for the parsimonious set of control variables. The observations **in bold** represent the tests given shortly before and shortly after summer break. Standard errors are in parentheses.

time was spent outside of school. On the raw scores, there is little difference before and after the summer break; to the extent there is any gap, it favors black students. With controls, black students lose slightly relative to Whites over the summer on math (the gap rises from -.097 to -.134), but the null hypothesis of no change cannot be rejected. The point estimates for reading show slight gains by black students relative to Whites over the summer. Thus, the empirical results lend little support to the hypothesis that differential summer setbacks explain the lost ground of black students in our sample. We do observe Blacks losing ground during the school year in both subjects in both years, in direct conflict with Entwisle and Alexander.

CONCLUSION

Previous efforts to explain the black-white test score gap have generally fallen short—a substantial residual remained for black students, even after controlling for a full set of available covariates. Using a new data set, we demonstrate that among entering kindergartners, the black-white gap in test scores can be essentially eliminated by controlling for just a small number of observable characteristics of the children and their environment. Once students enter school, the gap between white and black children grows, even conditional on observable factors. We test a number of possible explanations for why Blacks lose ground. We speculate that Blacks are losing ground relative to Whites because they attend lower quality schools, though we recognize that we have not provided definitive proof. This is the only hypothesis that receives any empirical support. To convincingly test this hypothesis, we need more detailed data on schools, neighborhoods, and the general environment kids grow up in.

Compared to previous studies, our results provide reason for optimism. Research on earlier cohorts of children found much greater black-white test score gaps, both in the raw scores and controlling for observables. When we attempt to mimic the nonrandom sample frames in earlier research (for example only looking at low birth-weight babies as in IHDP), we continue to find much smaller gaps in our sample. One plausible explanation for the differences between the current sample and cohorts attending kindergarten ten to thirty years ago is that the current cohort of Blacks has made real gains relative to Whites. Recent cohorts show smaller black-white gaps in the raw data, across multiple data sets, which gives us reason for optimism.

DATA APPENDIX

The Early Childhood Longitudinal Study Kindergarten Cohort (ECLS-K) is a nationally representative sample of 21,260 children entering kindergarten in 1998. Thus far, information on these children has been gathered at four separate points in time. The full sample was interviewed in the fall and spring of kindergarten and spring of first grade. All of our regressions and summary statistics are weighted, unless otherwise noted, and we include dummies for missing data. We describe below how we combined and recoded some of the ECLS variables used in our analysis.

Socioeconomic Composite Measure

The socioeconomic scale variable (SES) was computed by ECLS at the household level for the set of parents who completed the parent interview in fall kindergarten or spring kindergarten. The SES variable reflects the socioeconomic status of the household at the time of data collection for spring kindergarten. The components used for the creation of SES were: Father/male guardian's education; Mother/female guardian's education; Father/male guardian's occupation; Mother/female guardian's occupation; and Household income.

Number of Children's Books

Parents/guardians were asked "How many books does your child have in your home now, including library books?" Answers ranged from 0 to 200.

Child's Age

We used the Child's Age at Assessment Composite variable provided by ECLS. The child's age was calculated by determining the number of days between the child assessment date and the child's date of birth. The value was then divided by 30 to calculate the age in months.

Birth Weight

Parents were asked how much their child weighed when he/she was born. We multiplied the pounds by 16 (and added it to the ounces) to calculate birth weight in ounces.

Mother's Age at First Birth

Mothers were asked how old they were at the birth of their first child.

Average Class Size

We computed each child's average class size over his/her kindergarten year by adding their class size in the fall and spring and dividing by two.

Teacher Has Master's Degree

We coded a dummy variable equal to one if the child's teacher has a master's degree or above.

Computer:Student Ratio

The number of computers in each school and the total enrollment of each kindergarten program is provided by the ECLS based on a survey given to each school. We divided the number of computers in each school by the total enrollment in kindergarten to produce this ratio.

Internet Hook-Up:Student Ratio

This was constructed similar to the Computer:Student ratio, except the numerator consists of Internet/LAN connections in the school.

Percent of Students in Child's School Eligible for Free Lunch

Schools provided the percent of students in their school who were eligible for free lunch.

Gang Problems

Schools were asked: "How much of a problem are gangs in the neighborhood where the school is located?" We coded this variable so that 1 implies "no problem," 2 implies "somewhat of a problem," and 3 implies "big problem."

Teacher Turnover

Schools were asked how much they agreed with the statement "teacher turnover is a problem in this school." Answers range from 0 to 5, 0 indicating they strongly disagree and 5 indicating they strongly agree.

Litter around School

The ECLS interviewer was asked to report the amount of litter around each school. The variable ranges from zero to three. Zero indicates no litter and three indicates "a lot."

People Loitering around School

The ECLS interviewer was asked to report the amount of loitering by nonstudents around the school. The variable ranges from zero to three, zero indicating no loitering and three indicating "a lot."

PTA Funding

Schools reported whether or not they receive supplemental funding from their PTA. We recoded this variable so that 1 implies yes and 0 implies no.

Hall Pass Required

Schools were asked: "Are hall passes required to ensure the safety of the children in your school?" This variable is coded 1 if yes and 0 if no.

NOTES

This chapter originally appeared as "Understanding the Black-White Test Score Gap in the First Two Years of School," *The Review of Economics and Statistics* 86, no. 2 (May 2004):465–480. We are grateful to Josh Angrist, Janet Currie, Michael Greenstone, Christopher Jencks, Alan Krueger, James Heckman, Susan Mayer, Derek Neal, Meredith Phillips, Barbara Schneider, and two anonymous referees for helpful comments and suggestions. Financial support was provided by the National Science Foundation (Fryer and Levitt). Correspondence can be addressed either to Roland Fryer, Jr., American Bar Foundation, 750 N. Lake Shore Drive, Chicago, IL 60611, or to Steven Levitt, Department of Economics, 1126 E. 59th Street, University of Chicago, Chicago, IL 60637. E-mail: roland@uchicago.edu, slevitt@midway.uchicago.edu.

1. See W. Baughman and W. Dahlstrom, *Negro and White Children: A Psychological Study in the Rural South* (New York: Academic Press, 1968); B. A. Braken, E. Sabers, and W. Insko, "Performance of Black and White Children on the Bracken Basic Concept Scale," *Psychology in Schools* 24, no. 1 (1987):22–27; Jeanne Brooks-Gunn et al., "Do Neighborhoods Influence Child and Adolescent Development?" *American Journal of Sociology* 99, no. 2 (1993):353–395; Jeanne Brooks-Gunn, Greg J. Duncan, and Pamela Klebanov, "Economic Deprivation and Early-Childhood Development," *Child Development* 65, no. 2 (1994):296–318 and "Ethnic Differences in Children's Intelligence Test Scores: Role of Economic Deprivation, Home Environment and Maternal Characteristics," *Child Development* 67 (1996):396–408; James Coleman et al., *Equality of Educational Opportunity* (Washington DC: U.S. Government Printing Office, 1966); Richard J. Coley, "An Uneven Start: Indicators of Inequality in School Readiness," *Educational Testing Service Report*, Princeton, NJ, March 2002; Richard J. Herrnstein and Charles Murray, *The Bell Curve: Intelligence and Class Structure in American Life* (New York: The Free Press, 1994); Lloyd Humphreys, "Trends in Levels of Academic Achievement of Blacks and Other Minorities," *Intelligence* 12 (1988):231–260; Arthur Jensen, "How Much Can We Boost IQ and Scholastic Achievement?" *Harvard Educational Review* 39 (1969):1–123 and *Educability and Group Differences* (New York: The Free Press, 1973); A. Kaufman and N. Kaufman, *K-ABC: Kaufman Assessment Battery for Children* (Circle Pines, MN: American Guidance Services, 1983); E. Krohn and R. Lamp, "Current Validity of the Stanford-Binet Fourth Edition and K-ABC for Head Start

Children," *Journal of Psychology* 27 (1989):59–67; J. Naglieri, "WISC-R and K-ABC Comparison for Matched Samples of Black and White Children," *Journal of Social Psychology* 24 (1986):81–88; Meredith Phillips et al., "Family Background, Parenting Practices, and the Black-White Test Score Gap," in *The Black-White Test Score Gap*, Christopher Jencks and Meredith Phillips, eds. (Washington, DC: Brookings Institution Press, 1998), pp. 103–145; Meredith Phillips, "Understanding Ethnic Differences in Academic Achievement: Empirical Lessons from National Data," in *Analytic Issues in the Assessment of Student Achievement*, David Grissmer and Michael Ross, eds. (Washington DC: U.S. Department of Education, National Center for Education Statistics, 2000), pp. 103–132; and Sandra Scarr, *Race, Social Class and Individual Differences in I.Q.* (Hillsdale, NJ: Lawrence Erlbaum Associates, 1981).

2. See Derek Neal and William R. Johnson, "The Role of Pre-Market Factors in Black-White Wage Differences," *Journal of Political Economy* 104 (1996):869–895 and June O'Neill, "The Role of Human Capital in Earnings Differences between Black and White Men," *Journal of Economic Perspectives* 4, no. 4 (1990):25–46.

3. To this effect, Jencks and Phillips write: "Reducing the black-white test score gap would do more to promote racial equality than any other strategy that commands broad political support."

4. See Herrnstein and Murray, *The Bell Curve*; Jensen, *Educability and Group Differences*; and Arthur Jensen, *The G Factor: The Science of Mental Ability* (Westport, CT: Greenwood Publishing Group, 1998); Greg Armor, "Why Is Black Educational Achievement Rising?" *Public Interest* (September 1992):65–80; Jeanne Brooks-Gunn and Greg J. Duncan, eds., *The Consequences of Growing Up Poor* (New York: Russell Sage, 1997); Susan E. Mayer, *What Money Can't Buy: Family Income and Children's Life Chances* (Cambridge, MA: Harvard University Press, 1997); Phillips et al. 1998; Michael Cook and William Evans, "Families or Schools? Explaining the Convergence in White and Black Academic Performance," *Journal of Labor Economics* 18, no. 4 (2000):729–754; Lisa Delpit, *Other People's Children: Cultural Conflict in the Classroom* (New York: The New Press, 1995); Ronald F. Ferguson, "Teachers' Perceptions and Expectations and the Black-White Test Score Gap," in *The Black-White Test Score Gap*, Jencks and Phillips, eds., 273–317; William Rodgers and William Spriggs, "What Does AFQT Really Measure: Race, Wages, Schooling and the AFQT Score," *The Review of Black Political Economy* 24, no. 4 (1996):13–46; Phillip Cook and Jens Ludwig, "The Burden of 'Acting White': Do Black Adolescents Disparage Academic Achievement?" in *The Black-White Test Score Gap*, Jencks and Phillips, eds., 375–400; Signithia Fordham and John Ogbu, "Black Students' School Successes: Coping with the Burden of Acting White," *The Urban Review* 18, no. 3 (1986):176–206; Roland Fryer, "An Economic Approach to Cultural Capital," 2002, Working Paper (Chicago: University of Chicago Press); C. Steele and J. Aronson, "Stereotype Threat and the Test Performance of Academically Successful African Americans," in *The Black-White Test Score Gap*, Jencks and Phillips, eds., 401–430.

5. On a test of general knowledge, a racial test-score gap persists. On a subjective teacher assessment of general knowledge, however, there is no difference between Blacks and Whites in fall of kindergarten.

6. Neither Hispanics nor Asians experience this widening test score gap over time. Indeed, Hispanic children systematically close the gap relative to Whites, pre-

sumably because their initial scores are artificially low as a consequence of limited English proficiency among some Hispanic parents.

7. Lyle V. Jones, Nancy Burton, and Ernest Davenport, *Mathematics Achievement Levels of Black and White Youth* (Chapel Hill: University of North Carolina, L.L. Thurstone Psychometric Laboratory, 1982); Phillips, "Understanding Ethnic Differences"; Meredith Phillips, James Crouse, and John Ralph, "Does the Black-White Test Score Gap Widen after Children Enter School?" in *The Black-White Test Score Gap*, Jencks and Phillips, eds., 229–272.

8. This pattern is also consistent with self-selection of low-achieving Whites into schools attended by Blacks. Casting doubt on this alternative explanation is the fact that Whites who go to school with Blacks have baseline test scores upon entering kindergarten that are similar to those who are in all-white classes (Humphreys, "Trends in Levels of Academic Achievement," documents a similar finding among high school students). When we eliminate from the sample Whites who have no black children in their class (more than 60 percent of all white children fall into this category), we obtain similar results.

9. In particular, Herrnstein and Murray's controversial book, *The Bell Curve*, published in 1994, ignited interest in the subject by arguing that genetic differences are the primary explanation for the differences between Blacks and Whites in achievement test scores. For excellent summaries of the book, see James J. Heckman, "Lessons from The Bell Curve," *Journal of Political Economy* 103, no. 5 (1995):1091–1120 and Arthur Goldberg and Charles Manski, "Review Article: The Bell Curve," *Journal of Economic Literature* 33, no. 2 (1995):762–776. Examples of the discussion that emerged include Bernie Devlin, Daniel Resnick, and Kathryn Roeder, *Intelligence, Genes, and Success: Scientists Respond to the Bell Curve* (New York: Copernicus Books, 1998); Steven Fraser, *The Bell Curve Wars: Race, Intelligence, and the Future of America* (New York: Basic Books, 1995); and Joe Kincheloe, Shirley Steinberg, and Aaron Gresson, *Measured Lies: The Bell Curve Reexamined* (New York: St. Martins Press, 1997).

10. See Brooks-Gunn and Duncan, *The Consequences of Growing Up Poor*; Mayer, *What Money Can't Buy*; Jeanne Brooks-Gunn, P. K. Klebanov, and Greg J. Duncan, "Ethnic Differences in Children's Intelligence Test Scores: Role of Economic Deprivation, Home Environment, and Maternal Characteristics," *Child Development* 67, no. 2 (1995):396–408; Jeanne Brooks-Gunn and Greg J. Duncan, "Family Poverty, Welfare Reform and Child Development," *Child Development* 71, no. 1 (2000):188–196.

11. David Grissmer, Ann Flanagan, and Stephanie Williamson, "Why Did the Black-White Score Gap Narrow in the 1970's and 1980's?" in *The Black-White Test Score Gap*, Jencks and Phillips, eds., 182–228; Larry Hedges and Amy Nowell, "Black-White Test Score Convergence since 1965," in *The Black-White Test Score Gap*, Jencks and Phillips, eds., 149–181; Humphreys, "Trends in Levels of Academic Achievement."

12. In addition, there is an ECLS birth cohort that tracks a nationally representative sample of over 15,000 children born in 2001 through the first grade.

13. The marginal benefit associated with one additional book decreases as more books are added. Beyond roughly 150 books, the marginal impact turns negative. Only 16 percent of the sample lies above this cutoff point.

14. Roland Fryer and Steven Levitt, "The Black-White Test Score Gap in the First Two Years of School," *The Review of Economics and Statistics* 86 (2004):447–464, test a more exhaustive set of possibilities.

15. We have also experimented with limiting the sample to the set of children for whom there is substantial overlap across races in background characteristics. More specifically, we ran probits with an indicator variable for black as the dependent variable and the full set of covariates as predictors. When we drop from the sample the roughly 30 percent of students whose predicted probability of being black is less than 10 percent or greater than 90 percent, the black-white gap on math rises slightly and the reading gap becomes closer to zero.

16. The exceptions we are aware of in which the black-white test score gap has been made to disappear are Jonathan Cane, "Race and Children's Cognitive Test Scores: Empirical Evidence that Environment Explains the Entire Gap," University of Illinois at Chicago (1994). Kai Li and Dale J. Poirier, "The Roles of Birth Inputs and Outputs in Predicting Health, Behavior, and Test Scores at Age Five or Six," 2001. Working Paper, University of British Columbia; and Pedro Carneiro and James Heckman, "Human Capital Policy," 2002, Working Paper, The University of Chicago. Li and Poirier, "The Roles of Birth Inputs and Outputs," using a Bayesian structural model, find no systematic differences between Blacks and Whites using the NLSY. Herrnstein and Murray, *The Bell Curve*, and Meredith Phillips, James Crouse, and John Ralph, "Does the Black-White Test Score Gap Widen after Children Enter School?" in *The Black-White Test Score Gap*, Jencks and Phillips, eds., 229–272, using different methods on the same data, find large gaps still persist. Using CNLSY, Crane (1994) and Carneiro and Heckman, "Human Capital Policy," find that on some tests, racial gaps disappear with controls, although large gaps remain on other tests designed to capture similar sets of skills.

It is important to note that on the test of general knowledge in ECLS, the black-white gap does not fully disappear. Black students test almost one full standard deviation behind Whites in a raw comparison of means. That gap falls to .3 when controls are included. On the subjective teacher assessments, the raw gap in general knowledge between Blacks and Whites is much smaller (.25 standard deviations) and does shrink almost to zero with the inclusion of controls.

17. Our results are also unchanged when we limit our ECLS sample to low birthweight babies, who are oversampled in IHDP, another data set analyzed by Phillips, Crouse, and Ralph, "Does the Black-White Test Score Gap Widen?"

18. Similar results (not shown in the table) are obtained when we include the full set of nearly 100 covariates. In those specifications, black students lose .136 standard deviations on math and .109 standard deviations on reading. Including the fall kindergarten test score as a covariate predicting the spring first grade test score also has little impact on the results: black students lose .192 (.140) standard deviations in math (reading).

19. Fryer and Levitt, "The Black-White Test Score Gap," test a more exhaustive set of possibilities.

20. Black students may attend these schools, but just not be in the classrooms sampled.

21. Because elementary school students attend schools close to home, there is no

way for us to distinguish between the impact of neighborhood and school quality in our data set. Note, however, that we are able to explain racial gaps upon entry to school without using controls for the neighborhood environment. For neighborhoods rather than schools to explain the racial divergence in test scores, the quality of the neighborhood would need to have a large impact on test scores after entry into school, but not before.

22. This finding in some ways parallels the findings in Janet Currie and Duncan Thomas, "School Quality and the Longer Term Effects of Head Start." *Journal of Human Resources* 35, no. 4 (2000):755–774, that early gains for students who attend Head Start tend to disappear due to low-quality schools that these students later attend. Consistent with Currie and Thomas, we do not find a positive effect of Head Start on student test scores even in kindergarten, once other factors are controlled for. This finding is also related to Alan Krueger and Diane Whitmore, "Would Smaller Classes Help Close the Black-White Achievement Gap?" 2001, Working Paper #451 Industrial Relations Section, Princeton University and Phillips, Crouse, and Ralph, "Does the Black-White Test Score Gap Widen?," who find that the black-white gap widens as a result of poorer quality schools.

23. Indeed, from a theoretical perspective, one might expect that the opposite hypothesis would hold true: the importance of parental inputs declines with age. Prior to reaching school age, the relative share of educational inputs provided by parents is very large. Once school starts, much of the burden for educating is shifted to the schools. Our empirical evidence does not, however, provide much support for this conjecture either.

24. An alternative explanation for the shrinking coefficient on the SES variable is that socioeconomic status varies over time. Therefore, using the kindergarten value of the SES variable in the first grade regression induces measurement error. That explanation cannot explain the declining coefficients on age at school entry and mother's age at birth. Moreover, for other variables that are time varying, like number of books and WIC participation, the coefficients do not shrink in the first-grade regression.

25. Doris Entwisle and Karl Alexander, "Summer Setback: Race, Poverty, School Composition, and Mathematics Achievement in the First Two Years of School," *American Sociological Review* 57 (1992):72–84 and "Winter Setback: The Racial Composition of Schools and Learning to Read," *American Sociological Review* 59 (1994):446–460; Barbara Heyns, *Summer Learning and the Effects of Schooling* (New York: Academic Press, 1978).

5

Lessons Learned from School Desegregation

David J. Armor, George Mason University

Many educators and civil rights activists had high hopes that the end of state-mandated segregation signaled by *Brown* would improve black learning and eliminate the black-white achievement gap. Despite some improvements in black achievement during the 1970s and 1980s, the achievement gap actually grew slightly during the 1990s and remains very large more than fifty years after *Brown*. As a consequence, the concern and debate over the achievement gap has also grown over the last several years, particularly following the No Child Left Behind Act and its demand to eliminate all achievement gaps by the year 2014. This legislation has catapulted racial achievement gaps to one of the highest priorities of federal, state, and local education agencies.

Why has the achievement gap been so hard to eliminate? Did school desegregation help reduce the gap, and if so why was its impact limited? Perhaps we do not fully understand the ways in which school segregation affects black achievement. Given their history, do desegregation policies have a future role in efforts to close the achievement gap?

Assuming the ultimate goal is to reduce the achievement gap, it is critical to understand the specific causal mechanisms behind low black achievement and whether desegregation plays a role in the overall strategy to eliminate achievement gaps. In this respect, this chapter focuses not just on the relationship between desegregation and achievement, but also on theories about why desegregation should improve black achievement. Research on desegregation can be useful not only for discovering the effects of desegregation per se, but also for revealing conditions that may improve black achievement even within the context of segregated schools.

After reviewing the most prominent theories relevant to desegregation and the achievement gap, I will discuss existing and new evidence on the role of desegregation and other factors that might help reduce the achievement gap. My goal is to recommend educational policies that promise to reduce the gap and to evaluate whether school desegregation needs to be part of those policies.

THEORIES OF THE GAP

There are four major theories that try to explain why desegregation or certain types of racial composition should improve black achievement. Each of these theories posits a specific mechanism that is responsible for the achievement gains. The first is the classic self-esteem theory, the second is an educational input theory, the third is peer group theory, and the fourth is the theory of family risk factors.

Self-esteem Theory

The self-esteem theory was developed by psychologists during the 1940s and 1950s, and it led to the well-known "psychological harm" thesis mentioned in the *Brown* decision.[1] The theory was given added weight by a statement for the Supreme Court signed by thirty-two social scientists.[2] Briefly, the theory stated that school segregation—especially when enforced by law—harms black children's self-esteem. Segregated black children internalize the inferior status conferred upon them by the dominant white society, which in turn interferes with their ability to learn. It was thought that desegregated schools would eliminate this judgment of inferiority, improve black self-esteem and motivation, and raise black achievement.

Generally, research from the late 1960s onward has found few black-white differences in either self-esteem or educational aspirations regardless of desegregation status; I will mention some recent evidence later.[3] There are, however, modern versions of the psychological harm theory, what I call the "harm and benefit thesis." For example, one version sees teachers as the active agent for low self-esteem rather than segregated schools. The argument is that some teachers, even those in desegregated schools, have low expectations for black students, and low teacher expectations can cause low black achievement via lowered motivation and self-esteem.[4] Under these newer versions, black achievement can still fail to improve even when schools are desegregated.

There are other differences between the old and new theories, mostly in conditions that must be present if desegregated schools are to raise black achievement. These conditions were outlined in a modern statement signed by sixty-four social scientists and submitted as part of a brief in *Freeman v. Pitts* (DeKalb County, Georgia).[5] In addition to teacher and staff attitudes, the conditions include parental involvement, cooperative learning strategies, elimination of tracking and grouping practices, and many other educational policies and practices. For these theorists, the absence of these conditions is often invoked to explain the lack of black achievement gains in desegregated schools.

Educational Inputs Theory

The educational inputs theory employs concepts from economics to emphasize the amount of school resources such as school facilities, expenditures, teacher quality, class size, and curriculum. According to classic economic production theory, as school resources (inputs) increase, so should academic achievement (output). As late as the mid-1960s, most educators and social scientists believed that the resources and programs in black schools were inferior to those in white schools, and this resource inequality explained lower black achievement. Given this assumption, if desegregation equalizes school resources, it follows that black achievement should improve.

In 1966 the Coleman report on the Equality of Educational Opportunity strongly challenged this theory.[6] Not only did black and white schools have relatively equal school resources (once regional differences were factored in), school resources had very weak correlations with academic achievement (although teacher characteristics were the most important of the school factors). This implies that even if unequal resources were found in some states or school districts, they would not explain very much of the achievement gap.

The Coleman conclusions were controversial in 1966, and the debate over the importance of school resources continues to the present time.[7] Many education researchers invoke school resource inequality to explain the achievement gap, particularly with respect to the quality of teachers. Some policy experts believe that more black than white students attend schools with lower-quality teachers, and this explains at least part of the achievement gap. This is one of the reasons why the No Child Left Behind Act places such a strong emphasis on raising teacher quality in low-achieving schools.

Most recent research, however, tends to confirm Coleman's finding that school resources and most measured teacher characteristics have fairly weak and inconsistent correlations with academic achievement, with the possible exception of teacher subject-matter mastery (as indicated by certification, college major, or test scores). Therefore, even if desegregation helped to equalize resources, we would not expect a large reduction in the achievement gap from this fact alone.

Peer Group Theory

Peer group theory is grounded in the sociological concept of group influences. Peer group theory holds that academic performance is influenced by the dominant norms of a school or classroom. The potential influence of peers on academic achievement can be positive or negative. According to this thesis, school desegregation should improve black achievement because it increases the exposure of lower-achieving black students to higher-achieving white students. School segregation could worsen black achievement by minimizing contact with white students. The notion of "concentration of poverty" represents a similar concept; school environments with high concentrations of poverty are thought to have adverse effects on educational and social outcomes above and beyond the effects of individual poverty itself.[8]

Peer group theory was given a boost by findings in the original Coleman report, and the Coleman report was used in early desegregation litigation to support the view that desegregation would improve academic achievement. Coleman himself, however, cautioned that it was not racial desegregation per se but rather socioeconomic desegregation that provided benefits. Thus desegregating low-income white children with low-income black children would not be expected to have any particular benefit. Later analyses of the Coleman data found an error in the original analysis and concluded that the peer group effect was not statistically significant.[9]

In recent literature about the achievement gap, peer group theory has resurfaced in a somewhat different form. Rather than emphasizing the positive effects of a majority white school environment, authors such as McWhorter and Ogbu have emphasized the negative effects of "black culture," particularly in secondary schools, whereby a black peer culture discourages high black achievement on various grounds (e.g., it is tantamount to "acting white").[10] Thus, even in desegregated schools the potential benefits of having a majority white environment may be negated by the adverse effects of black peers.

Another variant of peer group or "black culture" theory has been put forward by the Thernstroms.[11] They endorse the potential anti-academic effects of black culture, reinforced by a complacent school faculty and staff. But they go even further to argue that a school administration and faculty can create a school culture that challenges the conventional black culture by setting very high academic standards and demanding high performance. This new school culture, they claim, can successfully overcome low performance norms among black students even when a school is predominantly black. In fact, virtually all of the schools they cite as successful examples are predominantly black (e.g., KIPP Schools). Clearly, this type of school culture effect, if validated, would not require school desegregation in order to improve black achievement. Indeed, it might be difficult to implement such a strategy in schools that enrolled both low SES Blacks and high SES Whites.

Clearly, peer group effects cannot be the only cause of the achievement gap, because the gap is very large during the early school grades when peer effects would be minimal. For example, the NCES Early Achievement study shows that the achievement gap in mathematics is about .7 standard deviations in the spring in first grade, and NAEP data show an achievement gap of .7 in grade four.[12] It seems unlikely that the type of peer effects described by Ogbu and McWhorter would be operating this early in elementary school. Of course, black peer culture may contribute to low black achievement patterns when black students get into middle and high school.

Family Risk Factors

A fourth theory of the achievement gap from child development research postulates a set of critical family risk factors.[13] Most of these factors operate during infancy and early childhood and explain why there is a cognitive skill gap before children start school. These risk factors include parent IQ, parent education, family income, number of parents at home, number of children, birth weight, nutrition, mother's age at first birth, number of books (or reading materials) in the home, and the parenting behaviors of instruction (cognitive stimulation) and nurturance (emotional support).

Some authors have identified these family risk factors as components of black culture.[14] It makes sense, however, to distinguish these demographic and behavioral factors from strictly cultural attributes such as attitudes, values, and beliefs. Family risk factors are valid for all children regardless of race or ethnicity, although some factors may have different degrees of influence depending on a child's race.

More will be said about the validity and applicability of these theoretical perspectives following a discussion of the evidence on desegregation and black achievement.

EVIDENCE OF THE GAP

Most studies on desegregation and achievement were undertaken before 1990, and most of these were small studies within a single school district. I will mention just one early study before moving to more recent evidence that provides a fresh opportunity to revisit questions once thought settled.

The NIE Review

The most comprehensive review of the relationship between desegregation and black achievement was carried out by the National Institute of Education (NIE) in 1984. A panel of seven experts conducted meta-analyses of the most methodologically sound studies of desegregation and black achievement available at that time. The selected studies (nineteen total) were longitudinal and included a nondesegregated control group. Six of the experts conducted independent meta-analyses and wrote separate reports; one panelist (Thomas Cook) reviewed the six analyses and attempted to synthesize the results.

Some panelists found no significant effects of desegregation, some found large positive effects, and yet others were somewhere in between. Cook's synthesis stressed the large variation in results from the nineteen studies, and he concluded that desegregation had no effect on math achievement and a small positive effect on reading achievement. He also felt that the wide variation in results made it difficult to offer reliable policy recommendations.[15]

Recent Studies

There were few studies of desegregation and achievement during the 1990s.[16] Interestingly, the most important book on the achievement gap during the 1990s was Christopher Jencks and Meredith Phillips, *The Black-White Test Score Gap*, yet it did not contain a single chapter dedicated to the effects of segregation or desegregation on the achievement gap. However, one chapter in that volume used aggregate NAEP data to suggest that desegregation was one of several possible explanations for rising black achievement during the 1970s and 1980s.[17] Although the results were suggestive, the analyses did not include any individual-level data showing that black students in desegregated schools had higher test scores than those in segregated schools once other factors were taken into account.

In 2002, I published a review of desegregation and black achievement based on both national and school district data. The national data consisted of individual test scores from the 1992 NAEP, and the school district data was drawn from five large cities or counties that had undergone desegregation of varying degrees (Charlotte-Mecklenburg, North Carolina; Dallas, Texas; Kansas City, Missouri; Minneapolis, Minnesota; and Wilmington-New Castle, Delaware). In my opinion, the school district studies offered some of the most compelling evidence; I will review some of those results later. Overall, this review found little evidence that desegregated schools or desegregated school systems had reduced the achievement gap by a significant degree.[18]

The most recent comprehensive study on desegregation and black achievement is by Hanushek, Kain, and Rivkin (HKR), and it comes to quite the opposite conclusion.[19] The analysis is based on achievement test scores in Texas schools, grades three to seven, from 1993 to 1997. It is a complex model based on annual changes in student test scores, and one with some unusual results that are not readily explained. The HKR findings are summarized in table 5.1.

The key finding is shown in the last row of table 5.1 (labeled gain score 3), and it shows the effect of a 1 percent change in black classmates on annual achievement gains with the maximum number of control factors removed. The annual estimated effect of black classmates, $-.0025$, seems small but is actually very large. It means that an increase of 1 percent black classmates decreases black achievement by .0025 standard deviations *each year*. This implies that black students who experience a decrease of 40 percent black classmates (e.g., who go from a 80 percent black school to a 40 percent black school) and remain in that school for five years would gain one-half a standard deviation in their test scores—or a reduction in the achievement gap by more than one-half. If the time span of desegregation was ten years, then the gap should be completely eliminated. Importantly, black composition had no significant effects on white achievement.

Note that the model assesses percent black (on black achievement), and not the percent white that corresponds to the usual definition of desegregation. In so doing, it treats Hispanics, Asians, and other minorities as equivalent to Whites. Tacitly, this model assumes a black peer group effect; that is, the percentage black rather than white peers is the driving force for black achievement. If percent white does not have a large positive effect on black achievement, then one might conclude that segregation lowers black achievement not because of white absence but because of black concentration.

While this study and model constitutes an important advance on earlier work, it has several limitations. First, the model of achievement gains controlling only for student background characteristics (labeled gain score 1) shows a large and *positive* effect of a change in percent black classmates. This means that, controlling for student and family characteristics (but not school

Table 5.1.   Annual Effect of Percent Black on Black Math Achievement* Dependent

Variable	Effect (prob)	Controls
Math score	$-.0007$ (ns)	Gender, grade-by-year, community type
Gain score 1	$+.0029$ ($<.001$)	Free lunch, grade-by-year, student fixed effects, type of school move
Gain score 2	$-.0030$ ($<.001$)	Add to 1: school-by-grade fixed effects
Gain score 3	$-.0025$ ($<.001$)	Add to 2: attendance zone fixed effects, teacher experience, class size, and student turnover

Source: Hanushek et al. 2004, table 5.1

*Effect estimates changed to reflect percentage black instead of proportion black. Effect is the expected increment in math or gain scores, in sd's, from a 1 percent change in percentage black students (in a student's school grade) in one year.

effects), an increase in percent of black classmates leads to an *increase* in achievement scores (or vice-versa), and the magnitude is even larger than the negative effect in model three.

HKR claim that this positive effect is spurious, arising from students who matriculate from elementary to middle schools. Middle schools usually have a lower percent black because of larger attendance areas, and the authors argue that temporary adjustment problems cause test scores to decline, giving rise to a positive relationship. However, the study provides no summary data to back up this argument.

Second, the inclusion of school fixed effects raises concerns. It is an understandable step, because it removes any unmeasured between-school effects to compensate for the relatively sparse measures of school resources and teacher quality (apparently only teacher experience and class size are available). But given that racial composition is also a between-school characteristic, removing school fixed effects means that achievement gains are not being compared between segregated and desegregated schools. Rather, achievement gains are being analyzed only in relation to changes from one year to the next at specific schools, which could reflect demographic or other changes that are also affecting test scores. A school might lose white students because of turmoil in the surrounding neighborhood, or a school might gain white enrollment because of middle-class movement to that area.

Another possible interpretation arises from the common practice of reassigning students with behavior problems to special (alternative) schools that frequently have higher minority composition. Such reassignments might lead to declines in student achievement regardless of other school characteristics.

Finally, my greatest reservation is the sheer magnitude of the HKR effect in the absence of concrete examples showing that an increase in long-term desegregation is associated with a very substantial reduction or even elimination of the achievement gap. There are school districts with desegregation plans which have changed racial composition by 40 or 50 points for long periods of time, and yet I do not know of a single case, including cases in Texas, where this level of desegregation has led to large reductions in the achievement gap.

Accordingly, the rest of this section presents some new analyses based on national and state data that examine the relationship between racial composition and black achievement. The goal is to test whether the HKR findings apply to other states or to the nation as a whole.

New National and State Data

If black concentration is a major cause of low black achievement (under whatever theory might apply), and if school desegregation is a remedy and does not adversely affect white achievement, then schools that undergo substantial desegregation should show black achievement gains and a corresponding reduction of the achievement gap.

In the dozens of school districts I have studied, I have not observed this phenomenon, even when the desegregation is extensive and occurs under ideal conditions. These studies are consistent with my cross-sectional analyses of the 1992 NAEP data, which found little relationship between school percent white and black achievement (or the achievement gap) after controlling for student background. However, results from the 1996 NAEP using percent black instead of percent white reveal some interesting differences, some of which are consistent with the HKR findings.

The new analysis uses individual math scores for eighth graders (thirteen-year-olds) from the 1996 national administration. Math scores were adjusted for student background (free lunch, parent education, family status, and household reading items), and then the effect of percent white was compared to the effect of percent black for both black and white achievement.

Figure 5.1 shows the relationship between school percent white—the conventional measure of desegregation—and SES-adjusted white and black eighth-grade math scores.[20] There is no consistent relationship between the percent white in a school and either black or white achievement, once student socioeconomic factors are removed. Although the lowest black scores are observed for those in 0–10 percent white schools, black scores in 11–30

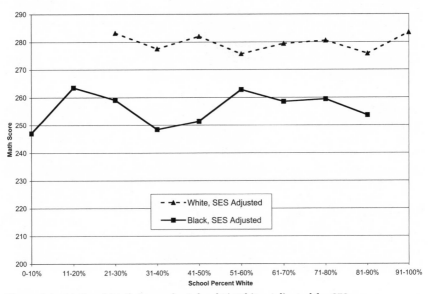

Figure 5.1   National Math Scores by School % White, Adjusted for SES (1996 NAEP Age 13)

percent white schools are as high or higher than those in 61–80 percent black schools. Of course, the sample sizes are small in some categories, so considerable variability is expected.

In figure 5.2, I follow HKR by assessing the effect of percent Black on math achievement. Strikingly, there is a significant negative relationship between school percent Black and both black and white math achievement; the results for black students are consistent with the HKR findings in Texas. There appear to be two thresholds in this relationship. After adjusting for student SES, black students in schools 80–100 percent black score about 10 points lower than Blacks in racially mixed schools, which corresponds to about one-third of a standard deviation. It should be noted that since white achievement is affected in about the same way, the black-white gap remains at about 20 points regardless of racial composition (about two-thirds of a standard deviation).

The fact that school percent White and school percent Black have different relationships with black achievement is important. Under classical psychological harm theory, the benefits of desegregation for black students derive from increasing exposure to Whites, not decreasing exposure to other Blacks. The possibility that black achievement may be affected more by black than white composition has important theoretical implications, especially regarding the role of black peer effects.

Although the NAEP correlation between percent Black and SES-adjusted

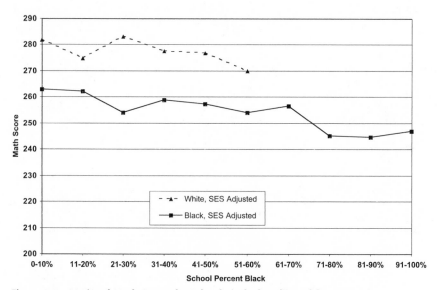

Figure 5.2   National Math Scores by School % Black, Adjusted for SES (1996 NAEP Age 13)

achievement is clear, more analysis is needed before even tentative causal inferences can be drawn. The NAEP scores have been adjusted for only a limited number of student SES factors; there are many other student, school, and programmatic factors that could be causing the correlation between test scores and racial composition shown in figure 5.2. What causal mechanisms might be operating here? Is the correlation spurious because of uncontrolled student or school variables? Can the correlation be replicated using school-district or state-level data? Which of the theories discussed earlier offer the best explanation? I will try to give preliminary answers to each of these questions.

First, I examined regional and state-to-state variations within the NAEP data itself. There was no North-South explanation for the correlation in figure 5.2; that is, predominantly black schools (81 percent black or higher) were located in both the North and the South, and the regional means were nearly equal. There was, however, considerable variation from one state to another. Although the 1996 NAEP samples are relatively small for each state, the state variable had a strong and statistically significant effect on SES-adjusted black achievement.

Figure 5.3 shows the adjusted black scores for the nine states that had predominantly black schools. The predominantly black schools in Ohio and Tennessee had the lowest scores, while the predominantly black schools in New York and Texas had the highest. The New York score of 267 is espe-

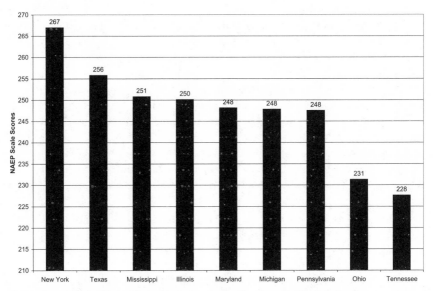

Figure 5.3   Black 8th Grade Math Scores in Predominantly Black Schools

cially striking, since it is substantially higher than the national average for black students in predominantly white schools. Even the Texas score of 256 is noteworthy, because it is not unlike the national mean of students in desegregated schools (21–60 percent Black). Although these results are strictly provisional because of small sample sizes, they do suggest that the disadvantage of predominantly black schools might be location dependent, possibly because of curriculum or other school program differences.

The NAEP results led me to undertake an analysis of state testing data. So far I have been able to examine the relationship between racial composition and math achievement in four states: New York, North Carolina, South Carolina, and Texas. Like the NAEP results in figure 5.3, the state analyses reveal substantial and so far unexplained variations in the potential effect of predominantly black schools on black math achievement.

The available data differ somewhat for each state, so a few comments on approach and methodology are in order. Since black students in predominantly black schools may have lower SES than black students in desegregated schools, ideally test scores should be adjusted for student SES (in this case free lunch status). Unfortunately, individual SES data are available only for New York and South Carolina. The North Carolina and Texas data are available only at the school level, and while test scores are calculated separately by race, adjustments for individual student SES are not possible.[21] Accordingly, the New York and South Carolina analyses show both adjusted and unadjusted math scores. Further, eighth grade math scores are analyzed in North and South Carolina and Texas, but the available New York test scores were for sixth graders.

Figure 5.4 illustrates the relationship between racial composition and sixth grade math scores for the New York State math test. There is a very weak relationship between racial composition and actual black scores, mostly due to higher scores for Blacks in predominantly white schools. Adjusting for student free lunch status generally raises black scores, as expected, but now there is virtually no effect of racial composition. Interestingly, there is a significant correlation between school percent Black and actual white achievement, but after adjusting for free lunch status the relationship becomes quite weak. These results are consistent with and validate the NAEP results shown in figure 5.3; attending a predominantly black school in New York State does not appear to have adverse effects on sixth grade math achievement for either race.

Figure 5.5 shows an analysis for North Carolina eighth-grade students using their 2002 state End of Grade proficiency tests. The test scores are actual percent passing according to North Carolina state standards; no adjustment is made for student SES. In contrast to New York, there is a substantial relationship between racial composition and black achievement; the pass rates for Blacks in predominantly black schools are 30 percentage points

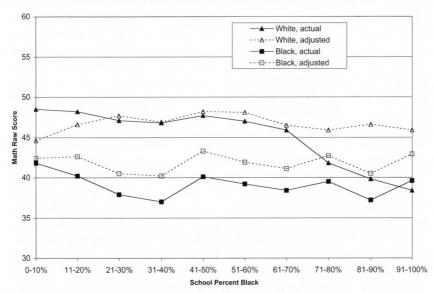

Figure 5.4   New York Math Scores by School % Black (1998 Grade 6)

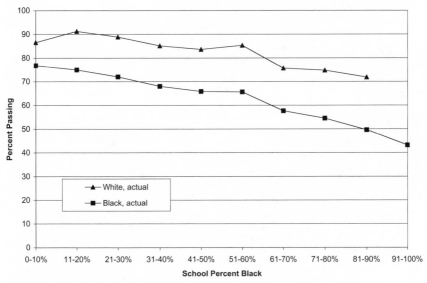

Figure 5.5   North Carolina Math Scores by School % Black (2002 Grade 8, actual scores)

lower than those in predominantly white schools. Since no adjustments can be made for free lunch, it is possible that black students in predominantly black schools have lower SES than those in desegregated schools (e.g., see the results for Charlotte-Mecklenburg in figure 5.8). Fortunately, because North Carolina is more desegregated than the nation as a whole, less than 10 percent of all North Carolina black eighth graders are enrolled in schools greater than 80 percent black.

Figure 5.6 summarizes the analysis for South Carolina eighth-grade students using their 2003 state test scores (PACT). Like New York, South Carolina allows a comparison of actual math scores with scores adjusted for student SES. Unlike New York, there is a modest negative relationship between school percent Black and actual black math scores. Black students in predominantly black schools score about 4 points lower than Blacks in predominantly white schools (the standard deviation of these scale scores is about 13 points). After adjusting for student free lunch, however, the effect of black concentration is very small (about 1 point between majority black and majority white schools). A somewhat stronger negative relationship remains for white students after SES adjustments—the point spread for white students in majority black vs. majority white schools is about 2 points.

The Texas analysis uses school-level results from their 2003 TAKS testing program, and the results are summarized in figure 5.7.[22] Since student free lunch data are not available, only actual eighth-grade math scores are shown.

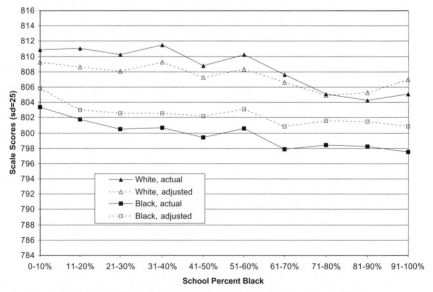

Figure 5.6   South Carolina Math Scores by School % Black (2003 Grade 8)

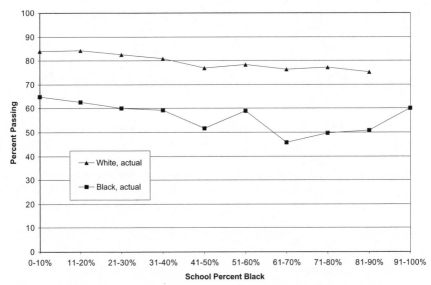

Figure 5.7   Texas Math Scores by School % Black (2003 Grade 8, actual scores)

The relationship between racial composition and the percent of Blacks passing the math test is complex. The relationship is curvilinear, with a modest negative relationship for schools 10–40 percent and a positive relationship for schools 61–100 percent black. Scores in schools over 90 percent black and 51–60 percent black resemble the scores of Blacks in 11–40 percent black schools.[23] It must be emphasized, of course, that student poverty is not taken into account in figure 5.7, and this modest relationship might be reduced or even eliminated if individual student SES could be introduced as a control.[24]

An illustration of the possible impact of variations in poverty rates in predominantly black schools is shown in table 5.2. Dallas and Houston enroll about two-thirds of all black eighth graders in Texas who are enrolled in middle or junior high schools that are more than 80 percent black. While the average percent black is nearly identical in these schools (88 and 89 percent black, respectively), the average poverty in Dallas is thirteen points lower

Table 5.2.   Black Passing and Poverty Rates in Schools >80% Black

	Dallas	Houston
% Passing 8th Grade math	60	51
% Poverty	75	88
No. students	1,664	926
No. schools	5	5

than the Houston schools. This lower poverty rate may explain why Dallas eighth grade pass rate in these schools is nearly ten points higher than Houston's (60 percent vs. 51 percent).

The lack of a strong effect of racial composition in the 2003 Texas state data is inconsistent with the HKR findings based on earlier data. Of course, the results shown in figure 5.7 are based only on a simple cross-sectional analysis, while the HKR study uses student change scores and a very sophisticated model. But if the HKR findings reflect a fundamental causal process, there should be a stronger cross-sectional correlation than found here. Moreover, the vast majority of black students in Texas attend schools with less than 50 percent black enrollments and have done so for many years, yet the achievement gap shown in figure 5.7 is just about as large for those schools as majority black school. This does not square with the implications of HKR findings.

Before leaving the state studies, one of my studies at the school district level is relevant to the discussion here, especially in view of the results for North Carolina in figure 5.5. One limitation of state or national studies is that racial composition is not linked to actual desegregation. That is, the racial composition of schools may simply reflect the natural demographic composition of cities and neighborhoods rather than policies adopted because of a desegregation objective. When school systems adopt desegregation plans, especially when ordered by a court, many things can change other than the racial composition of schools including teacher assignments, curriculum, and resource allocation. Thus, when analyzing statewide test scores, the effects of racial composition do not necessarily reflect the effects of desegregation policies as distinct from demographic effects.

Charlotte-Mecklenburg was under a court-ordered desegregation plan from 1971 to 2000. During the first twenty years or so, Charlotte maintained a high degree of racial balance using extensive cross-district busing. In the early 1990s Charlotte shifted to more choice options including magnet schools. Through a combination of white losses in the urban center and white gains in the suburbs, by the late 1990s its elementary and middle schools had substantial variations in racial composition. Although the majority of black students still attended desegregated schools (30–70 percent black), there were significant numbers of black children in predominantly white and predominantly black elementary schools.

Figure 5.8 shows the relationship between percent Black and unadjusted math scores for Charlotte third, fourth, and fifth graders in 1998. There is virtually no correlation between black achievement and racial composition (the actual correlation coefficient is .02), but there is a small negative correlation for white achievement (−.13).[25] When the scores are adjusted for free lunch status, there is no difference for black students, but the correlation for white students is reduced to less than −.1.

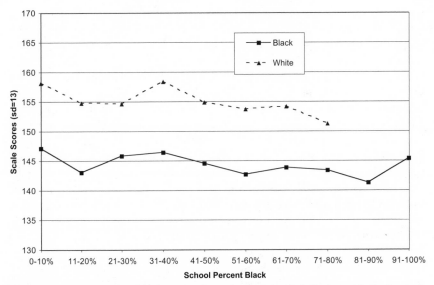

Figure 5.8   Charlotte-Mecklenburg Math Scores by School % Black (1998 Grades 3–5; unadjusted scale scores)

The implication is that, while North Carolina as a whole shows a negative correlation between black concentration and black achievement, its largest city does not. This finding underscores the variability and inconsistency of black concentration effects.

Whatever might be causing the relationship between racial composition and black achievement in the NAEP data, it appears to be a conditional correlation—it occurs in some states or school districts but not in others. How do we explain this? Is there any information from NAEP that might give us some clues about why the relationship appears in some locations but not others?

Investigating the NAEP Correlation

Can the 1996 NAEP math assessment be used to shed light on possible causal mechanisms that explain the lower black achievement in predominantly black schools? The 1996 NAEP math assessment includes a large number of student, teacher, and school program characteristics; an examination of these characteristics could suggest whether one or more of the theories reviewed earlier help explain this racial composition effect.

A few caveats are in order about this analysis. First, while the ultimate goal is to explain the black-white achievement gap, the focus here is comparing black students in segregated vs. desegregated schools to develop explanations for variations in black achievement. Second, much of the student data comes from self-administered questionnaires with all of their inherent limitations (e.g., socially desirable response bias). Accordingly, references to other research will be made as appropriate.

Student characteristics include self-rated math ability, educational aspirations, absenteeism, and hours of TV watched per day. Teacher characteristics include advanced degrees, experience, certification for junior high math, study of math in college, and race. Curriculum characteristics include class size, type of math class (algebra, pre-algebra, etc.), and teacher's rating of how much algebra is taught in the class. Two types of analyses were carried out to test whether any of these characteristics could help explain the relationship between racial composition and black achievement. First, the relationship between each characteristic and racial composition was examined; second, if a relationship with racial composition was found, a regression was run to estimate the effect of that characteristic on black achievement after controlling for student SES.[26]

The relationships between these characteristics and school racial composition are shown in table 5.3 for black students in the 1996 NAEP. A few of these characteristics are related to racial composition; the question then becomes whether they are related to SES-adjusted black achievement in such a way that helps explain the correlation in figure 5.2.

Considering the student characteristics, two are relevant to the psychological harm thesis—self-concept and educational aspirations. The self-concept question asked about agreement with the statement, "I am good in math," and the aspiration question asked how far students plan to go in school. Neither characteristic is reliably related to racial composition for black students. Although not shown in the table, there is virtually no black-white difference in either self-concept or educational aspirations; for example, 77 percent of Whites and 76 percent of Blacks plan to graduate from college. Not only do black self-concept or college aspirations fail to explain racial composition effects on achievement, more fundamentally they contribute little to explaining the black-white achievement gap. The findings on self-concept have been replicated in dozens of studies over the past several decades.[27]

The other three student characteristics could reflect potential adverse effects of black culture. These include discussing schoolwork at home (parental involvement), absenteeism, and hours of watching television (often cited as a cultural factor). Neither frequency of discussing homework with parents nor hours of watching TV had a significant relationship with racial composition, and neither of these student characteristics was related to SES-adjusted black achievement.

Days absent from school was significantly related to racial composition. Black students in predominantly black schools were absent an average of twenty days during the school year compared to thirteen days for those in

Table 5.3. Student and School Characteristics for Black Students by Racial
Composition of School (1996 Naep Math, Age 13)

	Percentage Black in School				
Characteristic	1–20%	21–50%	51–80%	81–100%	All
STUDENT CHARACTERISTICS					
% Agree "I am good at math"	63	65	63	68	64
% Plan to graduate from college	78	76	77	74	76
% Discuss school at home daily	41	39	38	42	40
Days absent (per year)	13	17	16	20	17
Hours of TV per day	3.9	4.2	4.4	4.3	4.3
TEACHER CHARACTERISTICS					
% MA degree or higher	40	53	54	51	50
Years teaching math	12	12	13	15	13
% Certification in math	84	69	78	56	69
% College major/minor in math	82	68	67	65	69
% Black	4	19	24	70	35
CURRICULUM					
% in algebra class	16	15	22	25	20
% Emphasis on algebra: "a lot"	63	45	32	47	46
Math instruction hours/week	3.1	3.3	3.2	3.2	3.2
Minutes of homework/day	54	54	55	48	52
Class size	25	25	24	27	26
Weighted Ns	135	219	216	262	832

predominantly white schools and about sixteen days for those in racially mixed schools.[28] Not surprisingly, regression analysis shows that absenteeism is related to SES-adjusted black achievement; five days of absence is associated with a reduction of about one point in black achievement.[29] Therefore, assuming that the causal direction runs from absenteeism to achievement rather than the other way around, the racial composition differences in absenteeism shown in table 5.3 could explain a small portion of the black achievement differences between predominantly black and predominantly white schools.

Regarding teacher characteristics, racial composition is not significantly associated with teachers having higher degrees, years of teaching math, or having a math major or minor in college. Racial composition is, however, significantly related to teacher's race and having a certificate in math. Teachers in predominantly black schools are 70 percent black (versus less than 25 percent in other schools) and are less likely to have a certificate in math than their counterparts in desegregated schools. According to a regression analysis, both of these characteristics have significant effects on SES-adjusted black achievement, −8 points for black teachers (controlling for certification) and +2 points for having a math certificate (controlling for race).

There is, however, a significant and puzzling interaction between these two factors. Black students in classes with certificated black teachers have the lowest scores at 244 points. In contrast, black students with noncertificated teachers of either race score about 6 points higher, and black students with certificated white teachers score the highest at 259 points. Furthermore, when state is examined to help clarify this pattern, an even more complex interaction emerges which makes these two teacher characteristics very difficult to interpret.

Table 5.4 shows the relationship between race of teacher and black math achievement for the nine states in the 1996 NAEP with predominantly black schools (81–100 percent black). Overall, there is no difference in SES-adjusted test scores for students with black or white teachers. In five states with teachers of both races, students with black teachers score higher or about the same as those with white teachers in four; the exception is Tennessee, where students with black teachers have extremely low scores.[30] Note that Ohio, with the second lowest black scores, has all white teachers. A similar complex and inconsistent pattern emerges when certification effects are examined by state; for example, for the two states with the lowest scores

Table 5.4. SES-Adjusted Black Achievement by Race of Teacher in Predominantly Black Schools (1996 Naep Math, Age 13)

	Race of Teacher	
	White[a] (N)	Black (N)
New York	b	267 (15)
Texas	253 (7)	254 (35)
Illinois	252 (10)	254 (32)
Maryland	248 (19)	b
Michigan	246 (22)	253 (4)
Mississippi	b	246 (20)
Pennsylvania	235 (13)	268 (7)
Ohio	230 (13)	b
Tennessee	249 (8)	223 (49)
Total	245 (92)	246 (162)

a All are white except PA, where five of thirteen non-black teachers are Hispanic.
b No cases

(Ohio and Tennessee), all but a few of the teachers in predominantly black schools hold junior high math certificates.

While the small numbers of students prevent a definitive conclusion, teacher's race and math certification appear to interact with state (or school district) factors to produce complicated and inconsistent effects on black achievement. It is quite possible that these complex results are due to differing state certification and licensing policies. Whatever the reason, the low test scores of black students in predominantly black schools does not appear due to the predominance of black teachers or the lower rate of teacher certification.

Next, the NAEP contains several measures of specific curriculum characteristics. These include type of math class, emphasis on algebra, amount of math instruction, amount of homework, and size of the math class. There are no important racial composition differences for emphasis on algebra or hours of math instruction per week (rated by teachers), and black students in predominantly black schools are somewhat more likely to be enrolled in algebra than their counterparts in more desegregated schools. Not surprisingly, type of math class has a strong relationship with black achievement; black students taking algebra score twelve points higher than those taking eighth-grade math. But given the lack of racial composition differences favoring desegregated schools, the type of math class cannot explain the lower black achievement in predominantly black schools.

The other two curriculum characteristics, homework and class size, do favor desegregated schools. Black students in predominantly black schools spend about six minutes less time on homework per day, and homework is significantly related to black achievement such that the six-minute difference could explain about one point or so of the lower math scores. There is also a small difference of two students in average size of math classes, and class size has a small negative relationship with black achievement such that each additional student is associated with decrease of .4 points in black math scores. So class size might also explain about one point of the lower scores in predominantly black schools.

So far, these student and school characteristics have been examined one at a time. When absenteeism, homework, and class size are considered jointly, they lower black achievement in predominantly black schools by a total of -2.5 points. Thus, these three characteristics taken together may explain about one-fourth of the difference in black scores between predominantly black schools and racially mixed schools. Two of these characteristics, absenteeism and time spent on homework, are arguably black culture effects arising from lack of parental involvement. Class size is clearly a school resource effect.

Finally, while the NAEP achievement scores have been adjusted for important SES characteristics, there are other family characteristics not measured by the NAEP that influence achievement, including certain parenting behaviors, number of siblings, birth weight, and health care.[31] The proportion of black students with these other risk factors might increase as the school percent Black increases.

THE FUTURE OF DESEGREGATION AND BLACK ACHIEVEMENT

What can be concluded from this review of recent evidence on the relationship between racial composition and black achievement? Does the evidence favor one theory over another, and do favored theories suggest any mechanisms that might help improve black achievement in the absence of desegregation? Finally, what policy recommendations are supported by this evaluation of current evidence and theories?

At the outset, I want to make clear that the evaluation of racial composition here is restricted to its impact on black test scores and the academic achievement gap. Other important social and educational outcomes might be influenced by school desegregation, such as race relations, educational attainment, occupational success, and enrollment stability (e.g., white flight). As such, this examination does not reach any major conclusions about the effect of racial composition on these other outcomes, although the issue of white flight is mentioned in connection with certain policy implications.

Summary of the Evidence

With respect to the evidence, the most striking aspect of this review is the variation and lack of consistency of results from one study or set of data to another. The HKR analysis of Texas data is not consistent with the relationship between black concentration and black achievement for 2003 Texas eighth graders. The strong relationship between racial composition and black achievement in the 1996 NAEP math scores is replicated with North Carolina state testing data but not with New York, South Carolina, or Texas state-testing data. The North Carolina statewide relationship is not replicated within Charlotte-Mecklenburg, the largest school district in North Carolina.

Of course, methodological issues could be part of the reason for the inconsistency, particularly because the state and local data are cross-sectional while the HKR data are longitudinal. Although methodological limitations no doubt exist, they do not tell the whole story. If desegregation has the magnitude of effect found in the HKR Texas study, then comprehensive and effective desegregation plans like those in Charlotte-Mecklenburg and many other school districts should have eliminated the achievement gap after ten years or so. Indeed, the achievement gap should have been largely eliminated for Texas Blacks by now, since most have attended desegregated schools for many years now. These results simply have not materialized.

The within-school racial composition effects in the HKR model may be qualitatively different from the large between-school changes in racial composition when a desegregation plan is implemented. I am unaware of any significant desegregation changes occurring in Texas during the time frame of the HKR study. The largest changes in within-school racial compositions probably arise from enrollment changes when school boundaries change, as when schools open or close, or when a black student shifts from one school to another for a variety of reasons. These types of enrollment or student changes could induce reductions in black achievement as students adjust to a new school environment.

Apart from the HKR study, there are inconsistencies between the NAEP and state-level data. Even within the 1996 NAEP there were substantial variations in the effect of black concentrations, with some states revealing high and some low black scores in their predominantly black schools. What mechanism or conditions might explain why black concentration has adverse effects in some states or school districts but not in others? One possible explanation is that states and/or school districts have different standards of instruction, or differing standards of teacher certification, and these standards may interact with racial composition in such a way that predominantly black schools have adverse effects in some states or school districts but not others. Information on standards of instruction or certification is not readily available and therefore cannot be introduced to explain the differences observed here.

Theories of Desegregation Effects

Turning next to the various theories about why desegregation should raise black achievement, some theories receive little support from the evidence reviewed here, while others are still viable. For example, the NAEP analyses offer little support for the psychological harm theory and only weak support for the education resource theory. Black students have about the same levels of self-confidence and aspirations for college in schools of all racial compositions, and, in fact, there is no black-white difference in either self-concept or college aspirations.

With regard to school resources, black students in racially isolated schools have math teachers with the same education and experience as those in racially mixed schools, and they are enrolled in math courses with similar content, emphasis, and hours per week. There is a small difference in class size that favors racially mixed schools, and there is also a difference in certification rates and proportion of black teachers. The interaction between state, certification, and race of teacher makes it very difficult to understand exactly what effect these latter two teacher characteristics have on black test scores. Overall, the NAEP data do not suggest that school resource differences can explain the lower scores of black students in predominantly black schools.

What about peer group or black culture theories? On the one hand, they are given a boost because percent Black rather than percent White seems to be the critical predictor of black achievement in the HKR study and in the NAEP data. On the other hand, one might expect to see more attitudinal and behavioral differences in predominantly black schools if a negative black culture is operating. But black students in predominantly black schools have aspirations, watch TV, discuss school work with parents, and enroll in eighth-grade algebra at about the same levels as those in racially mixed schools. They do have somewhat higher absenteeism rates and spend somewhat less time on homework, which might indicate a black culture effect that reduces motivation for school, but these differences could also reflect unmeasured family risk factors such as parents who are not requiring their children attend school or do their school work.

With respect to family risk factors, all of the family SES characteristics that are available in the NAEP data were used to create the SES-adjusted achievement scores shown in figure 5.2. There are other important family risk factors that are not assessed by the NAEP including parent IQ, number of children, parenting behaviors, and nutrition; some of these unmeasured family risk factors may be more prevalent in predominantly black schools. Accordingly, the full set of family risk factors cannot be tested with NAEP data, and they remain a potential explanation for the lower black scores in predominantly black schools.

Finally, if some type of peer group or black culture effect is operating here, it is dependent on state or local conditions that are not fully understood as yet. The puzzling interactions between teacher certification and race of teacher, coupled with the variations by state, suggest the possibility that negative effects of black peers may operate unless they are counteracted by specific curriculum approaches, teacher certification, academic standards, or a combination of all three. Some states may have been able to impose higher standards through increased accountability measures, such as New York, South Carolina, and Texas, while others have not. Of course, this is just a hypothesis at this point, and more research is required to test for this "interaction" effect. With accountability systems and higher standards being promoted by the No Child Left Behind law, there may well be opportunities to test this hypothesis with more comprehensive NAEP data collected in all of the states.

The Future of Desegregation Policies

What does all this have to say about the future of desegregation policy? When it comes to school desegregation policy, it is always risky to predict the future. The reason is that so much of desegregation policy is derived from Supreme Court decisions, which are often decided by narrow margins. During the 1960s, few experts thought that *Brown* would ultimately lead to large-scale mandatory busing for racial balance; during the 1980s, few experts thought racial balance policies could be ended with a unitary status declaration.

There is no question that the *Grutter* decision in Michigan will revive the debate about the educational benefits of desegregated schools. I think the relevance is not so much over comprehensive racial balance or busing policies—which may violate the requirements of narrow tailoring—but rather whether desegregated *experiences* might be defended on the basis of educational benefits.

I agree with one HKR conclusion, that there are limited opportunities for direct policy action to change racial composition of schools on a large scale. Most racial segregation now lies between school districts, and there is neither the political will nor a judicial mandate to produce the kind of multi-district desegregation plans that would be necessary to eliminate racial concentrations in urban centers. Moreover, the problem of white flight is still prominent, a phenomenon that can undermine the effectiveness of comprehensive racial balance plans.[32]

While broader desegregation policies might be ruled out, there are smaller-scale desegregation issues to ponder. If research ultimately confirms that, under certain conditions, black student achievement suffers in predominantly black schools, it is possible that a school district or a state could defend a policy of letting students in those schools choose desegregated alternatives such as magnet schools—and courts might permit race-conscious policies to maintain desegregation in a magnet school. However, since most predominantly black schools are located in large, urban, and predominantly minority school districts, it is clear that desegregated experiences cannot be offered to these black students without going beyond district boundaries and into suburban school systems.

If predominantly black schools have adverse effects on achievement, and if the effects cannot be ameliorated by boosting standards or teacher quality, some might favor a desegregation policy that allows interdistrict transfers to schools of choice, such as charter schools, voucher schools, or public magnet schools located in other districts. Of course, the racial composition of the choice school would have to be considered. Some predominantly black charter or magnet schools might not be eligible for transfers under a *Grutter*-type desegregation policy unless it was clear that potential peer effects had been ameliorated.

Obviously, these policy options assume that the Supreme Court will apply the *Grutter* doctrine to K–12 public schools; whether it will do so is purely speculation at this point. The Supreme Court has not yet ruled on this question, but it is likely that a K–12 desegregation case will reach the

Supreme Court in the near future. At that time, evidence such as that reviewed here will be relevant to its decision. It is hoped that by that time there will be more research that resolves the inconsistencies found here and clarifies why black concentration appears to have adverse effects on black achievement in some states or school districts but not others.

NOTES

1. *Brown v. Board of Education*, 347 U.S. 483 (1954).
2. Social Scientists, "The Effects of Segregation and the Consequences of Desegregation: A Social Science Statement," *Minnesota Law Review*, 37: 427–439 (1953); signed by thirty-two social scientists.
3. See, for example, Morris Rosenberg and Roberta G. Simmons, *Black and White Self-Esteem*, (Washington, DC: American Sociological Association, 1971) and Judith R. Porter and Robert E. Washington, "Black Identity and Self Esteem," *Annual Review of Sociology* 5 (1979):53–74.
4. This argument has been made by several social scientists, including expert testimony by William Trent.
5. Social Scientists, "School Desegregation: A Social Science Statement," brief in the *Freeman v. Pitts* case, signed by sixty-four social scientists.
6. James S. Coleman et al., *Equality of Educational Opportunity* (Washington, DC: U.S. Government Printing Office, 1966).
7. For example, see the debate over school resources by Eric Hanushek and Larry Hedges in Gary Burtless, *Does Money Matter* (Washington, DC: Brookings Institution Press, 1996).
8. William Julius Wilson, *The Truly Disadvantaged* (Chicago: University of Chicago Press, 1987).
9. See Marshal S. Smith, "Equality of Educational Opportunity: The Basic Findings Reconsidered" in Frederick Mosteller and Daniel Patrick Moynihan, *On the Equality of Educational Opportunity* (New York: Random House, 1972), pp. 230–342.
10. John McWhorter, *Losing the Race: Black Self-Sabotage in Black America* (New York: Free Press, 2000); John U. Ogbu, *Black American Students in an Affluent Suburb* (Mahwah, NJ: Lawerence Erlbaum Associates, 2003).
11. Abigail Thernstrom and Stephan Thernstrom, *No Excuses: Closing the Racial Gap in Learning* (New York: Simon & Schuster, 2003).
12. Roland G. Fryer, Jr. and Steven D. Levitt, "Falling Behind," *Education Next* (August 2004). From a longer article, "Understanding the Black-White Test Score Gap in the First Two Years of School," *The Review of Economics and Statistics* (May 2004).
13. David J. Armor, *Maximizing Intelligence* (New Brunswick, NJ: Transaction Publishers, 2003); Meredith Phillips et al., "Family Background, Parenting Practices, and the Black-White Test Score Gap," in *The Black-White Test Score Gap*, Christopher Jencks and Meredith Phillips, eds. (Washington, DC: Brookings Insitute Press, 1998), pp. 103–145.

14. Orlando Patterson, "Taking Culture Seriously: A Framework and an Afro-American Illustration, in *Culture Matters: How Values Shape Human Progress*, Lawrence E. Harrison and Samuel P. Huntington, eds. (New York: Basic Books, 2000), pp. 202–218.

15. Thomas Cook, *School Desegregation and Black Achievement* (Washington, DC: National Institute of Education, 1984).

16. Chapter 2 in David J. Armor, *Forced Justice: School Desegregation and the Law* (New York: Oxford, 1995) reviewed the NIE study, data from four school districts not previously published, and NAEP national trend data to conclude that there was little relationship between desegregation and black achievement

17. David Grissmer, Ann Flanagan, and Stephanie Williamson, "Why Did the Black-White Score Gap Narrow in the 1970s and 1980s," in *The Black-White Test Score Gap*, Jencks and Phillips, eds., pp. 182–226.

18. David J. Armor, "Desegregation and Academic Achievement," in *School Desegregation in the 21st Century*, Christine Rossell, David Armor, and Herbert Walberg, eds. (Westport, CT: Praeger, 2002), pp. 147–188.

19. Eric A. Hanushek, John F. Kain, and Steven G. Rivkin, "New Evidence about Brown v. Board of Education: The Complex Effects of School Racial Composition on Achievement," unpublished manuscript. An earlier version of this paper was published in January 2002 as NAEP Working Paper #8741.

20. These results are similar to the analysis of 1992 NAEP scores; see Armor, "Desegregation and Academic Achievement." That study did not assess the effect of percent Black.

21. Percent free/reduced lunch is available at the school level for North Carolina and Texas, but because it can be highly correlated with percent Black, such an adjustment might bias the effect of racial composition downward.

22. The analysis is confined to schools with middle or junior high grade ranges (lowest grade five and highest grade nine) to eliminate possible confounding effects of schools for special needs students. Middle/junior high schools account for about three-fourths of all schools with an eighth grade in Texas.

23. A linear regression of black achievement on percent Black shows a statistically significant coefficient of −.18 (an increase of 10 percent black enrollment is associated with a decrease of 1.8 percent in eighth-grade black pass rate).

24. If school percent free lunch is introduced as a control in the above regression analysis, the coefficient for percent Black drops to −.04 and is not statistically significant

25. These results are replicated in studies of numerous school districts, including Pasadena, California; Norfolk, Virginia; Wilmington-New Castle County, Delaware; Tampa, Florida; Minneapolis, Minnesota; and Kansas City, Missouri. Most of these studies are summarized in Armor, "Desegregation and Academic Achievement."

26. Only those student and school characteristics reliably related to racial composition and to black achievement levels could help explain the relationship in figure 2.

27. It is possible, of course, that these results are biased by social desirability effects that are sometimes found in self-report data, and equal aspirations does not necessarily imply equal information about how to get into a college. The lack of a relationship between self-esteem and desegregation has been documented in many

studies; see Judith R. Porter and Robert E. Washington, "Black Identity and Self-Esteem," *Annual Review of Sociology* 5 (1979):53–74; Walter Stephan, "The Effects of School Desegregation," in *Advances in Applied Social Psychology*, M. Saxe and L. Saxe, eds. (Hillsdale, NJ: Lawrence Erlebaum Associates, 1986), pp. 181–206.

28. The NAEP survey records days absent in past month; this value was multiplied by 9 to estimate days absent during a full school year.

29. The regression coefficient was − .21 with a robust standard error of .05.

30. The scores in table 4 are not quite the same as those in figure 3 due to some missing data for teacher's race.

31. See Armor, *Maximizing Intelligence*, and table 2 in the Neal chapter in this book for evidence about the influence of these other family characteristics on achievement.

32. Charles Clotfelter, "Are Whites Still Fleeing? Racial Patterns and Enrollment Shifts in Urban Public Schools, 1987–1996," *Journal of Policy Analysis and Management* 20 (2001):199–221.

6

Early Returns from School Accountability

Eric A. Hanushek and Margaret E. Raymond, Hoover Institution and Stanford University

One of the most vexing problems of the United States is the continuing gap in economic outcomes between Blacks and Whites. Despite extensive policy interventions aimed directly or indirectly at closing the gap, substantial economic differences remain. Part of these differences are traced directly to differences in schooling outcomes—and those too have been the focus of concerted policy attention for over a half century. The school desegregation efforts flowing from *Brown v. Board of Education* have been followed with increased resources (e.g., Head Start and Title I) and a variety of very specific programs, but the achievement gaps remain large.

We have entered into a new era both in focus and in policy perspective. The federal government in the No Child Left Behind Act (NCLB) of 2001 turned policy attention to student outcomes and the accountability of the schools. The U.S. Supreme Court, while supporting affirmative action in law school admissions, also reinforced improvements in outcomes and elimination of achievement gaps with its presumption that special actions would not be required for more than an additional quarter of a century.[1] Is there reason to believe that the new thrust of student accountability will lead to a narrowing of the black-white achievement gap?

Accountability systems, as developed by the states throughout the 1990s, are characterized by a combination of objective measures of student achievement with yardsticks for judging the performance of students. These systems always produce regular reports on a school-by-school basis and frequently apply rewards or sanctions to the schools based on various judgments about their performance The approaches of the states involve a wide range of approaches even though the objectives are essentially identical.[2]

The focus of this work is disentangling the potential impact of school accountability on achievement. This task is complicated because the move toward accountability by the states is correlated with a variety of other changes in schools and society. As a result we must consider the range of other structural and policy factors that might systematically affect achievement gaps.

Our approach uses information about state differences in mathematics and reading performance as identified by the National Assessment of Educational Progress (NAEP) over the 1990s. We pursue a number of strategies designed to isolate the effects of school accountability on performance. First, we look at growth in performance between the fourth and the eighth grades to eliminate fixed differences in circumstances and policies across states (whether they are readily measurable or not). Second, we include explicit measures for major categories of inputs to achievement that may vary over time: parental education, school spending, and racial exposure in the schools. Third, in estimating the achievement growth models, we allow for systematic differences across states (through state-fixed effects) to eliminate any other policies that lead to trends up or down in student performance in each state. Finally, to identify differences by race or ethnicity, we disaggregate the state results for Whites, Blacks, and Hispanics and compare any differential impacts.

A portion of this achievement analysis simply reinforces a variety of results common to past work. Parental education tends to influence growth in performance positively (although, because of the estimation approach, the effects are not always statistically significant). Attending schools with high concentrations of minorities also tends to harm black achievement growth while having no strong impact on either Whites or Hispanics. Finally, differences in school spending are unrelated to differences in student performance growth.

Much less work has focused on accountability, but it has demonstrated that the introduction of accountability systems into a state tends to lead to larger achievement growth than occurs without accountability.[3] The analysis here refines that work and provides more details. Importantly, whether a state accountability program attaches consequences to performance or simply relies on reporting results appears to make a difference. Just reporting results appears to have minimal impact on student performance.[4]

In looking further, however, we find that Hispanic students gain most from accountability, while Blacks gain least. States have disaggregated scores in order to focus attention on any persistent achievement gaps for different groups of students. This appears to have been important for getting gains by

Hispanics, but it does not seem to matter much for Blacks. (This is moot from a policy standpoint, however, because NCLB requires such disaggregation).

The overall implications for black-white achievement gaps are quite clear. While accountability has a positive impact on everybody's learning, it does not reduce any gaps in learning. In fact, because Blacks (and Hispanics) had generally lower achievement growth over the 1990s, the gap in achievement with Whites expands in accountability states as well as nonaccountability states.

This finding is consistent with having a shortage of policy instruments. In general it is not possible to achieve two separate objectives with a single instrument. Obtaining favorable joint objectives depends on the correlation or alignment of the objectives, which is not assured in this case. While some have thought that achievement gaps might have been simultaneously narrowed along with raising overall achievement—because accountability as currently followed concentrates on lower achieving students—the evidence does not suggest such a fortuitous result.

BLACK-WHITE ACHIEVEMENT GAP

A variety of measures of educational outcomes consistently point to a gap in the performance of Blacks and Whites. Early work on test scores used information from the Scholastic Aptitude Test (SAT), so the voluntary nature of the test and its varying participation rates makes interpretation of these results ambiguous.[5] A clearer picture is provided by NAEP, a federal testing program that has tested a random sample of students since roughly 1970. On a rotating schedule, students in fourth, eighth, and twelfth grades have been consistently tested approximately every four years in a range of subjects, including reading, science, and math.

Figure 6.1 shows the gap in NAEP scores between black and white seventeen-year-olds. In the aggregate, there are three distinct periods: a constant gap in the 1970s, a narrowing gap in the 1980s, and a reversal with constant or widening gaps in the 1990s. These patterns, with slight differences, hold across each of the three tests. The magnitude of the differences is also important. The gaps by test range from three-quarters of a standard deviation to over a full standard deviation. A standard deviation of 1.0 would imply that the average black student is performing at the level of a white student in the 16th percentile.

An interesting comparison is provided by Hispanics. In the mid-1970s, Hispanic students were separately identified. Figure 6.2 displays the Hispanic-white gap. Once again, a gap that narrowed in the 1980s reopened in the early 1990s. But in the late 1990s, the white-Hispanic gaps in all subjects

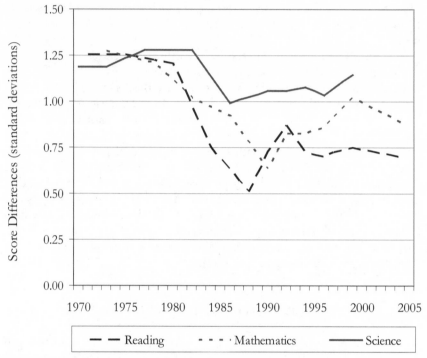

Figure 6.1   White-Black Differences in NAEP Scores, 17-year-olds

were at or close to their lowest levels ever. Moreover, the white-Hispanic gaps are noticeably smaller than those for Blacks. In short, there are signs that the Hispanic experience is beginning to diverge from that of black Americans and that we are observing something more complex than just a "minority" problem.

PERSPECTIVE OF PRIOR RESEARCH

Educational gaps between minorities and Whites have long been the subject of both research and policy concern. The majority of the early work concentrated on differences in the amount of schooling obtained (e.g., the analysis by James Smith and Finis Welch).[6] Prior to availability of achievement data such as provided by NAEP, the focus of any research on quality was on differences in inputs; more recently, the attention has shifted to issues of outcomes.

The studies that exist tend to fall into two basic categories: those concen-

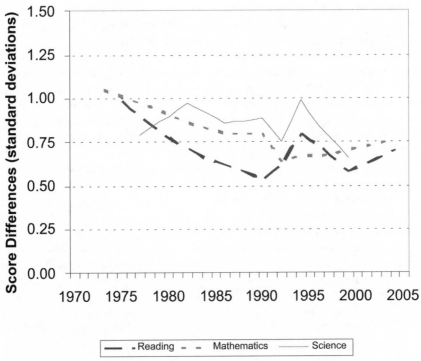

Figure 6.2   White-Hispanic Differences in NAEP Scores, 17-year-olds

trating on underlying structural factors that cause any gaps and those con-centrating on policy interventions or programmatic effects. The investigation of structural factors tends to concentrate on attributes of the students and seeks to identify and explain potential determinants of the difference in achievement. This body of work tries to identify factors that are statistically significant in explaining the difference by looking at attributes that might co-vary with achievement changes in a systematic way. The focus is on defining structural differences between groups, and in some cases to tie those differences to larger social disparities. Without going into detail, studies have ranged across such major categories as differences in parental education, cultural differences, distinct learning styles, different intellectual capacities, variations in self-esteem, and differences in expectations by parents and teachers. It has also had widely varying perspectives including suggesting that differences are immutable or that the school system has not (could not) have much effect on the outcomes.

The second body of work attempts to prescribe or evaluate policy solutions to the achievement gap. Of course, one major thrust of this policy work, consistent with this conference, concentrates on school desegregation. But through much of the period since *Brown*, there has been a parallel line of work on resources—where the distribution of resources has been seen as both a cause and a solution. Along this line, in addition to notions of simply increasing the total resources available to minorities, proposals have included increased teacher quality (though little consensus on how to achieve it), longer school days, reduced class size, a return to "traditional" education, greater diversity in staffing and a wide range of curricular changes. While this work, like the previous structural work, fits into the general topic of "determinants of achievement," the two lines of work are frequently quite separate.

More recently, in part driven by the failure of these previous policy factors to close the gap in achievement, attention has switched to new policy approaches. Two major policies stand out in this regard: improved school accountability and expanded school choice. Early experiences with school choice in Milwaukee and in private voucher programs give some hints that choice could help if employed on a larger scale.[7] Accountability experience also seems to point in the same direction.[8]

The important conclusion that we take away from the existing work is simply that a variety of factors may simultaneously enter into the observed achievement gap. As such, simple bivariate analyses of structural issues or of policy effects are potentially quite misleading.

ANALYTICAL FOCUS

The landmark federal legislation on accountability, the No Child Left Behind Act of 2001, codified a developing policy view that standards, testing, and accountability were the path to improved performance. Moreover, NCLB explicitly requires that the performance of students within specific ethnic subgroups be monitored and that schools be held accountable for raising the scores of all groups. Because Blacks (and other minorities) have traditionally scored much lower than Whites, a natural inference is that helping students at the bottom would disproportionately help Blacks and other minorities.

It is nonetheless not possible to investigate the impact of NCLB directly. First, and most importantly, the majority of states had already instituted some sort of accountability system by the time the federal law took effect. Thus, there is not a ready comparison group that can indicate what might have happened in the absence of NCLB. Second, as indicated, the law has many facets but there is no obvious way to identify and measure the impact of the different components. Third, because states introduced accountability systems simultaneously into all schools within a state, within-state variation in outcomes is unavailable to use to analyze state accountability.

The uneven adoption of pre-NCLB accountability across states, however, makes it possible to study the impact of accountability on student performance. Analysis of state differences is possible because of the extensive participation of states in NAEP. Importantly, in 1990 NAEP began a program of state representative testing for states that volunteered to participate. Because students in all states take the same test, NAEP provides an independent and consistent measure by which to compare academic achievement across states—something not possible using the states' own tests, which vary widely from one another. The influence of accountability policies can be discerned by tracking changes in student performance on NAEP as state accountability systems are introduced.

Understanding the impact of such accountability must, however, be put within the context of state educational policies. Both NCLB and state accountability operate within a larger world of other state policies and of differences in state populations.

The major questions addressed in this paper concern both the overall impact of school accountability and the equivalence of effects from accountability programs on students in different race/ethnicity groups. Investigation of the overall impacts extends prior work (based on more limited data) that suggested accountability states show higher achievement gains than nonaccountability states.[9] With more extensive data and using a different analytical strategy, we expand on an earlier analysis by Carnoy and Loeb that showed black and Hispanic students in states with accountability systems tended to improve even more than white students on the eighth-grade math NAEP after adjusting for other factors.[10]

We also provide further evidence on the competing theories about the operative mechanisms of accountability systems. One possible explanation, driven by microeconomic theory of markets, suggests that accountability systems may work by virtue of their disclosure of information about schools. Creating common measures of performance and making them available to affected constituencies rectifies a significant market failure—in this case, asymmetric information about school performance.

An alternative explanation draws from research on motivation and strategies to shape behavior via external influences. Work in the field focuses on which incentives are most effective to achieve desired actions from individuals. Individuals are theorized to have unobservable states of motivation, subject to influence, that drive behavioral choices. From this perspective, accountability systems could be effective if they impose both positive and negative consequences to the results of teacher and administrator behavior. In the context of theories of motivation, teachers and administrators might be attracted to the rewards and/or be repelled by the prospect of sanctions.

The current analysis offers the chance to test these two competing theories. If the operative mechanism is largely motivational, then lower gains in performance could be anticipated in those states that have no accountability systems or have report cards. (This assumes, of course, that disclosure of school performance without consequences is nonthreatening.) If, however, the repair of imperfect information leads to pressure to improve from a newly informed community, states with accountability systems that carry consequences would be expected to outperform other states.

DIFFICULTIES OF ANALYZING SCHOOL ACCOUNTABILITY

Analyzing the effects of accountability on student performance is difficult. First, because accountability systems are introduced across entire states, all local school districts in a state face a common incentive structure related to its state system. Thus, the only possible variation useful for analyzing the impacts of accountability systems comes from interstate differences. But states also differ in ways other than accountability. Second, several states have not participated completely in national testing programs, limiting the number of states for which information is available. Third, while NAEP seeks to test a representative sample of student, participation rates are uneven, and various exclusion rules are applied for special education students and for limited English proficient students. Further, the application of these rules has changed over time.

Extensive analyses of educational production functions have been conducted, and they form the relevant background for this work. Those studies have concentrated on describing how various inputs to schools enter into the determination of student outcomes. As described elsewhere, however, these studies have not provided any consistent picture of how schools affect student performance.[11]

Many different state policies, regulations, and incentives—although poorly identified and measured—enter into determining student performance. State educational policy encompasses a wide range of factors including financial structure, collective bargaining rules and laws, explicit regulations on educational processes, and the like. The complications for the analyst are multiple.

The objective is to separate the impact of accountability from other possible influences on student achievement. But, if these other influences cannot be readily measured and cannot be directly controlled for in any statistical analysis, they are likely to be correlated with accountability, making accurate identification of the impacts of accountability on achievement impossible.

The analysis here relies on three related approaches to the statistical disentanglement of the impacts of accountability. First, important components of general state factors that influence achievement—either from policy or from the character of the state population—will influence student achievement at multiple levels of schooling. Therefore, if we look at the growth of achievement over time—say, as used here, the change in student performance between fourth and eighth grades—common factors that have a constant impact on the level of achievement over the observation period will be fully captured in the early test score and thus will be implicitly controlled in the statistical analysis.[12] Second, from the multiple observations of performance in each state over time, it is possible to estimate a common state-specific growth rate for student performance. (Technically, this amounts to extracting a state-specific effect in the growth equations for student scores.) Third, a variety of time-varying factors can be entered directly into the analysis. For example, the pattern of spending on students in each state or changes in the adult (parent) population are readily measured and can be introduced to avoid any complications that might arise from correlations with the introduction of accountability measures.[13] (The details of this specification are discussed in appendix 6.1.)

This formulation provides much better control for other factors influencing performance growth, because the formulation effectively adds a trend in performance that is relevant for each state. Of course, other policies that are put into effect—and that are implicitly incorporated through the growth formulation and the introduction of state-fixed effects—may or may not be effective in raising achievement. No presumption is made about how they influence achievement, but similarly no information is available about these forces. Our estimates of the effects of accountability are identified and estimated entirely on the basis of the introduction of accountability systems within each state. In essence, the estimation relies on a state-specific prediction of performance gains and then considers how the addition of an accountability system affects outcomes.

The essential question throughout is whether the introduction of accountability into a state alters the achievement that would be expected due to parents, school characteristics, and other policies that have also been put in place.

DATA ON STATE ACCOUNTABILITY

The source of information on student performance employed in this analysis is the National Assessment of Educational Progress. Since the introduction of state-level testing in 1990, NAEP has tracked performance in mathematics and reading at regular intervals for participating states. The sampling/testing design of NAEP in each subject is particularly helpful because it has a basic four-year testing cycle that involves testing fourth and eighth graders. Thus, fourth graders in 1992 are tested as eighth graders in 1996. While not the same students, this approach allows tracking the same cohort, and thus takes into account the common experiences of the cohort. This regularity of testing also makes it possible to create a panel with two time periods of achievement growth in each subject, adding to our capacity to identify accountability effects.

Second, NAEP provides data separately by the ethnic groups of Whites, Blacks, and Hispanics. These consistent performance data permit direct investigation of performance gains for each ethnic group. (Note, however, that disaggregated data for Blacks or Hispanics within a state is not always available because student samples are insufficiently large. Thus, there are fewer state observations of black and Hispanic achievement than of white achievement.)

Because we are interested in performance growth over time, the number of observations of group test score gains by state thus depends both on the availability of achievement data for each group as well as participation of the state in testing during both of the relevant testing years (e.g., fourth-grade math testing in 1992 and eighth-grade math testing in 1996). The number of observations in the various relevant testing periods is shown in table 6.1. A total of 348 observations of group gains on the tests is available.[14] This total includes 135 white observations, 111 black observations, and 102 Hispanic observations. Note, however, that there are actually more distinct states (42) than appear for any of the time period-test breakdowns, because a varying group of states are available in each of the different years.

When assessing the effects of accountability, we adjust for three primary factors: state demographic composition, school resources, and school racial and ethnic composition. The key demographic factor included in our study is adult education, measured by the percent of the population twenty-five years old or more with at least a high school education.[15]

Table 6.1.   Number of States for Analysis by Race/Ethnicity, Test, and Sample Period

	White	Black	Hispanic	Total
Mathematics				
1992–1996	35	29	32	96
1996–2000	34	26	32	92
Reading				
1994–1998	32	27	16	75
1998–2002	34	29	22	85
Total	135	111	102	348

School resources are measured by the cumulative average state expenditure per pupil in real terms over the relevant time period for achievement growth. This measure varies by state and time but not by subgroup, as we have no separate measure of school expenditures for Whites, Blacks, or Hispanics.

To investigate the impact of racial concentration and trends over time, we include summary data on the racial and ethnic composition across the schools in each state. Specifically, for Whites, Blacks, and Hispanics, we calculate exposure to minority students in each school of the state (using the Common Core of Data of the U.S. Department of Education). The exposure measure indicates the proportion of schoolmates who are minority for the average white, black, and Hispanic student in the state in each year. These exposure rates are averaged over the relevant test growth periods. The pattern of concentration of minorities by school yields disparate results for the amount of minority exposure for each group. Whites attended schools that on average over the period have 16 percent minority students, while the comparable percentages for Blacks and Hispanics are 48 and 38 percent, respectively.

Data on accountability come from a survey and analysis of all states by CREDO.[16] For each state, information was collected on when a state introduced an accountability system for schools. For these purposes, an accountability system was defined as publishing outcome information on standardized tests for each school along with providing a way to aggregate and interpret the school performance.[17] States were classified by whether or not they attached consequences to school performance or simply provided a public report. Additionally, data were also collected on when a state began disaggregating test information by subgroups of the population. Note that these accountability measures pertain just to accountability for schools and do not include any accountability for students that may have been introduced at a different time.[18]

The estimation relies on the varying timing of introduction of accountability systems into the different states. Figure 6.3 displays the overall cumulative pattern of accountability across the states. The data are broken up into states that attach consequences to their systems and states that simply report on school achievement. To understand the estimation strategy better, the set of NAEP testing dates for eighth-grade math and reading performance is superimposed on the pattern of accountability. The varied introduction across time and across the different testing periods permits disentangling the impact of accountability.

Finally, while the NAEP testing provides a consistent sample of performance for the states, some variations might arise simply because of differences in the test-taking procedures in the states. Specifically, over the period a variety of students could be excluded from the testing because of special consideration, such as being identified as a special education or a Limited English

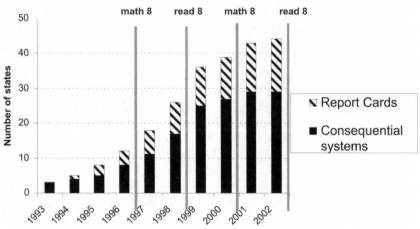

Figure 6.3   State Accountability over Time (with NAEP Testing Dates)

Proficient student. The common presumption is that, since these students usually fall near the bottom of the achievement distribution, excluding them will artificially raise average scores of the tested population. Fortunately, NAEP provides information on test exclusions by test and year. Over the relevant time period, special education placements rose for the nation as a whole and for the separate states—going from 11.4 percent in 1990 to 13.3 percent in 2001. Over that same time period, test exclusions also rose, but by amounts that exceed the overall growth in the special education population. The pattern, however, differs dramatically by state with some states actually reducing the NAEP exclusion rate while others saw very large increases. These data on NAEP exclusions permit us to adjust for whether exclusion rates increased or decreased across separate testing periods in each state (which we do in a regression framework).

STATE ACCOUNTABILITY IMPACTS

We begin with the overall effect of state accountability on NAEP performance in the eighth grade across the three racial/ethnic groups: Whites, Blacks, and Hispanics. The basic estimation pools the different time periods and tests but includes indicator variables for time period and test. The regression estimates predict eighth-grade performance based on fourth-grade performance of students in the state four years earlier. Table 6.2 provides a summary of the key results for the performance for all students across the states that appear at least once in the testing. A total of 348 observations with complete data across forty-two states forms that basis for the estimation. (Specific

Table 6.2. Determinants of Growth in State NAEP Performance in Mathematics and Reading between the Fourth and Eighth Grades

	(1)	(2)
Consequential accountability	3.237	3.460
	(1.123)**	(1.114)**
Report card system	0.554	0.758
	(1.787)	(1.770)
%pop(age 25 +) = high school	0.075	0.030
	(0.054)	(0.058)
School spending, $/ADM	− 0.001	− 0.001
	(0.002)	(0.002)
Change in exclusion rates	0.518	0.510
	(0.124)**	(0.122)**
Black	− 10.865	− 7.372
	(1.788)**	(2.098)**
Hispanic	− 9.748	− 10.065
	(1.896)**	(2.208)**
Minority exposure × white		1.815
		(6.210)
Minority exposure × black		− 8.478
		(4.035)*
Minority exposure × Hispanic		− 3.287
		(3.583)
Observations	348	348
Number of states	42	42
R-squared	0.95	0.95

* significant at 5%; ** significant at 1%

Notes: All models are estimated with state fixed effects. Models include NAEP fourth-grade scores for reading and math (lagged four years) and indicator variables for test and period. Robust standard errors are found in parentheses.

variable definitions along with descriptive statistics are found in appendix 6.1.)[19]

The estimates can be thought of as considering two sets of factors: those related to achievement determination in general and those related to accountability systems. We begin with the general factors and then turn to a detailed look at the impact of accountability.

General Achievement Factors

A key element of the estimation is the implicit elimination of a wide range of determinants of achievement through looking at growth models and through including state-fixed effects. The growth models eliminate the influence of common state factors (that enter into both fourth- and eighth-grade achievement). The state-fixed effects eliminate changes in educational policies and other factors that take effect smoothly over time, including, for example, movements in characteristics of parents of each cohort through immigration into the state. Eliminating these factors minimizes any bias that would be introduced into the estimates of the impact of accountability through imperfect measurement of other policies or inputs, but it makes it very difficult to identify other separate influences on achievement growth.

Throughout the analysis, the amount of parental education never has a statistically significant impact on achievement growth. Because this differs dramatically from most previous evidence about the importance of parental inputs, this undoubtedly reflects the inability to estimate the impact from just the changes in parents within states over the short period observed.[20]

The large differences in spending per pupil also never influence scores. Consistent with past evidence on the impacts of resources, the pattern of NAEP scores across states is not explained by spending. The impact of aggregate state spending is consistently small, negative, and statistically insignificant.[21]

Test exclusions always have the expected effect on tests: more exclusions from a test for special education or language increase the average growth in test score. The introduction of exclusions, however, does not impact the estimates of accountability—chiefly because the introduction of accountability was not associated with large increases in exclusions. In fact, when states introduce accountability measures, they tend simultaneously to reduce their exclusion rates by a small amount.

Table 6.2 also concentrates on the basic differences in performance by race. With disaggregation of achievement growth by ethnicity, we see distinct differences in gains by Blacks and Hispanics: Each subgroup shows growth that is roughly 10 points lower than Whites on NAEP between fourth and eighth grade, other things being equal. This finding of lower black and Hispanic achievement growth is particularly interesting in light of the narrowing of the achievement gap that occurred in the 1980s and the subsequent explanations for this improvement.[22] The analysis of state details here that controls for state policy, family backgrounds, and testing exclusions shows a clear reversal of the prior decade.

The second column of table 6.2 relates directly to the other major policy movement that had potential racial aspects: the influence of changing concentrations of minorities.[23] In this, we introduce measures of exposure rates of Whites, Hispanics, and Blacks to minorities (Hispanics and Blacks) across the schools in each state.[24] Higher minority concentrations have a statistically significant negative impact on Blacks but do not significantly affect either Whites or Hispanics. This finding is generally consistent with the analysis of racial composition in Texas by Hanushek, Kain, and Rivkin.[25] In that work, Blacks were quite sensitive to school composition—specifically the proportion of Blacks in the school negatively affected Blacks, but Whites and Hispanics were unaffected by student body composition.

Basic Accountability Effects

From table 6.2 we find consistent evidence that introduction of consequential accountability by a state had a positive impact on student math and reading performance during the 1990s.[26] Specifically, states that introduced consequential accountability systems early, tended to show more rapid gains in NAEP performance, holding other inputs and policies constant. This is consistent with our prior estimates of the effects of accountability for aggregations of all students in each state.[27] However, these estimates that are based entirely on changes in achievement growth within states after introducing consequential accountability provide considerable confidence that they are not simply the result of other policies or changes in the states.

Interestingly, the estimates suggest very little influence of simply reporting the results as opposed to attaching consequences to them. Report card systems are not significantly different from zero (i.e., no effect) at conventional levels of statistical significance, and are significantly different from consequential systems at more than the one percent level. Subsequent, more refined estimation finds even weaker evidence that report card systems have an impact unless they also carry rewards and/or sanctions.

Extended Investigation of Accountability Impacts by Ethnicity

The models discussed so far (and represented in table 6.2) consider the effects of accountability to be equivalent across the separate ethnic groups. For a variety of reasons, the effects may not be uniform. Thus, we estimate the same basic models but permit the effects of accountability to differ by race and ethnicity. Table 6.3 presents extended results of the achievement growth models. The first column is directly comparable to the previous table, but it now indicates distinct differences by subgroup. Specifically, we see in column 1 that Hispanics seem somewhat more affected than Whites by having accountability, while Blacks appear less affected than Whites. Both differences are statistically significant at the 5 percent level or better.

The last column provides further detail. When states introduce accountability systems they may or may not disaggregate the test results by racial group (as now required by NCLB). When disaggregated accountability information is provided, Hispanics again show a significantly greater reaction to accountability than Whites, while Blacks gain significantly worse than both Whites and Hispanics.

Table 6.3. Determinants of Growth in State NAEP Performance in Mathematics and Reading between 4th and 8th Grades with Heterogeneous Effects by Ethnicity

	(1)	*(2)*
Consequential accountability	3.420	3.541
	(1.218)**	(1.191)**
Report card system	0.734	0.727
	(1.695)	(1.692)
Accountability × black	−2.065	
	(1.044)*	
Accountability × Hispanic	3.076	
	(1.236)*	
Disaggregated × black		−2.349
		(0.978)*
Disaggregated × Hispanic		3.009
		(1.322)*
%pop(age 25 +) = high school	0.052	0.059
	(0.056)	(0.057)
School spending, $/ADM	−0.001	−0.001
	(0.002)	(0.002)
Change in exclusion rates	0.501	0.505
	(0.121)**	(0.123)**
Black	−6.268	−6.713
	(2.053)**	(2.065)**
Hispanic	−10.055	−9.726
	(2.089)**	(2.121)**
Minority exposure × white	1.325	0.964
	(6.066)	(6.053)
Minority exposure × black	−8.209	−7.889
	(3.944)*	(3.983)*
Minority exposure × Hispanic	−4.468	−4.674
	(3.746)	(3.726)
Observations	348	348
Number of states	42	42
R-squared	0.96	0.96

* significant at 5%; ** significant at 1%

Notes: All models are estimated with state fixed effects. Models include NAEP fourth-grade scores for reading and math (lagged four years) and indicator variables for test and period. Robust standard errors are found in parentheses.

PRELIMINARY CONCLUSIONS

Accountability is important for students in the United States (and in a variety of other countries that are pushing for better performance measurement). Despite design flaws in the existing systems, we find that they have a positive impact on achievement.[28] This significantly positive effect of accountability holds across the alternative specifications of the basic achievement model. However, the impact holds just for states attaching consequences to performance. States that simply provide better information through report cards without attaching consequences to performance do not get significantly larger impacts over no accountability. Thus, the NCLB move toward adding consequences to accountability systems is supported by looking at the historic introduction of consequential accountability systems.

It is useful to put the detailed subgroup impacts into perspective. Accountability significantly increases the state achievement gain, particularly for Hispanics. However, because both Blacks and Hispanics show lower gains relative to Whites on each of the tests, accountability by itself is insufficient to close the gap in learning. We also find that the effect varies by subgroup, with Hispanics gaining most and Blacks gaining least. Because Whites gain more than Blacks after accountability is introduced, their achievement gap actually widens with the introduction of accountability.

In addition to accountability, the analysis looks into other determinants of student performance. Most relevant for consideration of where we stand fifty years after *Brown v. Board of Education*, black students are hurt by greater minority concentration in the schools. This compositional effect has no significant influence on white or Hispanic scores, making the effects very similar to those found by Hanushek, Kain, and Rivkin.[29]

The finding of differential effects of accountability raises a clear policy dilemma. A prime reason for the U.S. federal government to require each state to develop a test based accountability system involved raising the achievement of all students. These results suggest a beneficial effect on overall achievement but some gaps across subgroups could widen. We conclude from this that additional policies are needed to deal with the multiple objectives. Again, as is frequently the case, a single policy cannot effectively work for two different objectives—raising overall student performance and providing more equal outcomes across groups.

TECHNICAL APPENDIX

The general issues behind the modeling are easy to demonstrate. Consider a simple model of achievement such as:

(1) $\quad O_{st} = f(X_{st}, R_{st}, \rho_s)$

where O is the level of student outcomes in state s at time t, X is a vector of family and nonschool inputs, R is a vector of resources, and ρ captures the policies of the state. (It does not matter for this discussion that we begin with aggregate outcomes for a state instead of building up from the individual student level, where the outcomes are presumably generated. The more general situation is discussed and developed Eric Hanushek, Steven Rivkin, and Lori Taylor.[30] Where the aggregation is important, we discuss the implications.)

If one attempts, say, to understand the implications of different resources on student performance by regressing O on explicit measures of families and schools, the estimated effects will be biased to the extent that ρ is correlated with the included measures (i.e., a standard model misspecification story).

This issue is nonetheless directly relevant to the analysis of accountability systems that we pursue here. While there are state data on student performance from NAEP, it is not possible to understand the impact of newly introduced accountability systems without considering the range of other possible impacts. A linearized version of this model is simply:

$$(2) \qquad O_{st} = \beta_0 + \beta_X X_{st} + \beta_R R_{st} + (\rho_s + \epsilon_{st})$$

where the β's are unknown parameters of the educational process.[31] If, however, ρ is not observed and the β's are estimated with just information on X and R, correlations with ρ obviously lead to bias in the estimation. When background factors (X) and/or school resources (R) are correlated with state policies (ρ), these variables will partially proxy for the other policies—leading to incorrect inferences about what would happen if just X or R changed.

Now consider just adding A, a measure of whether or not accountability affects incentives and thus student performance.

$$(3) \qquad O_{st} = B_0 + \beta_X X_{st} + \beta_R R_{st} + \gamma A_{st} + (\rho_s + \epsilon_{st})$$

The objective is to understand γ, but under almost all circumstances γ will also be biased through omission of relevant state policies, through either their direct correlation with accountability or with the other inputs into achievement.

Moreover, the bias in any estimation will generally increase with the level of aggregation in situations like this. Specifically, when the omitted variable is relevant at the state level, estimation of the model across states will have the most bias.[32] Note that this does not say anything about the direction of any bias, only that aggregation worsens the bias. In the case of measures of school resources, all evidence indicates that there is an upward bias from omitting state policies. It does not, however, give much indication of how any estimation of partial models of accountability would bias analyses of γ.

If, however, the state policies are constant over our observation period, a variety of estimation approaches becomes possible. In the simplest form, simply looking at outcome changes over time eliminates any state differences that are constant over the period t to t^*:

(4) $\Delta O_{s} = \beta_X \Delta X_s + \beta_R \Delta R_s + \gamma \Delta A_s + \Delta \epsilon_s$
$_{t,t^*}$

The key element is that effects of accountability systems are identified from changes in accountability across states over the sample period. Specifically, if all states introduced new accountability systems at the same time, ΔA would be constant, and γ would not be separately identified. This estimation relies on the variation in introduction of accountability systems over the period during which student achievement gains are observed.

But different states are frequently doing a variety of things to try to improve their schools—not just relying on accountability (or the absence of accountability). In order to allow for other policies that are occurring over time, we add a state-fixed effect (δ_s) to the estimation as in equation 5:

(5) $\Delta O_{s} = B_X \Delta X_s + B_R \Delta R_s + \gamma \Delta A_s + \gamma \Delta A_s + \delta_s + \Delta \epsilon_s$
$_{t,t^*}$

Such a model can be estimated when there are multiple observations of achievement growth for each state.

Appendix 6.1. Variable Definitions and Descriptive Statistics: Means and Standard Deviations by Race/Ethnic Group

		All	White	Hispanic	Black
Consequential accountability	Proportion of period with school accountability system that has consequences;	0.53 (0.44)	0.51 (0.44)	0.49 (0.44)	0.58 (0.43)
Report card system	Proportion of period with report card system;	0.14 (0.31)	0.14 (0.31)	0.14 (0.31)	0.14 (0.31)
Disaggregated	Proportion of period with school accountability system disaggregated by race/ethnic subgroups			0.37 (0.43)	0.4 (0.45)
%pop (age 25 +) = high school	% of population age twenty-five and older with a high school degree or greater; interpolation for period of decennial census data by race/ethnicity between 1990 and 2000	71.2 (11.8)	81.7 (5.1)	58.2 (8.3)	70.5 (7.3)
School spending, $/ADM	Average expenditure per pupil in average daily membership for growth period (2000 $)	6,109 (1,354)	6,005 (1,273)	6,202 (1,431)	6,149 (1,383)
Change in exclusion rates	NAEP exclusion rates: difference in eighth grade and fourth grade lagged four years by test	−0.16 (2.9)	−0.17 (2.8)	−0.25 (2.9)	−0.11 (3.0)
Minority exposure	Average exposure rate to minorities (black + Hispanic) by school averaged across growth period years	0.38 (0.24)	0.16 (0.17)	0.45 (0.21)	0.57 (0.17)
NAEP8	Average scale score, NAEP eighth-grade test	257.4 (16.2)	274.8 (8.5)	249.0 (9.6)	244.0 (6.4)
NAEP4	Average scale score, NAEP fourth-grade test	207.6 (16.0)	224.7 (6.2)	200.4 (10.5)	193.5 (7.3)

NOTES

Hoover Institution/Stanford University, University of Texas at Dallas, and National Bureau of Economic Research; CREDO and Hoover Institution/Stanford University, respectively. Lei Zhang provided valuable research assistance. This work was supported by the Packard Humanities Institute.

1. In the 2003 decision of *Grutter v Bollinger et al.*, Justice Sandra Day O'Connor stated clearly, "We expect that 25 years from now, the use of racial preferences will no longer be necessary to further the interest approved today" (p. 31).

2. Eric A. Hanushek and Margaret E. Raymond, "Improving Educational Quality: How Best to Evaluate Our Schools?," in *Education in the 21st Century: Meeting the Challenges of a Changing World*, Yolanda Kodrzycki, ed. (Boston: Federal Reserve Bank of Boston, 2003), pp. 93–224; Eric A. Hanushek and Margaret E. Raymond, "Lessons about the Design of State Accountability Systems," in *No Child Left Behind? The Politics and Practice of Accountability*, Paul E. Peterson and Martin R. West, eds. (Washington, DC: Brookings Institution Press, 2003), pp. 26–151.

3. Martin Carnoy and Susanna Loeb, "Does External Accountability Affect Student Outcomes? A Cross-State Analysis," *Educational Evaluation and Policy Analysis* 24, no. 4 (2002):305–331; Hanushek and Raymond, "Improving Educational Quality."

4. The increased precision of the estimation conducted here permits accurate separation of the effects of reporting versus attaching actual consequences to the decisions. Our previous analysis did not find significant differences between the two types of systems; Hanushek and Raymond, "Improving Educational Quality."

5. Congressional Budget Office, *Trends in Educational Achievement* (Washington, DC: Congressional Budget Office, 1986).

6. James P. Smith and Finis Welch, "Black Economic Progress after Myrdal," *Journal of Economic Literature* 27, no. 2 (1989):519–564.

7. See Cecilia Elena Rouse, "Private School Vouchers and Student Achievement: An Evaluation of the Milwaukee Parental Choice Program," *Quarterly Journal of Economics* 113, no. 2 (1998):553–602; and William G. Howell and Paul E. Peterson, *The Education Gap: Vouchers and Urban Schools* (Washington, DC: Brookings Institution Press, 2002).

8. Carnoy and Loeb, "Does External Accountability Affect Student Outcomes?"

9. *Ibid.*; Hanushek and Raymond, "Improving Educational Quality?"

10. Carnoy and Loeb, "Does External Accountability Affect Student Outcomes?"

11. See Eric A. Hanushek, "The Failure of Input-Based Schooling Policies," *Economic Journal* 113, no. 485 (2003):F64–F98. One frequently hypothesized reason for this lack of relationship relates directly to the prior discussion: without strong incentives, resources are not consistently and effectively transformed into outcomes. That fact provides the motivation for moving to greater accountability systems.

12. A variety of alternative approaches are available, including adding the early test to the right hand side of an empirical formulation and looking at the simple difference in performance on the left hand side. The trade-offs involved are discussed in Eric A. Hanushek, "Conceptual and Empirical Issues in the Estimation of Educational Production Functions," *Journal of Human Resources* 14, no. 3 (1979):351:388

Chapter 6

and Steven G. Rivkin, Eric A. Hanushek, and John F. Kain, "Teachers, Schools, and Academic Achievement," *Econometrica* 73, no. 2 (2005):417–458.

13. Note that including these measurable inputs is done in a more coherent manner in the context of the growth models. In general, if one were looking at the absolute level of performance instead of its change over a specific set of grades, it would be necessary to measure the entire past history of relevant inputs. In the specification used here, it is only necessary to include the inputs received over the relevant time period.

14. Because of missing data on exclusions from testing, the analytical samples are reduced to 348 observations from the 351 state observations with matched fourth- and eighth-grade testing for specific cohorts.

15. The analysis interpolates data from the decennial censuses in 1990 and 2000 for each state to get the appropriate annual data for each state. We use the percentage of high school or more adults at the midpoint for each testing period. We calculate this separately for each population subgroup and for the relevant years of testing. Not surprisingly, there are significant differences in average attainment across states and across groups. In terms of averages, Whites are 82 percent; Blacks are 74 percent; and Hispanics are 60 percent.

16. CREDO, formerly the Center for Research on Educational Outcomes) is a research center at the Hoover Institution of Stanford University. The information on state accountability is found in Stephen H. Fletcher and Margaret E. Raymond, *The Future of California's Academic Performance Index* (CREDO, Hoover Institution, Stanford University, 2002).

17. The survey further collected information on the method by which schools aggregated scores. The alternative approaches are discussed in Hanushek and Raymond, "Lessons about the Design of State Accountability Systems."

18. Carnoy and Loeb, "Does External Accountability Affect Student Outcomes?" use an index of intensity of accountability that covers both school and student accountability measures but do not consider differential times of introduction. Thus, they follow a very different strategy for uncovering the impacts of accountability. The ideas surrounding student accountability are discussed in John H. Bishop et al., "The Role of End-of-Course Exams and Minimal Competency Exams in Standards-Based Reforms," in *Brookings Papers on Education Policy 2001*, Diane Ravitch, ed. (Washington, DC: Brookings Institution Press, 2001), pp. 267–345.

19. All estimates come from models that include fourth-grade performance, indicator variables for the type of test (math or reading) and the specific time period, and individual state-fixed effects. The results are qualitatively similar if simply estimated with random effects for states, but the estimated effects of accountability are weaker, reflecting the difficulty in separating accountability from other state policies.

20. The general impacts of parental inputs are summarized in Hanushek, "The Failure of Input-Based Schooling Policies." When state-fixed effects are included, the impact of other factors is estimated solely from changes in them that occur within each state over time and incorporate no information on differences across states in education levels. Some indication of the importance of this comes from the strong and statistically significant impacts of parental education that appear if the models are estimated with random effects instead of fixed effects for states. (The same is not true, however, for school spending that is discussed below.)

21. For a general review, see Hanushek, "The Failure of Input-Based Schooling Policies." As discussed in the previous note, this is probably not simply a manifestation of the fixed effect estimator. Many states display large changes in spending over this time period, and the impact of spending in random effect models is never statistically significant.

22. Christopher Jencks and Meredith Phillips, eds., *The Black-White Test Score Gap* (Washington, DC: Brookings Institution Press, 1998).

23. Earlier discussion of the lack of progress in closing the black-white gap in the 1990s speculated that changing patterns in school composition due to school desegregation patterns influenced the aggregate time series pattern of scores (Eric A. Hanushek, "Black-White Achievement Differences and Governmental Interventions," *American Economic Review* 91, no. 2 (2001):24–28.

24. These exposure rates are calculated on an individual school basis within each state. The variable for minority exposure in column 2 calculates exposure relative to each subgroup in the pooled sample (i.e., the variable is the exposure of white students to minorities for the observations of NAEP scores of Whites and is the exposure of Blacks to minorities for the observations of black gains).

25. Eric A. Hanushek, John F. Kain, and Steve G. Rivkin, "New Evidence about *Brown v. Board of Education*: The Complex Effects of School Racial Composition on Achievement," Working Paper #8741, National Bureau of Economic Research (Cambridge, MA, 2002). To test the effect of intra-race influences, a further refinement of these models (not shown) considered black exposures to Blacks instead of to minorities (Blacks plus Hispanics). It is very difficult within these data to distinguish between the two alternative specifications. Using black exposure for Blacks produced slightly less precise estimates ($t = 2.0$) but did not alter the other conclusions.

26. The accountability measure indicates the timing during the period when consequential state accountability became effective (i.e., it ranges from 0.25 for accountability being in place for one year of the growth period for performance to 1.0 for accountability being in place for all four years). Similarly, the report card measure records timing for systems that provide school-by-school performance results but do not attach any rewards or sanctions to them. The data collection was designed to measure when the accountability system became effective, not when it was legislatively passed (Fletcher and Raymond, "The Future of California's Academic Performance Index"). Nonetheless, potential state-to-state differences in the phase in of accountability systems could effectively introduce measurement error into the accountability variable. An alternative approach is simply to measure whether or not the accountability system was in effect during the period (i.e., taking on the values 0 or 1). Pursuing this estimation yields qualitatively similar results, although a variety of the effects are not as precisely estimated (Eric A. Hanushek and Margaret E. Raymond, "The Effect of School Accountability Systems on the Level and Distribution of Student Achievement," *Journal of the European Economic Association* 2, nos. 2–3 (2004):406–415.

27. Hanushek and Raymond, "Improving Educational Quality"; Hanushek and Raymond, "Lessons about the Design of State Accountability Systems."

28. For a general discussion of alternative designs, see Hanushek and Raymond, "Lessons about the Design of State Accountability Systems."

29. Hanushek, Kain, and Rivkin, "New Evidence about *Brown v. Board of Education.*"

30. Eric A. Hanushek, Steven G. Rivkin, and Lori L. Taylor, "Aggregation and the Estimated Effects of School Resources," *Review of Economics and Statistics* 78, no. 4 (1996):611–627.

31. The linear form is not particularly crucial but simply makes the exposition easier. An alternative model where policies act as an efficiency parameter affecting the impact of resources is developed in Eric A. Hanushek and Julie A. Somers, "Schooling, Inequality, and the Impact of Government," in *The Causes and Consequences of Increasing Inequality*, Finis Welch, ed. (Chicago: University of Chicago Press, 2001), pp. 169–199. Within the limited data for this study, however, it is virtually impossible to distinguish between the alternative models. The results of estimating the alternative form, discussed below, are qualitatively very close to the included estimates.

32. Hanushek, Rivkin, and Taylor, "Aggregation and the Estimated Effects of School Resources."

7

School Choice by Mortgage or by Design

Patrick J. Wolf, Georgetown Public Policy Institute

Parental school choice has been available for centuries in the United States. Until relatively recently, schools have been chosen almost exclusively based on where parents decide to live, or by the self-financing of private schooling. Both of these traditional mechanisms of school choice depend heavily on the financial resources of families. As a result, better-performing public schools and private schools have been populated disproportionately by upper-income white students. Privileged students tend to thrive in such well-resourced schools, surrounded by similarly advantaged peers. Meanwhile, low-income minority students are often assigned by their residential address to low-performing schools, with fewer resources and peers who lack the home environment educational advantages of upper-income white suburbanites. Many inner-city public schools, and the low-income minority students who populate them, struggle to achieve acceptable levels of educational performance. This divide between the educational "haves" and "have-nots" is often cited as a significant contributor to the black-white test-score gap.

Why do African Americans achieve at levels significantly below Whites? Scholars have advanced a number of theories to explain the existence and persistence of the racial achievement gap.[1] They can be grouped broadly into four categories: equal access to quality schools, peer groups, social capital, and differential exposure to competition. These specific potential causes of the gap are analyzed in much greater detail in other chapters of this volume. For our purposes, it is important to acknowledge that traditional and policy-induced forms of school choice may have different effects on these four factors—reinforcing positive educational conditions for some students but negative educational conditions for others. If the gap is to be closed within one generation, more disadvantaged minority students will need to be exposed to more positive educational conditions. School choice might help to bring that about, depending on the scope and form it takes.

Recently, a number of policies have been developed and implemented to facilitate school choice opportunities for low-income and minority students. Generally referred to as "policy-induced school choice," these initiatives include public school choice—in the form of magnet schools, interdistrict choice, open enrollment, and transfer options out of underperforming schools—charter schools, and subsidized education in private schools. These various forms of parental school choice all have one thing in common: they sever the deterministic link between where a child lives and where that child goes to school. To what extent do these efforts to level the school choice playing field hold promise for reducing the test-score gap in the next generation of students? That is the question explored in this chapter.

I begin with a discussion of the theory of markets that drives school choices under both traditional and policy-induced school choice regimes. Then I consider the possible role of residential assignment to public schools in producing, magnifying, and perpetuating the test-score gap. Next, I review the various instruments of policy-induced school choice with an eye toward evidence about how well they are delivering on their promise to boost achievement, especially for low-income and minority students. I then discuss specific reasons why instruments of policy-induced choice hold promise for equalizing educational results for disadvantaged students. I conclude that choice initiatives tend to demonstrate modest—though somewhat inconsistent—advantages over traditional school choice arrangements in promoting educational equality and minority achievement. Although an expansion of policy-induced school choice by itself is unlikely to close the achievement gap in one generation, the evidentiary record to date supports the idea that well-designed and expanded school choice programs should be one of the policy weapons deployed in the effort to vanquish the test-score gap in one generation.

MARKET THEORY AND SCHOOL CHOICE

In *Politics, Markets, and America's Schools,* John E. Chubb and Terry M. Moe put forth a theory of educational markets as an alternative to politically directed education.[2] Political control of education, they reasoned, is driven by the particular interests of office holders, especially school board members. Political control results in inconsistency and fragmentation in the curricula and educational programs of schools, as well as rules and regulations that unduly constrain principals, teachers, and schools. Under such circumstances, school bureaucracies are limited in their abilities to adapt and innovate in ways that would promote educational achievement.

In theory, markets provide an attractive alternative to the political direction of schools. Educational bureaucracies are held accountable by the actions of their clients, who signal their support of or displeasure with schools by "voting with their feet." With market-based accountability as a check on school performance after-the-fact, schools are less constrained by front-end procedural requirements and regulations. They are permitted to operate more autonomously and thus are better able to focus on their critical task—effectively educating students.[3] The threat of losing students and subsequent organizational resources to more attractive schools will motivate school personnel and spur schools to perform better, the theory suggests. According to market educational theory, schools of choice will care as much about the achievement of students of color as they do about the success of white students, as all students bring comparable resources to the organization.[4] Competition is central to market theory in education, but so is equality of opportunity.

Moreover, not every educational environment will be "best" for various students with diverging educational needs. Market theory predicts that schools will specialize when school choice is widespread, seeking a niche that is not occupied by many of its competitors but is attractive to many of its potential customers. Schools will compete on quality, but also on distinctiveness. The availability of a wide variety of school environments permits well-informed parents to select the environment that they judge to be best for satisfying their child's educational and personal needs, promoting "allocative efficiency."[5]

Finally, market theory as applied to education suggests that schools of choice are more likely to be communal organizations that foster the development of "social capital." Sociologist James Coleman first made this claim in the 1980s and is credited with coining the term "social capital" to describe the general benefits that accrue to participants in organizations when people freely choose to be there and cooperate willingly in pursuit of shared goals.[6] Parents who have played a prominent role in selecting a school naturally feel a sense of ownership and investment in that school, and school officials welcome them and their children and seek to make them comfortable within their educational community.[7] The school is "their school" by voluntary choice, not by zip code, and that makes all the difference according to these theorists.

In summary, market theory and its proponents suggest that market-based educational arrangements boost student achievement relative to politically controlled neighborhood assignment systems due to enhanced school autonomy, competition for students and resources, the consumer equality of the market, better matches of student needs to educational programs and environments, and higher levels of social capital. These claims are contested, however, by a number of prominent critics of educational markets.

The critics counter that educational markets are highly prone to various forms of "market failure." Decision makers hesitate to relax the procedural constraints on schools even when they are subject to the discipline of market forces.[8] Competition for students tends to manifest itself in superficial resource-draining advertising campaigns instead of actual quality improvements, critics argue.[9] Even when schools are subject to market competition, and fail to respond in positive ways, there is a natural resistance to closing an underperforming school.[10] Market pressures sometimes force schools to converge on a single model of education that is in vogue, generating a sameness in educational environments that precludes the matching of diverse students to distinctive schools.[11] Even if a variety of different schools is available to low-income parents, disadvantaged families are not "natural consumers" of education and therefore are ill-equipped to make informed and effective school choices.[12] Finally, Anthony Bryk and his colleagues, while lauding Catholic schools for the social capital that they generate, argue that an increase in market pressures would commodify education in ways that would diminish the communal nature of Catholic schools, thus slaying the golden goose that lays the social capital eggs.[13] The best way to resolve these disputes is to consider the evidence regarding the actual performance of school choice programs, to determine if they have lived up to the market theory hype or have tended to succumb to the forces of market failure.

Before we proceed to the evidence regarding the performance of policy-induced school choice relative to traditional school choice, we need to consider one important theoretical idea. Chubb and Moe may have presented us with a false choice when they posed markets as the alternative to politics in shaping educational decisions. First, political decisions bound and regulate market arrangements as well as government operations. This is clearly the case in education, where policy-induced choice programs are guided by, well, public policy. The same particularistic interests that shape public schooling on a regular basis in public school systems tend to influence the design of school choice policies in ways that limit their free-market form and effects.[14] This is especially evident when public school systems authorize their own charter schools and subject them to a set of constraints similar to those faced by neighborhood public schools. Second, market considerations influence school assignments, resources, and operations even in the politically controlled public school system. Better school systems attract higher-wealth residents whose resources then catalyze the schools to perform even better. Thus, political versus market control of education is a matter of degree and not kind. Traditional and policy-induced school choice regimes are two alternative ways for political and market considerations to influence educational choices and outcomes.

TRADITIONAL FORMS OF SCHOOL CHOICE

American parents have exercised school choice in one of two ways. They have either selected a residence in the catchment area of the public school that they want their children to attend or paid for private schooling largely out of their own pockets. Both of these traditional forms of school choice track closely with family wealth and income—relatively well-off families have a better chance of securing a residence in the zone of a desirable public school and also have a greater ability to finance the tuitions of a wide variety of private schools. This is particularly the case in urban areas, where the cost of homes and apartments varies widely based on the quality of local public schools and where a large number and variety of private schools tend to operate. Family income and wealth also correlate disturbingly, though thankfully not perfectly, with race. Thus, traditional forms of school choice are more readily available to financially advantaged families who are disproportionately white.

Residential Assignment

Assignment to schools based on residence is a practice as old as the public school system itself. Horace Mann's vision for government-run public schools in every community relied heavily on residential assignment of a sort. Most towns in Massachusetts were small in the 1830s, and could, at best, support only a single public school. Residential assignment was a great convenience to education officials. It ensured that a relatively stable and predictable cadre of students would attend the new public schools. Residential assignment also relieved administrators of the burden of making potentially complicated and politically controversial decisions about which students should attend which schools. Mann's vision was for every elementary school to be of roughly equal and high quality, so assignment to schools by residence would seem to be inconsequential to the quality of education one received.[15] Moreover, a core purpose of Mann's public school system was to promote civic values of patriotism and communal spirit. At the time, assignment to public schools by residence seemed to dovetail nicely with the public purposes of education.

The shameful history of slavery and race-based discrimination proceeded almost coterminous with the tradition of public schooling in the United States. Even as supporters of public schooling justified their system as a means to provide equal educational opportunity to all children, the norms and practices in many localities tolerated and even mandated dramatic educational inequities by race. In the era of post–Civil War Reconstruction, systems of "Negro" schools sprang up within public school districts, providing a modicum of education to the children and grandchildren of former slaves who were either covertly or overtly barred from attending the "white" public schools in their own communities.[16] The clear recognition that such a separation inherently resulted in most black children receiving inferior educations and engendered limited prospects for upward mobility was the central motive for the seminal *Brown v. Board of Education* court ruling that invalidated all systems of government-sanctioned school segregation by race.

The policy decisions that assignment to public schools should be based on residence, but cannot be based on race, placed great educational import on a family's choice of residence. A family's chosen neighborhood has a significant impact on the peer group that will surround children during their formative educational years. All else equal, parents seek to live in a "good" neighborhood, populated by other children who they expect will have a positive behavioral and educational influence on their own children that will then be reinforced by assignment to high-quality neighborhood public schools.[17] Residential choice is a pivotal decision for the parents of school-age children. A recent survey by the U.S. Department of Education indicated that 74 percent of K–12 students are assigned to schools this way, and 24 percent of public school students moved to their current residence explicitly to attend a particular school.[18] With one stroke of the pen on a mortgage document or apartment lease, parents can obtain positive peer-group influences for their children as well as assured entry to a specific well-performing public school.

A new commercial for Century 21, one of the largest realtors in the United States, makes this point quite dramatically. A pregnant woman stands on the sidewalk of her suburban neighborhood quizzing students on a school bus about the features and performance of their school. The students are flummoxed. The woman chases the bus, in desperation, as it heads off to school. The commercial closes with a spokesman assuring viewers that Century 21 realtors have encyclopedic knowledge of the quality of schools in their region and are happy to share that important resource with eager home buyers.

If "good" neighborhoods with high-quality schools are the ticket to educational peace of mind, as conventional wisdom and realty commercials suggest, then how do African American families get there? The disappointing answer is that too few do. Several computer simulations and econometric studies have documented that income constraints operate to prevent most African American families from paying the extra money necessary to locate in "good" neighborhoods.[19] Analysts estimate that families pay a premium of 20 percent or more on the price of a home near a high-quality public school.[20] For example, Lisa Barrow concludes that white families with children in the Washington, DC, area are willing to pay an extra $7,335 per year in mortgage costs just to live in a school district with average Scholastic Achievement Test scores 100 points above the national norm of 903.[21] Based on the 1996 National Household Education Survey, in urban settings, only 32 percent of families with income of $10,000–$15,000 were able to exercise school choice by mortgage or self-finance private schooling for their children. For families with incomes over $75,000, over 71 percent practiced those traditional forms of school choice.[22] Family income and wealth are so important to residential location that, under conditions of pure assignment to schools by residence, with no public or private school choice options, public schools would be perfectly stratified by income.[23]

Is a lack of family income all that is keeping many African American families from gaining access to desirable student peers and schools through residential choice? Unfortunately, the answer is no. Barrow discovered that when they relocate, "African-American and white households do not choose the same communities . . . [due to] differences in income, differences in preferences, and housing discrimination."[24] These differences led Barrow to analyze the results of relocations separately by race throughout her report. White families in metropolitan areas such as Washington, DC, appear to be free to behave rationally in the face of residential assignment to schools, moving to new locations based on the quality of the local schools. African American families with children, however, are circumstantially constrained from selecting residences based on school quality. Barrow explains that a number of studies have documented the continued presence of racial discrimination in the housing markets in and around DC, and concludes that "the location decisions of African-American households reflect [and subsequently reinforce] the existing segregation in the area more strongly than the estimates for white households."[25] It is probably no coincidence that the Century 21 commercial contained no African Americans.

If school choice by mortgage is not permitting many African American families to expose their children to positive educational environments, perhaps the other traditional form of school choice—private schooling—provides more hope for closing the test-score gap.

Private Schooling

Families of means who choose not to exercise school choice by mortgage can often choose a private school for their children. Nationally, the percentage of K–12 students attending private schools has increased from 9.1 percent in 1993 to 10.8 percent in 2003, an increase of almost 19 percent in a decade, though still short of the post-war peak of around 15 percent in the 1960s.[26] The National Center for Education Statistics further estimates that

1.1 million students, composing 1.7 percent of the K–12 population, were home-schooled in 2003, a 29 percent increase in home-schooling in the past four years.[27] Consistent with market theory, private schooling is especially widespread in urban areas with poorly performing public schools. Barrow found that many high-income families remain in Washington, DC, when their children reach schooling age but spend extra money to purchase private school educations instead of paying inflated mortgage rates in the suburbs. By studying survey responses by census track, she determined that "45 percent of households with children in the Northwest section of D.C. have a child aged 6 to 17 enrolled in private school."[28] Private schools in urban areas are by no means the exclusive preserves of the rich—the average annual tuition of religious private schools in DC is less than $5,000. However, even though many inner-city African American students attend such schools as an alternative to local public schools, their numbers do not yet reflect their share of the school-age population. According to the U.S. Department of Education, in the 1999–2000 academic year, 9 percent of private school students were African American, compared to 17 percent of public school students who were of that race.[29] Moreover, at least some of the African American students who are attending private schools are doing so because of the availability of privately or publicly funded scholarships—policy induced school choice. If all African American families were required to finance private schooling entirely out of pocket, even less of them would have access to this traditional form of school choice.

In summary, market considerations are a key factor even in the functioning of traditional forms of school choice. Because a local address is the ticket into many good public schools, such addresses sell for a steep premium. Since access to quality public schools depends heavily on wealth and income, and African American families tend to have less of both than do Whites, school choice by mortgage is an educational market that likely contributes to and perpetuates the test-score gap. The same factors that often limit African American access to good public schools—wealth and income—also inhibit their ability to opt out of the system on their own and enroll in private schools. Educational markets "work" under traditional forms of school choice, but primarily to the benefit of advantaged white families.

WOULD CHOICE HELP?

Many social scientists and policy analysts recognize the shortcomings of the residential assignment system and the ways that school choice by mortgage might contribute to disparate outcomes such as the black-white test-score gap. But would policy-induced school choice produce educational outcomes that are less stratified by race? Even as market forces conspire to the benefit of relatively advantaged Whites under the traditional systems of residential assignment to public schools and unsubsidized private schooling, most policy-induced choice systems are explicit attempts to alter educational markets in ways that help disadvantaged families, many of them African American. Switching to a system of parental school choice targeted to low-income families holds the potential to transform in positive ways all four major likely contributors to the gap: equal access to good schools, peer groups, social capital, and overall school quality. In general, school choice is theorized to be capable of transforming this situation in positive ways because it (1) severs the link between residential location and both educational peer group and school assignment; (2) enhances parental responsibility for schooling; and (3) pressures the schools that serve African Americans to improve. The evidence regarding these theoretical assumptions that I review below is somewhat thin, and often contested. However, in general policy-induced school choice appears to hold more promise than traditional forms of school choice to at least narrow the achievement gap in one generation.

Parental School Choice within the Regular Public School System

The most common and oldest forms of policy-induced school choice permit parents to select a child's school while remaining within the public school system. This umbrella grouping of education policies includes magnet schools, interdistrict choice, open enrollment, and public school transfer options mandated by laws such as the federal No Child Left Behind Act (NCLB). The category excludes charter schools, which, in theory, operate within but independent of the public school system. Policy-induced public school choice (excluding charter schools) accounted for about 14 percent of K–12 school placements in 2003.[30]

Magnet schools were the first policy-induced form of school choice, and remain popular in many urban settings. Magnet schools are characterized by a distinctive school theme or pedagogical approach and admissions policies that permit students from outside the neighborhood to enroll so long as their attendance would improve racial balance at the school.[31] They represent an explicit attempt to undo the damage from the specific form of school choice by mortgage called "white flight" to the suburbs. However, as several researchers have established,[32] many public schools (even magnet schools) that are racially integrated on paper are actually heavily segregated by race in their daily operations. African American students are disproportionately assigned to the lower, less challenging "tracks" in schools, meaning that they are educated separately from other students throughout the school day. Clearly, such arrangements do not represent meaningful racial integration.

In response to this problem, many current public magnet school programs are converting to "whole-school" programs whereby the neighborhood members of the student body (predominantly minority) are more fully integrated into the magnet school environment.[33] Whole-school magnet schools are yet another example of how choice-induced deviations from strict residential assignment can better expose African American students to higher SES peers, with possible achievement benefits down the line.

How much does magnet schooling benefit students, especially if they are African American? In spite of more than thirty years of magnet schooling across the country, the evidence on this score remains somewhat thin. In a review of magnet school outcome studies from the 1970s and 1980s, Rolf Blank concludes that most studies report higher achievement levels and greater year-to-year gains for students attending magnet schools compared with those attending neighborhood public schools.[34] The evidence of magnet schooling advantages is merely suggestive, because none of the studies used random assignment to rule out self-selection as a driver of both higher achievement levels and achievement gains.

In the most comprehensive recent study of magnet schooling educational outcomes, Bruce Christenson and his colleagues collected data on the fifty-seven schools that were receiving financial assistance under the federally sponsored Magnet School Assistance Program.[35] They found that magnet schools were generating higher rates of gain in educational achievement than neighborhood public schools. However, after controlling for the changing demographic composition of the schools, they concluded that the adjusted gain levels for magnet schools were not significantly different from the gains being made by neighborhood public schools with comparable student characteristics.

A number of states and localities, such as Minnesota, Boston, and District 4 in New York City, permit exceptions to the norm of residential assignment beyond magnet and charter schools. These public school transfer programs take a number of forms, including specific "out-of-boundary" schools (which are often similar to magnet schools), intradistrict choice (a.k.a. "open enrollment"), interdistrict choice, and exit options from underperforming public schools. All such programs are governed by specific laws and regulations, so it is difficult to treat them as a class. However, in each case, at least some students are permitted to attend a "regular" public school based on parental preferences instead of based on residential assignment. A recent report on school choice estimates that as many as 500,000 students are attending public schools of choice in the United States under the various open enrollment and transfer programs in operation.[36]

Because transfer option programs are so diverse, often small, and cater to highly particular and self-selected populations, evidence of their effectiveness in improving educational achievement, especially for African American students, is scant. Most of the studies of these programs focus on their effects in better integrating schools by race and in permitting disadvantaged students to gain access to better educational environments. They typically report that the effects of the programs on integration and access for disadvantaged students depend heavily on the design of the program. For example, Armour and Peiser studied two interdistrict choice programs in Massachusetts.[37] They concluded that the general interdistrict choice program typically permitted middle-class white families to escape less desirable educational environments and gain access to more advantaged educational environments and communities.[38] The somewhat smaller METCO program, specifically designed to permit inner-city Boston minorities to attend suburban schools, clearly permitted highly disadvantaged students access to better educational environments.[39] Armour and Peiser did not evaluate the effect of switching schools on the subsequent achievement of choosers.

Mark Schneider and his colleagues performed extensive research on the intradistrict choice or "options" program in District 4 of New York City in the 1990s. They report that, all else equal, test scores in District 4 increased with the expansion of school choice. Their pooled time-series analysis over a twenty-five-year period indicated that "each 10 percent increase in the proportion of choice schools in District 4 increased reading scores by 8.5 percent and math scores by 7 percent, relative to the citywide average."[40] When combined with less extensive evidence of choice-induced achievement gains in Montclair, New Jersey, Schneider and his colleagues are left to conclude "in urban districts characterized by poverty and neighborhood blight, we should not lose sight of the many positive gains from public school choice."[41]

The accountability provisions of the federal NCLB education reform of 2002 have quickly become the source of the largest public school transfer program in the United States. According to the NCLB law, students in public schools that have not demonstrated "adequate yearly progress" in the achievement of their students or any of several specific sub-groups of students must be permitted to transfer to another public school in the district that is making adequate yearly progress, so long as space is available in such schools. The Citizens Commission on Civil Rights collected partial to complete information on the implementation of the NCLB student transfer policy in forty-seven states and 137 school districts; however, most of the complete data that they used for their analysis came from twelve states and the District of Columbia.[42] They were able to document the transfers under NCLB of nearly 70,000 students during the 2003–2004 school year.[43] Based on a close analysis of a subgroup of six states and forty-six districts in the remaining states, they estimate that about 2.4 percent of students eligible for transfer applied for it in 2002–2003 and 5.5 percent in 2003–2004.[44] However, only 1.3 percent of eligible students were actually placed in new schools in 2002–2003 and 1.7 percent in 2003–2004, primarily because of a dearth of available seats in better-performing public schools that were a manageable distance from the student's home.

A Louisiana study provided an extreme example of this availability problem, as over 33,000 students in Orleans Parish were eligible for transfer, 1,108 applied for it, and only thirty-seven (.11 percent of those eligible) were placed.[45] In communities with a high concentration of low-performing public schools, the few well-performing schools tend to be full or overcrowded already, because the families with the means to exercise school choice by mortgage have already done so. As a result, the transfer options under NCLB hold promise for more students than can actually be accommodated in the short run, at least until more interdistrict choice arrangements are made.

In spite of the limited options for public school transfers under NCLB, the Citizens Commission Report was largely favorable in its assessment of the program. They identified a number of school districts where the transfers that took place led to a much better integration of students in public schools by race and income.[46] There is a presumption that access to better-performing well-integrated public schools will increase the educational achievement of the students who transfer under NCLB, and could facilitate the closing of the achievement gap, but no study to date has analyzed the individual educational outcomes of this new policy.

Charter Schools

Charter schools are public schools that operate based on a contractual agreement with an education authority. That agreement usually provides the charter with greater autonomy to shape its educational environment in exchange for a commitment to meet or exceed certain performance standards. Admission to most charter schools is not determined by neighborhood of residence, although families face practical limitations regarding how far students can travel to attend a charter. The first charter school in the United States opened its doors as recently as 1992, initiating a veritable explosion in the availability of this particular school choice option. Nearly 3,000 charter schools operated in forty states and the District of Columbia in 2003, enrolling 600,000 students—close to 1 percent of the K–12 total.[47]

Just as the availability of charter schools is increasing dramatically, so are reports of the effects of charter schools on student achievement. Even for the empirical studies, both study findings and study quality are mixed. Bryan C. Hassel has systematically reviewed the existing studies of charter school effectiveness that meet a minimal standard for analytical rigor.[48] Hassel's meta-analysis indicates that researcher conclusions regarding charter school performance are influenced by the methods that they employ. Studies that rely on a one-year "snapshot" comparison of achievement levels of students in public charter schools versus students in neighborhood public schools are more likely to report lower levels of achievement in charters.[49] Such comparisons are likely biased against charters, since most charters are new schools that face an organizational learning curve and many of them specifically target underperforming and at-risk students for enrollment. Charter school evaluations that focus on gains in student achievement, control for the age of the charter, or that compare charters with specific neighborhood public schools with similar student demographics are much more likely to report comparable results for charter and noncharter public schools or even a charter school advantage in boosting achievement over time.[50]

For example, Solmon studied the performance of 60,000 students attending public charter or traditional schools in Arizona over a three-year period. He reported that, although the charter school students were more disadvantaged relative to the traditional public school students, once background demographics were controlled for, charter schooling boosted the achievement of students by an average of 3.3 percentile points per year beyond what they would have achieved in traditional public schools, so long as they remained in the charter school for a full three years. Solmon reported that the achievement gains were roughly similar by race of student. Since the African American students in the study began with lower levels of achievement, his finding suggests that Arizona charter schools are boosting achievement for all students but are not contributing to the closing of the test-score gap.[51] A major study of charter schools in California by the RAND Corporation reported mixed achievement effects of charter schooling. The cross-sectional comparison of achievement in charter versus traditional public schools indicated "that charter schools generally have comparable or slightly lower test scores than do conventional public schools."[52] Subsequent analysis of individual-level longitudinal data from six large school districts in California revealed "that charter school students are keeping pace with comparable students in conventional public schools."[53] Since less money was spent per pupil in charter versus traditional public schools in California, the RAND researchers concluded that the charter schools demonstrated a productivity advantage compared to the public schools.[54]

Robert Bifulco and Helen Ladd have released one of the few longitudinal charter studies thus far that reports significantly and consistently negative charter effects on student academic gains. They focus their analysis on North Carolina charter school students whose test-score performance was measured at least three times, either twice in a traditional public school and then once in a charter school or twice in a charter school and then once in a public school. They conclude: "The negative effects of attending charter school are large. Charter school students exhibit gains nearly 0.10 standard deviations smaller in reading and 0.16 standard deviations smaller in math, on average, than the gains those same students had when they enrolled in traditional public schools."[55] However, the authors fail to fully consider how the sample that they selected for analysis threatens study validity and should limit their ability to generalize their results to all charter students in North Carolina. Their selection decision limits the analysis to school switchers who already had two years of test-score data prior to switching. Since accountability testing does not begin until third grade in North Carolina, all of the students in Bifulco and Ladd's "preferred sample" must be in grades five and higher. Most charter schools admit the majority of their students in the elementary grades of K–4, where the opportunity to positively shape the child's early learning experience is greatest. Thus, the Bifulco and Ladd study merely suggests that the performance of a small and atypical subsample of North Carolina charter students compares unfavorably with that of former charter students in traditional public schools. Their study can tell us nothing about the effect of North Carolina charter schools in general on student achievement gains.

The most recent sophisticated analysis of charter school outcomes is the Wisconsin Charter School Study.[56] John Witte and his colleagues analyzed the performance of fourth and eighth graders in public charter and traditional public schools in Wisconsin in two panels, 2000–2001, and 2001–2002. In both panels of the study, the students in charter schools were more likely to be African American, with black students composing nearly 38 percent of the charter school population but less than 10 percent of the traditional public school student body.[57] Charter school students also were more likely to be participants in the free-lunch program than were the students in the traditional public schools. The demographic information suggests that "charter schools are clearly not educating the best students in the state of Wisconsin."[58]

The Wisconsin researchers controlled for the varying student demographics in the schools and made 120 careful comparisons between charter and noncharter achievement scores based on grade, panel, test subject area, and achievement hurdle (e.g., minimal, basic, or advanced). They found that either charter or traditional schools demonstrate a statistically significant advantage in seventy-two of the discrete comparisons, and in the vast majority of those cases (fifty-five) the advantage lies with the charter schools. After a more fine-grained follow-up analysis, they concluded *"that charter schools seem to be making their inroads by bringing students out of the minimal and basic levels in proportions higher than we would expect based on school characteristics."*[59] According to these researchers, Wisconsin public charter schools are serving a racially diverse and disadvantaged population and boosting the achievement especially of the students who are the furthest behind.

The results from empirical studies of public charter schools vary significantly but hints are emerging of some convergence regarding important conclusions. First, most charter schools disproportionately serve disadvantaged minority students. Second, new charter schools and the students in them tend to struggle in the first year of the charter school's existence. Thus, a study such as the recently released analysis from the American Federation of Teachers, which only examined achievement levels (not gains) in charter schools and included a disproportionate number of first-year charters, will naturally paint a negative and biased picture of charter school performance.[60] The many more sophisticated charter school studies have generally pointed toward a third important conclusion: once established, charters increase the performance of the students who persist in them beyond what they would have gained in a traditional public school. Finally, some charter school studies suggest that performance increases are strongest among disadvantaged students, while others conclude that the increases are roughly similar for advantaged and disadvantaged students.

Subsidized Private Schooling

The nascent empirical literature on private school choice generally supports the theoretical claims that parental choice would be better than residential assignment for educating many African American students. Coleman and his colleagues compared the achievement of white and black students in public schools with the achievement of roughly comparable students in private schools. They concluded that educationally disadvantaged students, including inner-city African Americans, appeared to benefit most from private schooling.[61] This preliminary finding has been confirmed by increasingly sophisticated test-score analyses by Neal,[62] Figlio and Stone,[63] Howell et al.,[64] and Barnard et al.[65]

For example, in their analysis of the test-score impacts of privately funded voucher programs in three cities after several years, Howell and his colleagues found that African American scholarship users improved their performance by an average of nearly seven National Percentile Rank points after two years, or approximately one-third of a standard deviation.[66] No test-score impacts of the scholarships were observed for the smaller subgroups of Latinos and Whites in the study. The voucher gains for African Americans were confirmed and extended in the third year of the New York City evaluation, which was the most evidence-rich of the three randomized field trials. The voucher results were not universally positive, however, as Howell et al.'s test-score results for Washington, DC, demonstrated no voucher effects in the third year, when voucher take-up rates dipped significantly.[67] Even the positive voucher effects for African Americans in New York City, reported by both Howell et al. and Barnard et al.,[68] have been contested in an alternative analysis by Krueger and Zhu,[69] which itself has been contested.[70] Still, when the smoke from the methodological dust-ups clears, there is an emergent body of evidence suggesting that African American students in particular benefit from policy-induced private school choice.

The cruel irony was and is that low-income inner-city African Americans seem to have the most limited access to private schools, even though private schooling appears to benefit them more than members of other ethnic groups. When school choice is made available to low-income families, through public policy or philanthropy, studies indicate that African Americans apply for such programs in numbers that greatly exceed their share of the eligible population.[71] Hoxby similarly reports that 21 percent of low-income families use public school choice programs compared to just 10 percent of high income families.[72] Low-income African Americans at the grassroots behave as if they know what social scientists are still trying to confirm conclusively: that policy-induced school choice is especially important for the future educational achievement of their children.

In summary, the empirical literature regarding the potential for policy-induced school choice to shrink the test-score gap in one generation is somewhat positive but far from consistent or conclusive. The best vehicles for using parental choice to boost the achievement of African American students appear to be means-tested private school scholarship programs, well-established charter schools, and open-enrollment programs (e.g., METCO) that are narrowly focused on expanding educational opportunities for low-income inner-city minority students. To the extent that policy-induced choice programs are limited in their ability to bring educational change to disadvantaged students, it is often because the interests of the winners in the school-choice-by-mortgage game are protected by the specific provisions of governmental choice programs or the limited availability of open seats in desirable neighborhood public schools. Just as policy-induced school choice is an alternative to traditional forms of choice, in certain respects the long-standing operation of school choice by mortgage has built a veritable mountain that often proves difficult for disadvantaged minorities to climb, even with the assistance of government-sponsored choice programs.

WHY DOES POLICY-INDUCED SCHOOL CHOICE SOMETIMES NARROW ACHIEVEMENT GAPS?

When policy-induced school choice operates to reduce the test-score gap, as it appears to in certain choice programs, why does it do so? What does breaking the link between residence and school bring about, specifically, to promote greater educational achievement especially for African American students? No study to date has been able to determine conclusively the basis for race-contingent choice impacts. African American students appear to face significant challenges to educational achievement due to economic and sociological factors that impact learning. It may be that school choice improves outcomes for African Americans in particular, and thus holds promise for closing the test score gap, because the transfer of African American students from residentially assigned public schools to schools of choice tends to bring with it greater equality in educational environments, a break from the inner-city peer group that discourages many African American students from achieving, an increase in social capital, and an improvement in the quality of schools in general.

School Choice and Educational Equity

As discussed above, the traditional forms of school choice—school choice by mortgage and family-financed private schooling—generate an educational landscape of schools that are separated by residential boundaries and highly stratified by income. Since income and wealth remain tied to race, they have produced the current version of "separate and unequal" schools with which many African American students must contend. Coons and Sugarman and Christopher Jencks initially made the case for policy-induced school choice on equity grounds.[73] They reasoned that equality of educational outcomes for African Americans could only be obtained if their families had school choice options comparable to those of relatively advantaged white families. Joseph Viteritti has pushed the claim further, arguing that school choice should be extended to low-income families as a simple matter of justice, regardless of its educational impacts.[74]

There is some evidence to support the claim that policy-induced school choice provides disadvantaged students with access to more effective schools. Purkey and Smith and Thomas Corcoran have summarized the research on effective schooling and identified a common set of characteristics of effective schools.[75] Schools that promote academic achievement tend to have strong principals with extensive discretionary authority, clear goals, high academic standards, expectations that all students will eventually meet those standards, an orderly school environment that is reinforced by strong discipline, and lots of homework. Many private schools, and the better charter, magnet, and public schools, share most of these characteristics. It would seem logical that closing the test-score gap in one generation should be an exercise in promoting greater access to effective schools for African American students. In that sense, policy-induced school choice that is targeted toward African American families, either explicitly or via income restrictions, should help to narrow the gap.

Moreover, at least some previous research has directly tied the exposure of African American students to an effective schooling environment to higher levels of student achievement. As Stephen and Abigail Thernstrom have documented, the KIPP Academy charter schools have attained fame for effectively educating inner-city African Americans and Latinos by following an educational model of strict discipline, school order, universally high educational expectations, and a focus on the mastery of basic skills before tackling more advanced material.[76] Private schools that participate in voucher programs, although they typically have access to lower material resources than do inner-city public schools, are given consistently strong marks by parents for their order and discipline and academic quality.[77] A follow-up analysis of the data from the experimental evaluation of the Washington Scholarship Fund privately subsidized choice program identified the level of dedication of the teachers in the choice schools and the amount of homework that they assign as two factors that apparently contributed to the higher levels of achievement exhibited by the African American students who exercised choice in the first two years of the evaluation.[78]

These results from experimental choice evaluations in the United States have been replicated in the nineteen countries in the Organization for Economic Cooperation and Development (OECD) studied by Dronkers and Robert.[79] They report that time spent on homework and time spent on reading and math activities in school are significantly higher in both government-supported and fully independent private schools in those countries. Time spent on homework is a substantially important and robust predictor of test-score achievement for students in OECD countries, even after controlling for an extensive set of family background, peer group, and educational environment factors. The authors conclude that government-supported choice schools, in particular, deliver clear value-added to their students, at least partly because they demand more of them academically than do typical government-run schools.

The research evidence linking equality of access to effective educational environments to a reduction in the test-score gap is promising but highly preliminary. In most cases, equal access to effective schooling practices only partially explains the achievement gains linked to the practice of policy-induced school choice. For a complete explanation, we also need to consider other factors.

The Influence of Residential Choice on Educational Peer Groups

In the sociological studies that preceded and followed in the wake of *Brown*, analysts concluded that coercive, state-sanctioned segregation of Blacks into all minority schools negatively impacted their self-esteem and thereby inhibited their ability to succeed academically. School choice holds the prospect to avoid such negative effects of coercive segregation in either of two ways. First, school choice may be an instrument for reducing the racial segregation of Blacks both among and within schools. Several careful empirical studies of school choice programs in the U.S. and abroad suggest that schools of choice are actually better integrated by race and socio-economic status than residentially assigned public schools.[80] For example, the RAND report on California charter schools reported that almost 42 percent of traditional public elementary schools in their sample had African American demographics that deviated significantly from the district-wide demographic, compared to about 29 percent of charter schools.[81] Like most school choice conclusions, these results have been disputed by other researchers using different analytic methods or studying different school systems,[82] but they are supported by common-sense logic. The evidence is overwhelming that low-income African Americans often are segregated into all-minority residential communities. As an alternative to the simple residential assignment of students to schools, which would inevitably reproduce residential segregation in the schools absent governmental intervention, school choice enables African American students to cross school boundaries and enroll in private or charter schools that are populated with students from a wider geographic area than neighborhood public schools. Since geography is not fate for schools of choice, they may serve as integrating institutions. For example, if an African American student leaves a neighborhood public school that is 90 percent African American, as many inner-city public schools are, and enrolls in an urban private school that is 40 percent African American, his/her exercise of choice improves the racial integration of both the school that he/she left and the school that he/she joined. African American students who leave all-minority assigned public schools will tend to arrive at schools of choice with student bodies that are at least somewhat higher in SES, although that is by no means guaranteed in all cases.

Important research has further explored the question of students "fitting into" peer groups within schools, and the implications for student achievement. Akerlof and Kranton recently published an important theoretical and empirical assessment of the effects of school identity and student attitudes on educational achievement.[83] Their research suggests that, under certain conditions, school choice will promote student achievement, especially for economically and educationally disadvantaged students who otherwise would have difficulty "fitting in" to the culture of a large public school. Student sense of belonging and educational effort depends on the extent to which a given school's student ideal matches their own background and preferences. A large public school is forced to choose between promoting a particular image of the ideal, and alienating many students who do not fit in, or promoting no particular image and becoming "Shopping Mall High." Neither strategy is productive for student outcomes and attitudes.[84]

School choice holds the prospect of improving the match between student attitudes and the school culture, and subsequently enhancing achievement for African American students, for several reasons. First, schools of choice are better able to define their culture in distinct ways, since they are not controlled by political authorities who are trying to satisfy the expectations of a broad political constituency.[85] Second, schools of choice are freer than are public schools to define their school culture in terms of high expectations for achievement. Third, schools of choice tend to be smaller in scale,[86] meaning that their internal constituency is likely to be more focused on the preferences and values of the school culture. Fourth, when given the opportunity, parents appear to choose schools at least partly based on a close match between the culture of the school and the needs of their particular child.[87] And fifth, schools of choice exhibit more frequent and meaningful communication between school and home, permitting both schools and parents to make accommodations in their preferences and cultural cues to arrive at a common standard that inspires students without alienating them.[88] Thus, it follows that schools of choice will tend to have cultures that are both more academic and a closer match to student attitudes and expectations than are assigned public schools. The close alignment of the prevailing culture of the school to the attitudes of students in choice schools, in theory, operates to reduce alienation among students, better integrate lower SES students with a higher SES peer group, spur effort, and increase achievement.

This application of Akerlof and Kranton's theory of identity and schooling to the case of school choice explains important empirical regularities regarding distinctive forms of schooling. For example, female students who attend single-sex schools appear to benefit academically from that special kind of educational environment, all else being equal.[89] Single-sex schools for females are better able to define their mission as promoting academic excellence for girls and women. Students who share such aspirations are more likely to choose to attend such schools. Once the choice has been made, if academic excellence is not a strong preference of a particular enrollee, she will be subject to constant cultural cues and pressures to change her attitudes to better conform to the school's culture. Especially if she began in a condition of educational or economic disadvantage, such an attitudinal change is likely to result in higher levels of achievement than she would have realized in a public school with a less distinct and less academic culture.

Just as school choice may increase the achievement of African American students by situating them within a school culture that rewards educational success, it also may increase their academic performance because it removes them from a neighborhood culture that discourages or distracts from learning. A number of sociologists and cultural anthropologists, most notably John Ogbu,[90] have argued that the street culture of low-income inner-city communities devalues educational performance. Crime and drugs, so rampant in many inner-city communities, promise easy money and pleasures as well as a means to "fit in" with a neighborhood crew that can age into a gang. The pressure to conform to the street culture and diminish educational striving may be especially intense if a student's neighborhood peer group is also his educational peer group. Since many schools of choice exist outside of a student's neighborhood, and socialize students into an alternative peer group, policy-induced choice could promote academic achievement for African Americans by providing them with greater exposure to a more advantaged peer group that values educational success and less exposure to a street culture that devalues education. The analysis of the potential causes of school choice gains for African Americans in Washington, DC, discussed above found that exposure to a more advantaged peer group was the third factor that appeared to matter, along with more dedicated teachers and homework.[91]

Although there are good reasons to think that policy-induced school choice can narrow the test-score gap by disassociating African American students from their neighborhood school and street culture, there is little hard evidence that changing a student's peer group by itself significantly boosts educational achievement.[92] Cook and Ludwig even challenge the claim that street culture diminishes the educational aspirations of African American youth.[93] Until more research can be done on the topic, little can be concluded regarding the extent to which school choice policies can narrow the test-score gap specifically by "upgrading" the school culture and peer group of African American students.

The Influence of School Choice in Improving Social Capital

One of James Coleman's many significant contributions to the theoretical literature on education was his claim that private schooling and school choice had the potential to affect parents and families in ways that enhanced the social capital and home environment to the benefit of student achievement.[94] Coleman's thinking about social capital and education built on the original conceptualization of Glen Loury,[95] and has been further developed by Brandl and Campbell,[96] among others.

This claim that school choice might enhance the social capital within and without the home highlights important conceptual differences between residential assignment and parental school choice educational systems. Under residential assignment, parents are not required to play the dominant role in arranging for and overseeing their child's education. Many do, particularly if their higher level of SES provides them with the resources and strong inclination to do so. However, inner-city parents who are struggling to get by, many of them African American, might be sorely tempted to cut corners regarding educational practices and information-gathering, comforted by the expectation that the educational professionals in their neighborhood public school will take care of things. Residential assignment to schools can become a sort of crutch for parents, with potentially dire implications for the test score gap.

The claim of Coleman and the other choice and social capital theorists is that, if you burden parents with more educational responsibilities, they will become more responsible. If it is up to them to select the schools that their children will attend, then they will go to the trouble of learning more about the schools in their community. This act, by itself, could represent a positive improvement in the home educational environment. Once parents have selected schools for their children, they should feel personally invested in the arrangement, and might become more involved in educational activities at home and at school. Some choice schools even require such parental involvement in their schools.[97] These predicted outcomes of choice hold the promise of reducing the achievement gap because they are likely to positively impact African American families, who on average suffer from a "social capital" deficit, more than white families, who already tend to engage in information gathering and supervisory activities through their relatively unrestrained exercise of school choice by mortgage.

Are the social capitalists correct to surmise that the extension of school choice will yield positive educational benefits, especially for African Americans, by transforming the behaviors of parents? The evidence to date on this question is decidedly mixed. Schneider and his colleagues report that the existence of universal school choice in Montclair, New Jersey, is associated with statistically significant positive gains in all four measures of social capital that they examined: PTA membership, voluntarism, parent networking, and trust of teachers.[98] Kim Metcalf and his colleagues, who evaluated the Cleveland voucher program over five years, suggested in a recent paper that parental school choice could be understood "as a decision intended to leverage the home and school social capital for the benefit of the child."[99] However, Howell and his colleagues report mixed social capital impacts from their three randomized field trials of privately funded scholarship programs in New York City; Dayton, Ohio; and Washington, DC.[100]

What are we to make of these disparate results regarding the effect of school choice on parental social capital and the home environment? The Montclair study involved universal "forced" choice: all parents were expected to select their child's public school, and there were no direct financial implications of the use of choice. Arguably, such conditions are ideal for identifying the social capital effects of school choice. Circumstances were different in the three-city study. The choice instrument in all three sites was a partial-tuition scholarship provided to low-income families. In focus group discussions, a number of parents described how they needed to work extra hours and scramble to finance their share of the private school tuition, and that they sometimes felt that they had less time to spend with their children. These mixed results on social capital should lead us to two tentative conclusions: (1) the design of the choice policy influences the impacts that it will produce; and (2) school choice's best prospects for closing the test score gap may be due to other factors besides social capital.

Choice-Induced Competition and System-wide School Quality

Finally, market theory predicts that choice-induced competition will spur schools to improve their quality and focus more on achievement. Any competitive effect of choice on school performance might be especially helpful to African Americans. As Barrow, Hoxby, and others have shown,[101] African Americans are more firmly anchored to low-income neighborhoods and low-performing public schools than are Whites. Traditional forms of school choice, including self-financed private schooling and school choice by mortgage, do not pressure the schools that largely serve African Americans to improve to nearly the extent that they pressure the schools generally serving white students to improve. School choice programs that provide African American students with easier school exit options hold greater promise for spurring the schools at risk of losing African American students to improve so as to retain them. Since most parents who participate in school choice programs, including African American parents who did not attend college, list academic quality as an important reason for their school choice,[102] schools that are pressured to change are likely to reform themselves in ways that boost academic achievement even for the students who do not switch schools.

An emerging but still incomplete research literature supports this competitive effects choice hypothesis. In her recent review of research on competitive choice effects in the United States, Hoxby describes how many of the schools in her analyses that were subject to the highest degree of competition, through the initiation and expansion of choice programs, improved their student test scores the most.[103] Jay Greene and his colleagues report similar results in such diverse locales as San Antonio, Milwaukee, and the state of Florida.[104] Armour and Peiser found that at least some of the schools impacted by interdistrict choice in Massachusetts took steps to improve the quality of their schools.[105] Schneider and his colleagues, reporting on competitive effects in District 4 of New York City, state that "Indeed, the academic performance of neighborhood schools has not declined after more than twenty years of option-demand choice, and in fact has improved, nearly across the board."[106] Although some researchers question the extent to which such school improvements are choice induced,[107] the evidence so far generally suggests that school quality in the public sector increases, perhaps especially for schools that serve African Americans, when more parents are permitted to choose their schools. To paraphrase Caroline Hoxby, school choice may be "a rising tide that lifts all boats," though its swells might especially buoy the schools that African American students typically attend.

CONCLUSION—WHAT ARE THE PROSPECTS?

It is important to acknowledge that this analysis of the potential for school choice to significantly shrink the persistent and disturbing black-white test score gap is necessarily speculative. Although an increasing number of rigorous school choice evaluations suggest that policy-induced school choice benefits choosers, and some find especially strong effects for African Americans, no single, careful, comprehensive, empirical study to date has confirmed all of the steps on the path that would take the existing population of African American students and deliver them, through school choice, to educational outcomes that more closely proximate those of the population of white students in the United States.

We can draw some conclusions based on the theoretical claims and evidence to date. The first is that traditional forms of assigning students to schools, through residence or unsubsidized private education, tend to operate to the advantage of many white students and to the disadvantage of many African American students. The primary reason is that residential assignment to public schools is a market system of education, but one that depends almost exclusively on the resources of families and the willingness of desirable communities to make themselves accessible to African Americans. Under such conditions, market theory predicts that African American students as a whole would be better off if parental choice, supported by government resources and policies, were targeted toward low-income families who tend to lose out under residential assignment to schools. The best empirical evidence to date tends to support the more cautious claims of market theorists that low-income African American students on average perform somewhat better over time if they are in a school of choice. The evidence supporting the efficacy of policy-induced choice ranges widely in quality, however, from suggestive in the case of targeted private school vouchers and established charter schools to rather thin in the case of public school transfers and magnet schools. No convincing empirical study of policy-induced school choice in the United States over the past thirty years has concluded that those who avail themselves of school choice tend to be harmed academically from the experience in the long run. Thus, we might conservatively characterize the evidence regarding the effect of policy-induced school choice on participants as neutral to moderately positive.

The evidence is even more speculative regarding specifically why policy-induced choice works for African Americans, when it works. It may be because it puts them on a more equal footing with advantaged Whites in gaining access to quality schools. Perhaps school choice helps African Americans succeed because it removes many of them from an anti-educational culture of the streets and situates them within the pro-achievement culture typical of many schools of choice. School choice could promote higher levels of social capital among African American parents by actively involving them in educational choices that previously were made by others, and thereby enhance student learning. Finally, reconnecting to market theory, school choice might narrow the test-score gap because competition for students pressures schools to improve their quality especially with regard to their academic program. If that proves to be the case, then African American students will benefit from the existence of more policy-induced school choice whether or not they actually exercise choice.

My answer to the question: "Can policy-induced school choice close the black-white test-score gap in one generation?" regrettably is "probably not." The gap is wide, and the evidence regarding choice effects to date merely suggests that modest gains are possible. If such gains accumulate over a long period of time, such as a generation, expanded school choice opportunities could possibly close the test-score gap in one generation. However, with the possible exception of District 4 in New York City, no school choice program has been evaluated over a sufficiently long stretch of time to accurately gauge its likely generational effects.

Policy-induced school choice certainly holds more promise to shrink the gap than does the traditional system of assigning students to public schools by residence. Still, residential assignment to public schools shows few signs of exiting the scene entirely, and, as we can see in the case of the implementation of the No Child Left Behind school choice provisions, advantaged families have scrambled to get to good public schools first and they are showing only limited signs of wanting to share their advantaged positions with those who cannot afford to live in their neighborhoods. That reality need not be a source of despair for education reformers, but does suggest that increasing the availability of school choice for disadvantaged students is a difficult undertaking. Nevertheless, policy-induced school choice is both expanding and demonstrating some promise for reducing the test-score gap. A reasonable person might count on school choice to reduce the black-white test-score gap in one generation, but not eliminate it entirely. Given the limits of the evidence to date, it would be somewhat foolhardy to assume that expanded school choice alone would forever vanquish the notorious test-score gap; yet, given the promise of the evidence so far, it would be perhaps more foolhardy to cease trying and learning.

NOTES

I gratefully acknowledge the research assistance of Daniel S. Hoople, Elizabeth Quilligan, Benjamin Traster, and Ashley Zollinger.

1. Christopher Jencks and Meredith Phillips, "The Black-White Test Score Gap: An Introduction," in *The Black-White Test Score Gap*, Christopher Jencks and Meredith Phillips, eds. (Washington, DC: Brookings Institution Press, 1998), pp. 1–51.

2. John E. Chubb and Terry M. Moe, *Politics, Markets and America's Schools* (Washington, DC: Brookings Institution Press, 1990).

3. James Q. Wilson, *Bureaucracy* (New York: Basic Books, 1989).

4. Milton Friedman, "The Role of Government in Education," in *Economics and the Public Interest*, Robert A. Solo, ed. (New Brunswick, NJ: Rutgers University Press, 1955), pp. 123–144.

5. Mark Schneider, Paul Teske, and Melissa Marschall, *Choosing Schools: Consumer Choice and the Quality of American Schools* (Princeton, NJ: Princeton University Press, 2000), p. 262.

6. James S. Coleman and Thomas Hoffer, *Public and Private High Schools: The Impact of Communities* (New York: Basic, 1987).

7. See John E. Brandl, *Money and Good Intentions Are Not Enough* (Washington DC: Brookings Institution Press, 1998); Anthony S. Bryk, Valerie E. Lee, and Peter B. Holland, *Catholic Schools and the Common Good* (Cambridge MA: Harvard University Press, 1993).

8. Frederick M. Hess, *Revolution at the Margins* (Washington, DC: Brookings Institution Press, 2002).

9. Kevin B. Smith and Kenneth J. Meier, *The Case against School Choice: Politics, Markets, and Fools* (Armonk, NY: M.E. Sharpe, 1995).

10. Patrick J. Wolf, "Comment on Joseph P. Viteritti," in *The Brookings Papers on Education Policy*, Diane Ravitch, ed. (Washington, DC: Brookings Institution Press, 2004), pp. 162–168.

11. Neville Harris, "Regulation, Choice, and Basic Values in Education in England and Wales: A Legal Perspective," in *Educating Citizens: International Perspectives on Civic Values and School Choice*, Patrick J. Wolf and Stephen Macedo, eds. (Washington, DC: Brookings Institution Press, 2004), pp. 91–130.

12. Bruce Fuller and Richard F. Elmore, *Who Chooses? Who Loses? Culture, Institutions, and the Unequal Effects of School Choice* (New York: Teachers College Press, 1996).

13. Bryk, Lee, and Holland, *Catholic Schools*.

14. Hess, *Revolution*.

15. Horace Mann, *First Annual Report of the Secretary of the Board* (Boston: Dutton & Wentworth, 1838).

16. David Rowell, "The Education of Jim Crow," *The Washington Post Magazine*, April 4, 2004: 18–21.

17. The effects of neighborhood peers on educational achievement and attainment may be somewhat exaggerated in the policy literature. In an analysis of national survey data, Caroline Hoxby has estimated that neighborhood demographics are only responsible for 4 percent of the explained variance in student test scores and 5 percent of the explained variance in the educational attainment of thirty-three-year-olds. See Caroline M. Hoxby, "If Families Matter Most, Where Do Schools Come In?" in *A Primer on America's Schools*, Terry M. Moe, ed. (Palo Alto, CA: Hoover Institution Press, 2003), pp. 89–125.

18. National Center for Education Statistics, "The Condition of Education 2004," U.S. Department of Education, Institute for Education Sciences, NCES 2004–077, June 2004, p. 74.

19. See Caroline M. Hoxby, "School Choice and School Competition: Evidence from the United States," *Swedish Economic Policy Review* 10 (2003):11–67; Thomas J. Nechyba, "Introducing Choice into Multi-district Public School Systems," in *The Economics of School Choice*, Caroline M. Hoxby, ed. (Chicago: University of Chicago Press, 2003), pp. 145–194; Dennis Epple and Richard Romano, "Neighborhood Schools, Choice, and the Distribution of Educational Benefits," in *ibid.*; Lisa Barrow, "School Choice through Residential Location: Evidence from the Washington, D.C., Area," *Journal of Public Economics* 86 (2002):155–189.

20. Nechyba, "Introducing Choice"; Shawna Grosskopf et al., "Allocative Inefficiency and School Competition," Federal Reserve Bank of Dallas Working Paper No. 97–08 (1997).

21. Barrow, "School Choice through Location," 184.

22. Hoxby, "If Families Matter Most," 107.

23. Epple and Romano, "Neighborhood Schools," 231.

24. *Ibid.*, 166.

25. *Ibid.*, 170. Other scholars confirm that the continued residential segregation of African Americans is not limited to the DC area. See Hoxby, "School Choice and School Competition," 48–49; Eric A. Hanushek, John F. Kain, and Steven G. Rivkin, *Disruption Versus Tiebout Improvement: The Costs and Benefits of Switching Schools* (Cambridge, MA: National Bureau of Economic Research Working Paper Series, 2001).

26. NCES, "The Condition of Education 2004," 74.

27. National Center for Education Statistics, "1.1 Million Homeschooled Students in the United States in 2003," U.S. Department of Education, Institute for Education Sciences, NCES-2004–115, July 2004.

28. Barrow, "School Choice through Location," 180.

29. NCES, "The Conditions of Education 2004."

30. My calculation from NCES, "The Condition of Education 2004," p. 74, and The Center on Education Reform website, www.edreform.com, accessed on August 25, 2004.

31. Rolf K. Blank, "Educational Effects of Magnet High Schools," in *Choice and Control in American Education*, Vol. 2, William Clune and John Witte, eds. (New York: Falmer, 1991).

32. See, for example, Blank, in *ibid.*; John E. Chubb and Terry M. Moe, "Politics, Markets, and Equality in Schools," in *Reducing Poverty in America*, Michael R. Darby, ed. (Thousand Oaks, CA: Sage, 1996), pp. 121–153.

33. Bruce Christenson et al., "Evaluation of the Magnet School Assistance Program, 1998 Grantees," in Report to the U.S. Department of Education, Office of Innovation and Improvement (Washington, DC: American Institutes of Research, 2004).

34. Blank, "Educational Effects of Magnet Schools."

35. Christenson, "Evaluation of Magnet School Program."

36. Citizen's Commission on Civil Rights, *Choosing Better Schools: A Report on*

Student Transfers Under the No Child Left Behind Act, Washington, DC, May 2004, p. 8.

37. David L. Armour and Brett M. Peiser, "Interdistrict Choice in Massachusetts," in *Learning from School Choice*, Paul E. Peterson and Bryan C. Hassel, eds. (Washington, DC: Brookings Institution Press, 1998), pp. 157–186.

38. *Ibid.*, 165–166.

39. *Ibid.*, 166.

40. Mark Schneider, Paul Teske, and Melissa Marschall, *Choosing Schools: Consumer Choice and the Quality of American Schools* (Princeton, NJ: Princeton University Press, 2000), p. 192.

41. *Ibid.*, 267.

42. Citizen's Commission on Civil Rights, 4.

43. *Ibid.*, 6.

44. *Ibid.*

45. Public Affairs Research Council of Louisiana, "NCLB: A Steep Climb Ahead," Baton Rouge, Louisiana, July 2004, p. 10.

46. Citizen's Commission on Civil Rights, 8.

47. Center for Education Reform website, www.edreform.com, accessed on August 25, 2004.

48. Bryan C. Hassel, "Studying Achievement in Charter Schools: What Do We Know?" Report prepared for the Charter School Leadership Council by Public Impact, January 31, 2005.

49. *Ibid.*, i. See also Tom Loveless, *The 2002 Brown Center Report on American Education: How Well Are American Students Learning?* (Washington, DC: Brookings Institution Press, 2002); F. Howard Nelson, Bella Rosenberg, and Nancy Van Meter, *Charter School Achievement on the 2003 National Assessment of Educational Progress*, Report of the American Federation of Teachers (Washington, DC: AFT, August 2004).

50. Hassel, "Studying Achievement in Charter Schools," i–ii; see also Jay P. Greene, Greg Forster, and Marcus A. Winters, "Apples to Apples: An Evaluation of Charter Schools Serving General Student Populations," Education Working Paper No. 1, Manhattan Institute for Policy Research, 2003; Lewis C. Solmon and Pete Goldschmidt, "Comparison of Traditional Public Schools and Charter Schools on Retention, School Switching, and Achievement Growth," Policy Report No. 192, Goldwater Institute, Phoenix, March 15, 2004; Lewis Solmon, Kern Paark, and David Garcia, "Does Charter School Attendance Improve Test Scores?" Report of the Goldwater Institute, Phoenix, March 2001; Timothy J. Gronberg and Dennis W. Jansen, "Navigating Newly Chartered Waters: An Analysis of Texas Charter School Performance," Report of the Texas Public Policy Foundation, April 2001; Margaret E. Raymond, "The Performance of California Charter Schools," CREDO report, Hoover Institution, Stanford University, Stanford, CA, June 2003; Tom Loveless, "Charter Schools: Achievement, Accountability, and the Role of Expertise," in *The 2003 Brown Center Report on American Education: How Well Are American Students Learning?* (Washington, DC: Brookings Institution Press, 2003), pp. 27–36; Erik A. Hanushek, John F. Kain, and Steven G. Rivkin, "The Impact of Charter Schools on Academic Achievement," unpublished manuscript, 2002.

51. Solmon and Goldschmidt, "Comparison of Traditional Public Schools and Charter Schools," 13.

52. Ron Zimmer et al., "Charter School Operations and Performance: Evidence from California," prepared for the California Legislative Analyst's Office, RAND Education, Santa Monica, CA, 2003, p. xxii.

53. *Ibid.*, 56.

54. *Ibid.*, 106.

55. Robert Bifulco and Helen F. Ladd, "The Impacts of Charter Schools on Student Achievement: Evidence from North Carolina," Terry Sanford Institute of Public Policy, Duke University, Working Paper Series SAN04–01, August 2004, p. 19.

56. John F. Witte et al., "The Performance of Charter Schools in Wisconsin," Report of the Wisconsin Charter Schools Study, August 2004.

57. *Ibid.*, 31.

58. *Ibid.*, 19.

59. *Ibid.*, 24, emphasis in the original.

60. Nelson et al., *Charter School Achievement*.

61. Coleman and Hoffer, *Public and Private High Schools*; James S. Coleman, Thomas Hoffer, and Sally Kilgore, *High School Achievement: Public, Catholic, and Private Schools Compared* (New York: Basic Books, 1982).

62. Derek Neal, "The Effects of Catholic Secondary Schooling on Educational Achievement," *Journal of Labor Economics* 15, no. 1 (1997):98–123.

63. David N. Figlio and Joe A. Stone, "Are Private Schools Really Better?" 1 *Research in Labor Economics* 1, no. 18 (1999):115–140.

64. William G. Howell and Paul E. Peterson, with Patrick J. Wolf and David E. Campbell, *The Education Gap: Vouchers and Urban Schools* (Washington, DC: Brookings Institution Press, 2002).

65. John Barnard et al., "Principal Stratification Approach to Broken Randomized Experiments: A Case Study of School Choice Vouchers in New York City," *Journal of the American Statistical Association* 98, no. 462 (2003):299–323.

66. Howell et al., *Education Gap*.

67. *Ibid.*, 147.

68. *Ibid.*; Barnard et al., "Principal Stratification."

69. Alan B. Krueger and Pei Zhu, "Another Look at the New York City School Voucher Experiment," *The American Behavioral Scientist* 47, no. 5 (2004):658–698; Alan B. Krueger and Pei Zhu, "Inefficiency, Subsample Selection Bias, and Nonrobustness: A Response to Paul E. Peterson and William G. Howell," *The American Behavioral Scientist* 47, no. 5 (2004):718–728.

70. William G. Howell and Paul E. Peterson, "Uses of Theory in Randomized Field Trials: Lessons from School Voucher Research on Disaggregation, Missing Data, and the Generalization of Findings," *The American Behavioral Scientist* 47, no. 5 (2004):634–659; Paul E. Peterson and William G. Howell, "Efficiency, Bias, and Classification Schemes: A Response to Alan B. Krueger and Pei Zhu," *The American Behavioral Scientist* 47, no. 5 (2004):699–717.

71. William G. Howell, "Dynamic Selection Effects in Means-Tested, Urban School Voucher Programs," *Journal of Policy Analysis and Management* 23, no. 2 (2004):225–250.

72. Hoxby, "If Families Matter Most," 107.

73. John E. Coons and Stephen D. Sugarman, "Family Choice in Education: A Model State System for Vouchers," *California Law Review* 59 (1971):321–438; Christopher Jencks, "Giving Parents Money to Pay for Schooling: Educational Vouchers," *New Republic*, July 4 (1970):19–21.

74. Joseph P. Viteritti, Choosing Equality: School Choice, the Constitution, and Civil Society (Washington, DC: Brookings Institution Press, 1999); "School Choice: How an Abstract Idea Became a Political Reality," in *The Brookings Papers on Education Policy*, Diane Ravitch, ed. (Washington, DC: Brookings Institution Press, 2004), pp. 137–173.

75. Stewart C. Purkey and Marshall S. Smith, "Effective Schools: A Review," *Elementary School Journal* 83 (1983):427–452; Thomas B. Corcoran, "Effective Secondary Schools," in *Reaching for Excellence: An Effective Schools Sourcebook*, Regina M. J. Kyle, ed. (Washington, DC: National Institute of Education, 1985), pp. 71–97.

76. Stephan Thernstrom and Abigail Thernstrom, *No Excuses: Closing the Racial Gap in Learning* (New York: Simon and Shuster, 2003).

77. Howell, *The Education Gap*.

78. Patrick J. Wolf and Daniel S. Hoople, "Looking inside the Black Box: What School Factors Explain Voucher Gains in Washington, D.C.?" *Peabody Journal of Education* 81 (2006).

79. Jaap Dronkers and Peter Robert, "The Effectiveness of Public and Private Schools from a Comparative Perspective," Working Paper, European University Institute, Political and Social Sciences Department, Badia Fiesolana, Italy, SPS No. 2003/13.

80. See, for example, Jay P. Greene, "Civic Values in Public and Private Schools," in *Learning from School Choice*, Paul E. Peterson and Bryan C. Hassel, eds. (Washington, DC: Brookings Institution Press, 1998), pp. 83–106; Stephen Gorard, "School Choice Policies and Social Integration: The Experience of England and Wales," in *Educating Citizens: International Perspectives on Civic Values and School Choice*, Patrick J. Wolf and Stephen Macedo, eds. (Washington, DC: Brookings Institution Press, 2004), pp. 131–156.

81. Zimmer et al., "Charter School Operations and Performance," 35.

82. See, for example, Edward B. Fisk and Helen F. Ladd, *When Schools Compete* (Washington, DC: Brookings Institution Press, 2000).

83. George A. Akerlof and Rachel E. Kranton, "Identity and Schooling: Some Lessons for the Economics of Education," in *Journal of Economic Literature* 40 (2002):1167–1201.

84. *Ibid.*, 1169–1170.

85. Chubb and Moe, *Politics, Markets and Schools*.

86. Howell, *The Education Gap*.

87. Mark Schneider et al., "Shopping for Schools: In the Land of the Blind, the One-Eyed Parent May Be Enough," *American Journal of Political Science* 41 (1998):1201–1223.

88. Akerlof and Kranton, "Identity and Schooling"; Howell, *The Education Gap*.

89. Bryk, Lee, and Holland, *Catholic Schools*.

90. John Ogbu, "Opportunity Structure, Cultural Boundaries, and Literacy," in

Language, Literature, and Culture: Issues of Society and Schooling, Judith Langer ed. (New York: Ablex, 1987), pp. 149–177; "Racial Stratification in the United States: Why Inequality Persists," *Teachers College Record* 96, no. 2 (1992):264–298.

91. Wolf, "Looking Inside the Black Box."

92. Hoxby, "If Families Matter," 98–101.

93. Philip J. Cook and Jens Ludwig, "The Burden of 'Acting White': Do Black Adolescents Disparage Academic Achievement?" in *The Black-White Test-Score Gap*, Jencks and Phillips, eds., 375–400.

94. James S. Coleman, "Social Capital in the Creation of Human Capital," *American Journal of Sociology* S. 94 (1988):95–120.

95. Glenn Loury, "A Dynamic Theory of Racial Income Differences," in *Women, Minorities, and Employment Discrimination*, P. A. Wallace and A. Lemund, eds. (Lexington, MA: Lexington Books, 1977), pp. 153–186.

96. See John E. Brandl, *Money and Good Intentions*; David E. Campbell, "Making Democratic Education Work," in *Charters, Vouchers, and Public Education*, Paul E. Peterson and David E. Campbell, eds. (Washington, DC: Brookings Institution Press, 2001), pp. 241–267.

97. The KIPP Academy charter schools require parents to sign an agreement that commits them to high levels of involvement in their child's school and educational activities outside of school. See Thernstrom and Thernstrom, *No Excuses*.

98. Schneider et al., *Choosing Schools*, 235.

99. Kim K. Metcalf, Natalie A. Legan, and Kelli M. Paul, "Do School Vouchers Offer Families Opportunities for Expanding Their Social Capital?" Paper presented at the Hawaii International Conference on Education, Honolulu, January 2005, p. 19.

100. Howell et al., *The Education Gap*.

101. See Barrow, "School Choice through Location"; Hoxby, "School Choice and School Competition."

102. See especially Schneider et al., *Choosing Schools*, 264; Howell et al., *The Education Gap*.

103. Hoxby, "School Choice and School Competition."

104. Jay P. Greene and Greg Forster, "Rising to the Challenge: The Effects of School Choice on Public Schools in Milwaukee and San Antonio," Manhattan Institute for Policy Research, Civic Bulletin 27; Greene and Winters, "When Schools Compete."

105. Armour and Peiser, *Learning from School Choice*.

106. Schneider et al., *Choosing Schools*, 269.

107. See, for example, Hess, *Revolution*; Bifulco and Ladd, "The Impacts of Charter Schools"; Gregory Camilli and Katrina Bulkley, "Critique of 'An Evaluation of the Florida A-Plus Accountability and School Choice Program,'" *Education Policy Analysis Archives* 9, no. 7 (2001):1–10.

8

Many Causes, No Easy Solutions

Chester E. Finn, Jr., Thomas B. Fordham Foundation

1954's *Brown* decision undid a grave moral and legal evil and led to enormous changes in American education. Yet its implicit promise has not been kept: the educational advancement and social good that should have flowed from it remain more hope than reality. If we're serious about finally keeping that promise for tomorrow's children, we will need a transformation of today's education policies and school practices as wrenching and bold as *Brown* was half a century ago.

Desegregating the schools can only be termed a partial victory if black youngsters emerging from them are ill prepared to succeed in American society and thus destined to remain at the "back of the bus," not because laws and policemen confine them there but because they aren't learning enough to move to the front. In 2004, the main education problem faced by black Americans is not state-enforced racial segregation. It is unacceptably weak academic achievement.

But why? What are the sources of today's vexing learning gaps? Heated, heartfelt arguments have raged for decades, arguments that we cannot resolve here. We can, however, note that most analysts settle on one (or more) of these six explanations:

1. The legacy of segregation and slavery. Nobody could reasonably be expected to bounce up quickly after centuries of being held down. Those favoring this explanation hold that Blacks differ fundamentally from newer immigrants and other minorities, due to their disparate histories. Not enough time has passed for them to recover from earlier deprivations and persecutions and come into their own in terms of educational achievement and other marks of success.

198

2. Continuing discrimination, poverty, unemployment, family erosion, shoddy health care, crime, troubled communities, and a host of other explanations largely beyond the reach of the formal education system. The key assumption here is that children with difficult lives, disrupted homes, and angry neighborhoods are apt to learn less. In chapter 2 of this volume, Derek Neal suggests that "underinvestment" in developing the "social capital" of black children, due to an array of societal circumstances and familial influences (including single-parent homes and dismaying "rates of idleness and incarceration" among young adult black men), explains the persistence and intransigence of the "achievement gap."

3. The short-changing of schools and other educational institutions attended by black children, as manifested in crummier facilities, less experienced teachers, fewer special programs, lower spending levels, etc. When combined with continuing—some say worsening—de facto segregation of schools and classrooms, and the attendant deprivations of mostly-black schools, this is believed by many to account for the weak educational attainment of African American youngsters. (There is, however, a body of contrary evidence indicating that school integration has actually advanced since 1970, particularly in the South.[1])

4. Low academic standards and weak expectations for black students turning into self-fulfilling prophecies. Some say this is the unintended result of a well-meaning "double standard" that emerged post-*Brown* lest black youngsters be made to feel inferior or fail because too much was demanded of them too soon. Others contend that educators really do expect less from poor and minority students, either because of racist attitudes or because they judge that children from disadvantaged homes simply cannot gain as much knowledge and skill in school as those surrounded by books and college-obsessed parents who douse the TV and read them bedtime stories.

5. The grip of many black children by a "culture" (peers, gangs, parents, etc.) that doesn't adequately value educational achievement and may even deprecate it. Such analysts as John Ogbu, Ron Ferguson, John McWhorter, and Abigail and Stephan Thernstrom contend that youngsters can scarcely be expected to study hard, behave properly in school, and learn a lot from teachers if their friends and sometimes their families send contrary signals about what's important.[2]

6. The victimization of poor and minority children by a public education monopoly that accords them fewer accessible schooling options than other youngsters have and that, like any monopoly, is thus freer to pursue its own ends and advance the interests of its adult "stakeholders" rather than attend to the needs of its youthful customers and their parents. The essential point: families lacking political clout, purchasing

power, and viable alternatives are singularly vulnerable to being stuck
in bad schools and instructed by people who lack incentives to teach
them well.

There's some truth in all of those explanations, and no doubt others can
be added to the list. It is of little use to spend vast energy trying to settle on
the causes of today's learning gap, considering that its roots are numerous
and tangled and that our real challenge is not to argue about its sources but
to narrow and in time eliminate it. Still, we do well to bear in mind, when
looking ahead to the politics of solving this problem and the policy options
available to us, that people's preferred—and abhorred—solutions tend to
align with their chosen explanations of the problem's sources.

In this chapter, I concentrate on possible remedies to be found primarily
within the bounds of education policy. I cannot deal here with solutions that
focus on larger cultural or societal conditions, save to note that any school-
centered remedy would naturally be more apt to succeed if parallel changes
were also made in other influential elements of the lives of black children and
their families.

But remedies and solutions to what, exactly? Let's be precise. The core
problem is an unacceptably wide black-white learning gap at the same time
that America's overall academic achievement level also needs to be raised. We
can defer to Congress, which in enacting the No Child Left Behind (NCLB)
act in 2001 stated that the purpose of the radically altered Title I program at
NCLB's heart is "to ensure that all children have a fair, equal, and significant
opportunity to obtain a high-quality education and reach, at a minimum,
proficiency on challenging State academic achievement standards and state
academic assessments." Two goals are thus joined: the "equal opportunity"
target that has been familiar since *Brown* and the bold new proposition that
this incorporates for all children, a serious shot at attaining academic "proficiency."

That's the law of the land. It's also an economic, social, and moral impera-
tive. And to no part of the U.S. child population does it apply more power-
fully than African American boys and girls. It should, therefore, be the goal
of education policymakers and analysts.

How to attain that ambitious goal insofar as can be done with the levers
available to education policymakers and institutions? Nobody knows for
certain, since it's never been done before in the United States—and in those
lands where something like it has been accomplished, there is usually either
markedly less diversity (e.g., Japan) or a powerful and near-universal education ethic (e.g., Singapore). (Sometimes there's also a lot less personal freedom.) Perhaps 100 percent proficiency is unrealistic for America. But I know
no one who thinks we cannot get a lot closer to it or who believes that

today's learning gaps cannot be substantially narrowed. Where disputes arise is over the surest way to do this.

Five broad strategies have adherents today. I review these, then double back and appraise some of their virtues and defects.

1. Expect educational results to improve if we succeed in breaking down the remaining walls of de facto segregation by taking effective government action to introduce more black youngsters into predominantly white schools and more white children into black schools, usually via elaborate desegregation schemes. These may be voluntary, involuntary or both and they typically include urban-suburban transportation of pupils, magnet schools, and suchlike. Further reduce barriers by assuring that black pupils can enter "gifted" classes and honors programs, that they are not overassigned to "special ed," and taking other steps to afford them complete access to the best that today's schools can offer. This approach is prominently associated with Harvard's Gary Orfield and some civil rights groups.

2. Compensate for present-day inequalities of outcome by deploying an arsenal of "affirmative action" policies and programs that enable black youngsters (and not-so-youngsters) to scale the education and career ladders of American society even if their current attainments would not otherwise make that possible. Assume that, in the fullness of time, this will yield truer equality of results such that special preferences will cease to be needed. In the Supreme Court's majority opinion in the most significant of the recent affirmative action cases, *Grutter v. Bollinger* (2003), Justice Sandra Day O'Connor wrote that "The Court expects that 25 years from now, the use of racial preferences will no longer be necessary to further the interest approved today."

   Affirmative action is not, to be sure, a strategy within the control of K–12 education policy makers, and it brings plenty of controversy. But because it is widespread in university admissions and in the hiring and promotion decisions of employers (including educational institutions), it inevitably reverberates in the high schools and beyond. Within K–12 policy circles, however, it tends to be resisted by those who rue double standards—and is plainly barred by NCLB—even as it is favored by some who believe that a single lofty standard will cause more minority youngsters to falter or drop out.

3. Improve the schools attended by black students by supplying them with better teachers, more minority teachers, additional professional development, stronger (or more "relevant") curricula, dynamic leadership, smaller classes, newer textbooks, powerful technology, tutoring, after-school programs, preschooling, etc. This approach is cherished by many educators and a host of public and private funders. As a result,

one can point to hundreds of resource-boosting schemes for schools attended by poor and minority children (including the federal Title I and Head Start programs) and to innumerable special projects and policies meant to augment the schools' capacity, extend their reach, and strengthen their performance.

4. Use standards, testing, and accountability to leverage improvement in schools and narrow the "learning gap," not by directly adding to their resources and services but by rewarding them for improvement and intervening to change them in sundry ways if they fail. Favored by many business leaders and elected officials, this is the core NCLB approach and the premise on which standards-based reform rests in many states. It sometimes includes high-stakes testing for individual pupils (e.g., passing the New York Regents exams or the Massachusetts Comprehensive Assessment System), meant to "incentivize" girls and boys along with those who run and teach in their schools. It may also include nudging colleges and employers to raise the stakes for doing well in primary-secondary schooling, as recommended by the American Diploma Project.[3]

5. Give black (and other needy) children different and better schools to attend by enabling more good schools to come into being and assisting youngsters to gain access to them while escaping from the faltering schools in which they are now enrolled. But do this voluntarily. Thus have arisen numerous market-style and choice-based strategies, including vouchers, charter schools, tax credits, interdistrict public school choice, home schooling, virtual schooling, etc. Some of these focus mainly on the "demand side" (i.e., assisting students to move among extant schools). Others concentrate on the "supply side" by creating more schools (e.g., KIPP Academies, Edison schools, "early college" high schools) or enlarging the capacity of those that already exist. It's important, however, to ensure that the alternative schools are truly superior, else little is gained by transferring into them. Broadly termed "school choice" and controversial in some of its forms, this is the preferred approach of some policy thinkers and elected officials and a growing number of black (and Hispanic) leaders.

Which of these five strategies is apt to have the greatest success? To be the most amenable to implementation? One reason the answer to those basic questions eludes us is that we never see any of them operating in isolation, much less in an experimental mode with proper controls and comparisons. Hence, we have scant data about the effectiveness of any strategy in its pure form. Rather, we find several of these reform plans functioning concurrently in real communities and states, often in muddy or compromised fashion. That's often a byproduct of multiple policies being put into place by different policymakers or in different political eras, challenging the analyst to undertake a veritable archeological dig through layers of accumulated programs. A further source of blurring is that some ambitious policy initiatives (e.g., the federal NCLB law) combine more than one strategy. Yet implementation is nearly always incomplete—the result of political compromise, institutional inertia, public apathy or resistance, and shortages of talent or money. The upshot is that one seldom observes a fully fledged version of a single strategy, properly implemented in its own right and uncontaminated by other reform schemes.

Where, then, to place one's hope, invest one's political capital, and expend the taxpayer's dollars? Social science and recent history offer no sure guide, though aficionados of each strategy offer their own forms of "evidence" that it "works." But neither resources nor time nor opportunity is infinite. So it's important, as one selects among strategies or devises combinations of them, to opt for whatever is apt to accomplish the greatest good in the most practical way (i.e., a mix of feasibility, affordability, and likely efficacy—assuming, of course, that constraints are relaxed and implementation is reasonably thorough and deft). Let us, therefore, now appraise some of their merits and uncertainties.

Further Efforts at Racial Integration

This certainly extends the spirit of *Brown*. It hinges on the expectation that black students will learn more if they go to school with white students—and that the schools they'll attend together will be better because they'll draw more experienced teachers, nicer facilities, more money, etc. But it also rests on two dubious assumptions. The first is that integrated classrooms will per se be places of greater learning, even if little else changes. A vast dispute has raged for four decades over the evidence adduced in support of this proposition; I do not, myself, find that evidence terribly persuasive.[4] Perhaps more importantly, even if integration's track record with respect to academic achievement were more convincing, I don't believe it's politically feasible to make this happen on a large scale via coercive means. Which is to say that this strategy fails to meet the practicality test, even if it were better proven.

The fact is that many Blacks are no longer keen for integration as an end in itself and more than a few Whites seem willing to go to lengths to avoid it. In any case, few American cities today have demographics that make serious integration possible and no court will order a "metropolitan" solution. Of late, in fact, we've seen many communities struggling to get out from under earlier desegregation orders, usually with the assent of black as well as white residents. Though nothing will cool the ardor of earnest integrators, as early as 1965 Kenneth Clark himself wrote (in *Dark Ghetto*) that it's at least as important to strengthen the offerings and standards of the schools in which black children find themselves as to focus on their racial composition. Some people think it racist to imply that black kids cannot learn satisfactorily in schools of their own—and point to some minority schools that display plenty of learning. As for integration per se, perhaps housing and income policies will gradually produce more of it on a voluntary basis, but in an era of ethnic consciousness and multiculturalism I'm not sure that will result in truly mixed schools. All one need do is observe our meticulously "diverse" colleges and universities to realize that integrating the freshman class does not necessarily lead to much mixing of social, educational, or residential life among students. Race-based enclaves seem to arise even where they need not.

Affirmative Action

This is its own debate, conducted largely outside the boundaries of primary-secondary education policy. It evokes strong feelings and endless litigation because it leads to a race-based "double standard" that many believe does almost as much violence to the doctrine of "equal protection" as school segregation did. As yet, we have no evidence that its long-term "theory of action" is correct (i.e., that schools—and their academic results—will spontaneously change for the better once black Americans have been lifted across the obstacles that they currently face). In terms of immediate K–12 education policy, however, I view this strategy as a counsel of despair that is plainly at odds with NCLB.

Improve the Schools that Black (and Other) Youngsters Attend Today

The encouraging element of this strategy is that we can point to stirring examples of schools that succeed in educating minority students, thus demonstrating that it's no pipedream—though it must also be noted that such schools typically have remarkable staffs, powerful cultures and, sometimes, extraordinary resources. One must wonder where we will find the talent and commitment to operate thousands more schools of this kind, particularly when one realizes that dramatically altering a failing school is one of the toughest challenges around.[5] (Admiral Rickover once compared it to "moving a graveyard.") The intervention-and-makeover strategy built into NCLB assumes that a local school system, often limited in its own capability and shaky in its governance, can successfully "reconstitute" the very schools that it has long been responsible for running. As for lesser interventions, a thousand programs seek to strengthen schools in a hundred ways and some of them work some of the time. But their track record is spotty, in large part because single-shot changes introduced into, or clamped onto, schools are not apt to succeed very often, not, at least, if everything else about the school remains as before. Moreover, many of these programs still focus on augmenting a school's resources rather than altering what it does with them. Simple resource boosting almost never yields stronger pupil achievement. As an essayist summarized the matter in *U.S. News*:

> In 1966, sociologist James Coleman found that school budgets had little effect on academic performance. The point has been hotly argued ever since. Kansas City famously poured millions into expensive magnet school programs, trying to spend its way to academic excellence. Such efforts did not succeed. Today, many reformers say that while denying the importance of money is foolish, how a school spends its money is as important as how much it spends. D.C. spends about $10,000 per student, putting its spending slightly above nearby Montgomery County, Md., a wealthy suburb known for its top-notch schools. By contrast, Charlotte [which scores significantly higher than the District of Columbia] currently spends $7,288 per student. Washington "doesn't suffer from a lack of resources," says Paul Ruiz, the city's former chief academic officer.[6]

High-stakes Testing and Standards-based Reform

This strategy is here to stay for the foreseeable future, as NCLB is now law and many states were previously committed to its theory of change— including more and more jurisdictions now deploying high-stakes tests for students. Indeed, President Bush has signaled that extending the NCLB umbrella more completely over high schools is at the top of the education agenda for his second term. There's promise in this general approach, as we've seen in a few jurisdictions that have steered a steady course, such as Texas, Florida, and Massachusetts. But while this strategy tends to lift all boats, some analysts find that it lifts white (and Hispanic) achievement more than black, thus potentially widening the black-white achievement gap. Moreover, NCLB is off to a rocky start. The data so far from the National Assessment show scant gains in math and reading, even as a steady flow of international comparisons shows the United States sagging well below other industrial nations, particularly at the high school level. Meanwhile, many states are responding to the accountability "backlash"—and NCLB's mandates—by quietly lowering their standards or deferring the day when these become binding.

How well such remedies can work will depend on many factors, not least the unanswered question of how schools will respond to sunlight, pressure, and embarrassment. That may turn out to work better on paper than in practice, particularly in locales where bureaucratic inertia and rigid union contracts limit the freedom of action of those leading individual schools. My hunch is that NCLB will do a fine job of identifying low performing schools (and groups of students) but prove less effective at repairing the "broken" ones. The efficacy of high-stakes testing will depend on political fortitude—the capacity of elected officials, community leaders, and educators to stick to a painful course despite dismaying failure at first—and the mustering of resources and resolve to help more kids pass these exams.

New Schools, Competition, and Choice

This is being tried in a variety of forms in dozens of places, but here, too, the available evidence is mixed. Of course, one whopping reason for the inconclusive results is that this reform strategy, being as fiercely resisted (albeit from different directions) as "busing," has not yet had a proper test anywhere in the United States. Still, there is evidence from limited trials and evaluations that black youngsters given access to different schools are more apt than other children to see palpable (if usually small) gains in academic performance. In other words, choice tends to narrow the achievement gap. What's more, we have seen that a "supply side" strategy *can* cause more good schools to come into existence—from scratch or replication more readily than through intervention and reconstitution—although the political obstacles to this remain great. Unfortunately, we have also seen that new schools are not necessarily good schools; they, too, can worship the wrong pedagogical gods, be run by incompetent people, and be chaotic, undisciplined places where little learning occurs. Also remaining to be determined: how deep is the pool of extraordinary people willing to shoulder the risks and burdens of starting, leading, and teaching in extraordinary schools?

※   ※   ※

By now it's evident that none of these strategies is a sure thing educationally or a slam-dunk politically. Each has enemies, each brings its own backlash, and any that is seen as intended solely to benefit black children could trigger stiffer recriminations, especially if seen as a zero-sum game in which brighter prospects for African American youngsters are believed to come at the expense of other kids.

This is no fantasy. One need not look far to see white objections to affirmative action and suburban resistance to interdistrict school choice. That Title I financial assistance has been spread across so many schools—and that so many youngsters are now covered by the federal "special education" program—further illustrates the difficulty in a pluralistic democracy of "targeting" special help on any narrowly defined population or set of schools. Moreover, we need from time to time to remind ourselves that, while our immediate focus is on the educational plight of black Americans, in fact the entire nation is at risk and almost everyone's academic outcomes need a boost. (Those who need reminding should look at the "PISA" and "TIMSS" results that came out in December 2004.[7])

Politically and programmatically, this says to me that the surest formula for progress is to identify a "rising tide" that can reasonably be expected to lift all education boats but especially those in which black children sail. In other words, a broad-based strategy for boosting achievement across the society that also incorporates measures from which African American youngsters will particularly benefit.

For that reason, I place little hope in strategies one and two—integration per se and affirmative action—though I do not doubt that their boosters and believers will continue to advance them. I welcome integration, so long as it's voluntary, but I think it's more apt to follow from other social changes than to cause them. As for affirmative action, it may, as Justice O'Connor and other observers conclude, be a necessary evil at the present time, but a "double standard" is inherently un-American and this cannot be the core of a long-term reform agenda.

I willingly stipulate that strategy three—improving today's schools through sundry additions, augmentations, and reform ideas—should be pursued, but great care must be taken to concentrate its energies and resources on interventions with the greatest evidence of success. These include (to name four well-proven examples): academically rich preschooling; research-based curricula and pedagogies in core academic subjects, including those—such as Direct Instruction—that appear to work especially well with disadvantaged children; recruitment and deployment of knowledgeable and committed teachers via multiple pathways; and identification of highly effective school principals.

Because existing schools are so difficult to change, however, strategy three alone, brightly though it gleams in the eyes of educators, politicians, and philanthropists, cannot be expected to meet the challenges we face. Which brings us to strategies four and five; that is, standards-and-accountability and new schools-and-choice.

Fortunately, we need not choose between them. Though their theories of action diverge and their political support comes from different directions, both hold promise, both have traction in the policy arena and enjoy strong public approval, and, perhaps most important, far from clashing, they actually reinforce and strengthen one another.

We have evidence of this from charter schools, which must simultaneously contend with state-imposed standards and market forces and which generally manage to balance these. We also find an interesting example in Florida, whose standards-based accountability system uses exposure to the marketplace as the ultimate "consequence" that can befall a failing school. Enacted in 1999, Florida's "A+" plan assigns a letter grade to every public school based primarily on its performance on statewide tests. If a school gets an "F" for two years, its students become eligible for vouchers (i.e., can take their state dollars to schools of their choice, including private schools).[8]

(NCLB contains weakened versions of this in its provisions for students to opt out of faltering schools or use a portion of their school's federal dollars to purchase "supplemental services" from other providers.)

Some analysts of Florida's program judge that the threat of choice—i.e., of students departing—has caused many of that state's troubled public schools to tug hard on their own bootstraps. In other words, exposure to the marketplace—even a whiff of the marketplace—is an action-forcing consequence that can play a constructive role within a regimen of standards-based reform.[9] Especially pertinent to this discussion, whatever is working in Florida is showing success with black pupils, too. Though the achievement gap remains wide, African American fourth graders in the Sunshine State made strong gains in reading between 1998 and 2003 on the National Assessment of Educational Progress.[10]

There *should* be synergy between standards-based and market-style reforms, because each offers a promising solution to a major problem besetting the other. Standards-based systems are better at spotting failing schools than at fixing them. In most jurisdictions, the list of low-performing schools doesn't change much from year to year, despite valiant efforts to improve them. Bad schools are famously difficult to transform into good ones, particularly when the main agents of their transformation are government bureaucracies working within a political environment where myriad interest groups can block changes that they dislike.

The upshot is that children enrolled in failing schools are apt to linger for years in classrooms where they learn little. What's happened is that a pure standards-based accountability system has succeeded in revealing shortcomings that it cannot set right.

What to do? Bring market forces to bear. Move the children to more effective schools, including new schools created for this purpose, or free families to move themselves. This can yield educational gains for those who do move—at least so long as there's a decent supply of superior schools to move to. As we have seen in Florida, Albany, Milwaukee, and elsewhere, it may also trigger needed changes in the schools they leave, which betters the lot of those youngsters who don't exit. No, we don't have solid, large-scale data. We *couldn't* have, until it's tried more comprehensively. But we have suggestive research by Caroline Hoxby and others, indicating that school systems produce somewhat stronger results when they face competition and we have lots of case studies and small-scale research on charter schools that generally point in the same direction.[11]

The converse is also true. School-choice reforms benefit from standards and tests. That's because the education market is flawed. Consumers have inadequate information about providers. Private schools, for example, are often coy about their actual academic results because they prefer to rely on their reputations and to shun statistical comparisons. Those reputations may be justified—or not. Without a transparent marketplace based on uniform standards and replete with comparable and readily accessible achievement data, one must trust every school to tell the truth and to do so in language that low-income parents can parse. Thus we often face a situation where schools are formally answerable to the marketplace yet their consumers are unable to make wise choices among them—a problem apt to be exacerbated for families without a lot of relevant experience or access to educationally savvy advisors. That leads to market failure, especially for those consumers who most need market success.

How can people know what school to choose—and resist false claims and unwarranted reputations—if they don't have comparative performance data from a system of uniform standards and statewide (or national) tests? How will educators know which schools are most worth teaching in? How will prospective school founders know which education niches cry out to be filled with high-quality alternatives?

The answer, of course, is better information about schools' effectiveness (and other attributes). And the surest path to that desirable situation is for the state to create a universal regimen of sound academic standards for core subjects uniform (or comparable) assessments; and a transparent, publicly accessible reporting system, whereby every school and other instructional provider can be carefully scrutinized by quality-minded shoppers in the education marketplace. (We'll leave for another day the contentious matter of whether this would be better accomplished via a single set of uniform national standards rather than by state-specific variants.)

The marketplace is bound to work better if standards, tests, and reporting systems are in place. But standards-based reform will also work better when there are bona fide alternatives for children otherwise cornered in schools known to be failing. Because such children are disproportionately minority, such a reform strategy is certain to serve them well.

But the "bona fide" alternatives need to be highly effective schools that can successfully meet the educational needs and match the challenges posed by the youngsters entering them. Simply being a "school of choice" does not assure this, nor do contented parents (who may, for example, be so grateful that their children have made it into a safe and friendly place that they fail to notice how little reading, writing, and arithmetic are being learned there). I've outgrown the hope that nailing a "charter" or "private" sign over a schoolhouse door guarantees its educational efficacy, any more than the label "district-operated public school" destines it to educational inadequacy.

Which brings us to the place where reform strategies four and five loop back to join with strategy three: making certain that these are good schools, whatever flag they fly.

My observation is that schools that prove most successful with poor and disadvantaged children (of every race) are schools that immerse the children in a sea of learning—and teach them to swim and to strive to reach the other side. These are schools that create their own culture, a micro-climate of learning, composed of standards, discipline, high aspirations, confidence in children's potential, expert teaching of a sound curriculum, and so much constructive attention to kids that the dysfunctional parts of their lives get squeezed down to manageable proportions. That means the day, week, and year are typically far longer than the American norm. Teachers and other staff members are often reachable (by cell phone or e-mail) around the clock—a prospect that carries all sorts of costs (e.g., can such teachers do right by their own families?) and should carry commensurate rewards. The school also has a spirit—a credo, really, a set of beliefs, behaviors, habits, and interpersonal relations—that both signals the attainability of success and shows the path to it. In a sense, the school becomes a virtual family for its students as well as the source of a healthier culture than they encounter in the 'hood. But it doesn't shun their real families; indeed, even the best of schools cannot overcome the effects of families that cannot or will not cooperate. Yet it can supply nearly everything that its pupils need for educational success.

Abigail and Stephan Thernstrom describe several such schools in their penetrating and hopeful 2003 book, *No Excuses: Closing the Racial Gap in Learning*. Others appear in the 2000 Heritage Foundation study, also entitled *No Excuses*.[12] Still more can be found in the pages of the March 2004 "unequal education" issue of *U.S. News & World Report*. But almost everyone who is serious about education reform has read such accounts and visited such schools over the years. We know they exist. It's just that until now we've supposed that they must always be the exceptions that prove the rule, the mavericks, the rarities, places that can happen only when extraordinary people engage in heroic measures and defy the "system."

Thus we come to the great challenge ahead, the challenge that I said at the start of this chapter will entail "a transformation of today's education policies and school practices as wrenching and bold as *Brown* was half a century ago." It is, quite simply, the challenge of turning such exceptional schools into the norm. Of altering the system itself.

How, you ask, can we do that which has defeated so many earlier reformers? By building a sturdy framework of high standards, sound assessments, and effective accountability around every school; by fostering the creation and replication of effective schools of many kinds as well as the reconstitution of existing ones; by giving every family the right to choose its children's schools from high-quality options that are transparent to their clients and to the larger public; by slashing the red tape—and overcoming the interest group resistance—that impedes these steps from being taken; by acknowledging that all-encompassing educational environments are bound to cost more than schools that play a lesser role in children's lives; but by also insisting that every education dollar—and every educator and school—be judged not by the nobility of its intentions but by the soundness of its results. Ambitious? Yes, indeed. Revolutionary, even. But so was *Brown*. The reform agenda I have sketched will strike many as implausible, daunting, unworkable. But so did *Brown*. I contend that it will lift all of America's education boats—and that this will do the greatest good for their black passengers.

But may it please not take us fifty more years.

NOTES

1. See, for example, Charles T. Clotfelter, *After Brown: The Rise and Retreat of School Desegregation* (Princeton, NJ: Princeton University Press, 2004).

2. See, for example, Abigail Thernstrom and Stephan Thernstrom, *No Excuses: Closing the Racial Gap in Learning* (New York: Simon & Schuster, 2003), especially pp. 120–147.

3. http://www.achieve.org/dstore.nsf/Lookup/ADPsummary/$file/ ADPsummary.pdf.

4. Hanushek, Kain, and Rivkin have examined the interaction of academic achievement with schools' racial composition (and concomitant "peer effects") in Texas and conclude that "a higher concentration of black schoolmates has a strong adverse effect on the achievement of Blacks." See their paper at http://edpro.stanford.edu/eah/papers/jpe.resubmission.feb04.PDF

5. Ronald C. Brady, *Can Failing Schools Be Fixed?* (Washington, DC: Thomas B. Fordham Foundation, 2003). http://www.edexcellence.net/doc/failing_schools.pdf.

6. Julian E. Barnes, "Unequal Education," *U.S. News & World Report*, March 22/ March 29, 2004, p. 73. It may also be noted that Coleman's resource measures were districtwide averages that masked possible school-level differences and may have understated their effects on building-level outcomes.

7. See http://nces.ed.gov/timss/Results03.asp for 2003 "TIMSS" results and http://nces.ed.gov/surveys/pisa/PISA2003Highlights.asp?Quest=2 for U.S. 2003 "PISA" results.

8. This feature of the Florida program is being litigated in the state's courts.

9. Jay P. Greene and Marcus A. Winters, *When Schools Compete: The Effects of Vouchers on Florida Public School Achievement* (New York, Manhattan Institute, 2003) http://www.manhattan-institute.org/html/ewp_02.htm.

10. Florida was the only state to post significant gains on the NAEP fourth-grade reading test in 2003, gains that spanned the ethnic spectrum. See http:// www.firn.edu/doe/sas/naep/pdf/naep03-readgap.pdf.

11. Caroline M. Hoxby, "School Choice and School Productivity (or, Could School Choice Be a Tide That Lifts All Boats?)" (Cambridge, MA: National Bureau of Economic Research, 2001). See http://www.educationnext.org/unabridged/20014/ hoxby.pdf.

12. Samuel Casey Carter, *No Excuses: Lessons from 21 High-Performing, High-Poverty Schools* (Washington, DC: Heritage Foundation, 2000). Available at http:// www.noexcuses.org/reports.html.

About the Contributors

David J. Armor is a professor of public policy in the School of Public Policy at George Mason University, Fairfax, Virginia, where he is also director of the PhD Program in Public Policy. He teaches graduate courses in statistics, culture and policy, and social theory and policy. He received his BA in mathematics and sociology from UC Berkeley and his PhD in sociology from Harvard University where he also taught as assistant and associate professor. From 1975 to 1982 Dr. Armor was a Senior Social Scientist at the RAND Corporation, and from 1986 to 1989 he was Principal Deputy Assistant Secretary and Acting Assistant Secretary of Defense for Force Management and Personnel. He has conducted research and written widely in the fields of education, race and civil rights policy, and military manpower. He has also served as an expert witness in many school desegregation and educational adequacy cases. In 1999 he was appointed to the National Academy of Science Committee on Military Recruiting. Some of his recent publications include *Forced Justice: School Desegregation and the Law*; "Race and Gender in the U.S. Military" (*Armed Forces & Society*, 1996); *Competition in Education*; *Maximizing Intelligence*; and *Attitudes, Aspirations, and Aptitudes of American Youth* (contributor).

Chester E. Finn, Jr. has devoted most of his career to improving education in the United States. As Senior Fellow at Stanford's Hoover Institution, President of the Thomas B. Fordham Foundation and Thomas B. Fordham Institute, and Senior Editor of *Education Next*, his primary focus is the reform of primary and secondary schooling. He is also a Fellow of the International Academy of Education and an Adjunct Fellow at the Hudson Institute, where he worked from 1995 through 1998. For more than 20 years, he has been in the forefront of the national debate about school reform. His participation in seminars, conferences, and hearings has taken him to colleges, education and civic groups, and government organizations throughout the world. Author of 13 books, Finn's most recent is *Rethinking Special Education for a New Century*, co-edited with Andrew Rotherham and Charles Hokanson (2001). In 2000, Princeton University Press published *Charter Schools in Action: Renewing Public Education*, co-authored with Bruno V. Manno and Gregg Vanourek. In 1999, with William J. Bennett and John Cribb, he wrote *The Educated Child: A Parent's Guide from Pre-School through Eighth Grade*. A native of Ohio, he holds an undergraduate degree in U.S. history, master's degree in social studies teaching, and doctorate in education policy, all from Harvard University.

Roland G. Fryer, Jr. is a Junior Fellow in the Harvard University Society of Fellows and an assistant professor of Economics, also at Harvard. He has served as a Faculty Research Fellow at the National Bureau of Economic Research since 2003. His research topics include affirmative action, discrimination, and social economics. He earned his BA in Economics with Departmental and University Honors from the University of Texas in 1998 and his PhD in Economics from Pennsylvania State University in 2002.

Eric Hanushek is the Paul and Jean Hanna Senior Fellow at the Hoover Institution of Stanford University. He is also chairman of the Executive Committee for the Texas Schools Project at the University of Texas at Dallas and a research associate of the National Bureau of Economic Research. He is a leading expert on educational policy with an emphasis on the economics and finance of schools. His books include *The Economics of Schooling and School Quality, Improving America's Schools, Making Schools Work, Educational Performance of the Poor, Education and Race, Assessing Policies for Retirement Income, Modern Political Economy, Improving Information for Social Policy Decisions*, and *Statistical Methods for Social Scientists*, along with numerous articles in professional journals. He previously held academic appointments at the University of Rochester, Yale University, and the U.S. Air Force Academy. Government service includes being Deputy Director of the Congressional Budget Office, Senior Staff Economist at the Council of Economic Advisers, and Senior Economist at the Cost of Living Council. He is a member of the International Academy of Education and was awarded the Fordham Prize for Distinguished Scholarship in 2004. He is a Distinguished Graduate of the United States Air Force Academy and completed his PhD in economics at the Massachusetts Institute of Technology. He served in the U.S. Air Force from 1965 to 1974.

Ron Haskins is senior fellow in the Economic Studies Program at the Brookings Institution and senior consultant at the Annie E. Casey Foundation in Baltimore. From February to December of 2002 he was the Senior

Advisor to the President for Welfare Policy at the White House. Prior to joining Brookings and Casey, he spent 14 years on the staff of the House Ways and Means Human Resources Subcommittee, first as welfare counsel to the Republican staff, then as the subcommittee's staff director. From 1981 to 1985, he was a senior researcher at the Frank Porter Graham Child Development Center at the University of North Carolina, Chapel Hill. Haskins has also co-edited several books, including *Welfare Reform and Beyond: The Future of the Safety Net*, *The New World of Welfare* and *Policies for America's Public Schools: Teachers, Equity, and Indicators*, and is a contributor to numerous books and scholarly journals on children's development and social policy issues. He holds a bachelor's degree in History, a master's in Education, and a PhD in Developmental Psychology, from UNC, Chapel Hill.

Stephen D. Levitt is the Alvin H. Baum Professor of Economics and Director of the Initiative on Chicago Price Theory at the University of Chicago. He also an Editor of *The Journal of Political Economy*. He has written over fifty research papers that have appeared in peer-reviewed journals. His recent book, *Freakonomics* (co-authored by Stephen Dubner), has spent months on the *New York Times* bestseller list. He earned his bachelor's degree from Harvard University in 1989 and his PhD in economics from the Massachusetts Institute of Technology in 1994.

Derek Neal is professor and chair in the Department of Economics at the University of Chicago. He is also a research associate of the National Bureau of Economic Research. He received his PhD in economics from the University of Virginia and began his academic career as an assistant professor at the University of Chicago in 1991. From 1998 to 2001, he served on the faculty of the University of Wisconsin before returning to Chicago. His most recent work documents the stability and possible widening of black–white skill gaps over roughly the past two decades and explores the causes and consequences of this development. In 2006, he will begin directing the Chicago Workshop on Black–White Inequality, a series of biannual conferences funded by the Searle Freedom Trust that will explore black–white differences in the United States. Professor Neal has served as an Advisory Editor for *Economics Letters* and as a co-editor of the *Journal of Human Resources*. He now serves as the Editor-in-Chief for the *Journal of Labor Economics*.

Paul E. Peterson is the Henry Lee Shattuck Professor of Government and director of the Program on Education Policy and Governance at Harvard University, a Senior Fellow at the Hoover Institution at Stanford, and Editor-in-Chief of *Education Next*, a journal of opinion and research on education policy. He is a former director of the Center for American Political

Studies at Harvard University and of the Governmental Studies program at the Brookings Institution. Peterson is the author or editor of over one hundred articles and twenty-two books, including most recently *No Child Left Behind? The Politics and Practice of School Accountability*; *The Future of School Choice, Our Schools and our Future . . . Are We Still At Risk?*, and *The Education Gap: Vouchers and Urban Schools*. Peterson chaired the Social Science Research Council's Committee on the Urban Underclass and has served on many committees of the National Research Council of the National Academy of Sciences. He is a member of the American Academy of Arts and Sciences, the National Academy of Education, and has also received fellowships from the Guggenheim Foundation, the German Marshall Foundation, and the Center for Study in the Behavioral Sciences. He has also been appointed to a Department of Education independent review panel to advise the agency in evaluating the Title I program for disadvantaged students. He earned his PhD and MA in political science from the University of Chicago.

Margaret Raymond is a Research Fellow at the Hoover Institution and director of CREDO. Previously, she was a senior scientist in the department of economics and adjunct associate professor of political science and public policy analysis. She joined the faculty of the University of Rochester in 1992, and assumed the position of director of the Center for Research on Education Outcomes in 1999. Dr. Raymond has twenty years' experience in conducting program evaluations for federal, state, and local governmental agencies. Previous evaluation assignments have examined federal welfare demonstrations, statewide impacts of legislative changes in criminal and juvenile justice policy, analyses of organizational shifts following regulatory changes, and comparative fiscal gains in post secondary professional curricula. She has extensive public policy experience, and has provided guidance to public and private organizations on strategic information systems.

Patrick Wolf is associate professor of public policy at Georgetown University. He is director of Georgetown's School Choice Demonstration Project and principal investigator for the official evaluation of the new Opportunity Scholarship school choice program in Washington, DC. Wolf is lead editor of the Brookings book *Educating Citizens: International Perspectives on Civic Values and School Choice* and was a contributing author to *The Education Gap: Vouchers and Urban Schools*. In addition, Wolf has authored or co-authored more than twenty articles and book chapters on school choice, special education, public management, and campaign finance. He was a member of the Gates-Brookings National Working Commission on Choice in K–12 Education and is a faculty associate of the Program on Education Policy and Governance at Harvard University. He received his PhD in political science from Harvard in 1995 and previously taught at Columbia University.